An Economic History
of the United States

An Economic History of the United States

Conquest, Conflict, and Struggles for Equality

Frederick S. Weaver

ROWMAN & LITTLEFIELD
Lanham • Boulder • New York • London

For Sharon

Executive Editor: Jon Sisk
Associate Editor: Natalie Mandziuk
Marketing Manager: Kim Lyons
Production Editor: Janice Braunstein

Published by Rowman & Littlefield
A wholly owned subsidiary of The Rowman & Littlefield Publishing Group, Inc.
4501 Forbes Boulevard, Suite 200, Lanham, Maryland 20706
www.rowman.com

Unit A, Whitacre Mews, 26-34 Stannary Street, London SE11 4AB, United Kingdom

British Library Cataloguing in Publication Information Available

Library of Congress Cataloging-in-Publication Data
Weaver, Frederick Stirton, 1939–
    An economic history of the United States : conquest, conflict, and struggles for equality / Frederick S. Weaver.
    pages cm
    Includes bibliographical references and index.
    ISBN 978-1-4422-5519-7 (cloth : alk. paper) — ISBN 978-1-4422-5723-8 (pbk. : alk. paper) — ISBN 978-1-4422-5520-3 (electronic)
    1. United States—Economic conditions. I. Title.
    HC103.W374 2016
    330.973—dc23
    2015031856

Contents

Introduction

Some Initial Definitions and Organizational Strategies

I seek to illuminate the constant, irrepressible historical movement and transformation of the United States. My approach, which I call political economy, emphasizes the relationships among economic forces, alterations in social-class structure, and government policy. At times changes in one of these aspects govern changes in others, and the direction of influence can vary. My emphasis on political economy is often deliberately provocative, but this does not mean that I believe that political economy is all there was and is to historical explanation. Nevertheless, without a sound grasp of the historically changing character of the political economy, it is extremely difficult to figure out, say, the roles of institutions, culture, individual attitudes, contingency, and their significance.

A second conviction expressed in this book's organization and analysis is the need for comparative history. Much of U.S. history is written in terms of national exceptionalism and uniqueness, an approach I consider to be self-aggrandizing and misleading. U.S. history is exceptional, but no more than any other nation's history. Moreover, the United States has been and continues to be firmly embedded in the world, and although many U.S. leaders have tried to deny or reduce this embeddedness, there is no getting away from it. Comparative perspectives are critical for controlling generalizations about the United States and for identifying the significance of events and tendencies.

As I have argued in different contexts, the character of capitalist industrialization changes historically. Nevertheless, there are basic, enduring features that are integral to capitalism's very definition. **Capitalism** does presuppose markets for the exchange of commodities (goods and services produced for sale on markets rather than for direct use). But commodities, whether circulating in world or local markets, have been produced over the centuries under conditions of almost every imaginable set of social relations between producers and nonproducers; for example, slaves dealing with masters, serfs dealing with lords, independent peasants and craftspeople dealing with merchants and political elites, and wage workers dealing with owners/employers. Since each relationship between producer and nonproducer possesses distinctive contradictions and sources of motion, mistaking the presence of commodity markets as evidence of the existence of capitalism is likely to misdirect analysis concerning the key points of conflict and change.

Three sets of social and political relations underlie capitalist social and economic orders. The central relationship and major source of contradictions and change in industrial capitalism is the wage-labor system, the capital-labor relationship. This is the perpetual struggle between propertyless workers, who have only their labor services to sell, and the propertied classes and their agents who control the means of production (for example, plant, equipment, land, mines) and purchase labor services, which had become commodities bought and sold in markets.

The second major source of dynamism and change in industrial capitalism is the capital-capital relationship: profit-motivated private firms compete with each other in product markets to realize profits. Are firms in direct and immediate price competition with each other? Do some firms have state-enabled protections from domestic and foreign competition? Do three or four large firms dominate the market for a particular product and compete mostly through product differentiation and advertising? Each one of these types of market competition expresses a particular industrial organization and a distinctive style of capital-capital relationship.

Contradictions and conflicts within the capital-labor and capital-capital relationships are the main driving forces of capitalism. The two sets of relationships are set in national political frameworks with shifting Public Sector–citizen interactions—the third set of social and political relations capable of altering power balances and affecting the directions of social and economic change.

Again, contradiction and conflict, not harmony, are inherent in capitalist societies and are the moving forces behind social, political, and economic change. A frequent way to avoid acknowledging conflict and struggle is to use the nation as a unit of analysis. For example, introductory economics textbooks assure us that the benefits from national specialization and international trade among nations are parallel to the argument that specialization among individuals within a nation leads to mutually beneficial exchange. The theory of **comparative advantage** treats nations as indivisible units, comparable to an individual. But the reality is that nations are not harmonious collections of individuals; they comprise groups with conflicting and contradictory interests. This means that a nation does not benefit or lose through international commerce but rather that some groups in the nation benefit at the expense of others. To deny such complexity is to risk conclusions that serve some groups and disadvantage other groups. Winners may gain enough from vibrant international trade to be able to compensate losers and still be ahead, but without political mechanisms able to achieve this compensation, such a calculation could easily degenerate into winner-supporting apologetics. Arithmetic models based on relative prices and national units are not adequate for a rigorous analysis of the benefits and losses from international trade.

Within the economy, I focus on manufacturing activity—on the way that it has developed and affected and been affected by social structure and government policy. It was only during the nineteenth and twentieth centuries that a strong consensus of intellectuals and political leaders thought a successful program of industrialization was necessary for national strength and prosperity. That is, they looked to the development of a manufacturing sector capable of self-generating expansion and stimulating activity in other sectors. While use of the term "industry" often includes construction, utilities, and even mining, my focus is on manufacturing—the economic activity that transforms physical goods into other goods. This may be raw cotton turned into yarn, turned into textiles, turned into apparel, or it may be iron ore and coal turned into steel, turned into washing machines, lawn mowers, automobiles, and GPS-guided bombs. Manufacturing does not include the production of the raw cotton (agriculture) or of iron ore and coal (mining), nor does it include the transportation (transport and communication) and sale of the clothing (retail) or the use of the lawn mower by a landscaping company (service).

Since the central characteristic of manufacturing is the physical transformation of physical goods, there is no deep mystery about why this economic activity was regarded as necessary for a modern, progressive, and prosperous economy. It has been in manufacturing that the greatest successes of applying science to production have taken place, creating the most dramatic and sustained technological advances. These technological changes have, in general, been the principal bases of increases in the productivity of human labor—raising the value of what can be produced with a given amount of time and effort by human labor. Rising productivity of human labor is the most secure basis for rising levels of material welfare and is the very definition of economic development.

In addition, the effects of a vigorous manufacturing sector have not been limited to those directly involved in manufacturing; manufacturing sectors supply products that directly increase workers' productivity in other sectors. For example, chemical fertilizers and mechanical harvesters enhance productivity in agriculture; drills, explosives, hydraulic pumps, and conveying equipment facilitate production from mines; telephones, computers, and vehicles are fundamental for communication and transportation; and electronic scanners and inventory control devices make retail stores more efficient.

Manufactured products themselves are also significant in other, more direct ways. Modern industrial sectors supply most of the goods desired by people who are becoming prosperous, thus increasing a government's popularity and legitimacy in the eyes of its citizens (or subjects). A domestic manufacturing capacity is essential for producing the materiel of warfare and thus for military power. And in a different vein, the organization of manufacturing production, by bringing large numbers of workers together, often in urban worksites, has historically been an important source of political mobilizations that broadened political participation and literacy.

While I emphasize industrial development, the book also contains subthemes that surface in almost every chapter—for example, the use of violence for social control and shifting but omnipresent real-estate speculation. But more fundamental is the underlying concept that general prosperity is not the creation of the efforts of a few gifted entrepreneurs but rather the consequence of much broader qualities of the social system. It is more complex to think in this manner, but consider the following: carpenters, taxicab drivers, college professors, leaders of organizations, and just about everyone else in the U.S. labor force earn many times more than people in the same occupations in, say, Ecuador. Does this mean that U.S. workers are that much more skillful, hardworking, decent, and effective than are Ecuadorian workers in corresponding occupations? Even the most nationalist xenophobe would consider that a stretch (although I am occasionally surprised). The most important differences are that U.S. workers work in a context of social capital, general prosperity, and opportunity that enhances the value of their work. In a comparative perspective, it is not principally, and certainly not exclusively, differences in individual merit that account for such broad disparities in national earnings or in how national earnings are distributed within the nation.

A truly egalitarian nation would indeed be exceptional, but we are not there yet. Understanding that our past is characterized by conquest, conflict, and struggles for equality will help us move toward that goal.

THE PLAN OF THE BOOK

Part I (chapter 1) focuses on precapitalist formations in the British North American colonies, and it includes a background discussion of European colonial empires in general, of which the British North American colonies were a part. In describing the demographics of the early colonies, the chapter pays special attention to indigenous peoples and the recurring struggles over land. The French and Indian War was a turning point in those conflicts. Throughout the chapter, the "Indian problems" in North America are contrasted with those of colonial Spanish America, including the tensions that led to conservative political independence in both colonial empires rather than to social revolutions.

Part II (chapters 2 and 3) goes through the first half of the nineteenth century. Chapter 2 describes the Northwest Ordinance and the difficulties that led to replacing the Articles of Confederation with a new Constitution and the angry debates around the process that included revolts by impoverished farmers. While this is going on at the political level, construction of transport infrastructure—roads, canals, the telegraph, and increasingly the railroad—made progress in knitting together the geography of the new nation, which the Louisiana Purchase expanded considerably. The chapter concludes with an analysis of manufacturing growth in the northeastern United States, a process led by a large number of small firms producing principally wage goods—standardized products for working people—in diffuse and competitive product markets. A thumbnail sketch of the English Industrial Revolution from the mid-eighteenth century to the early nineteenth century highlights some key similarities with and differences from the U.S. experience.

Chapter 3 describes the divergent regional patterns of economic growth and development in the early nineteenth-century United States. Wage labor was becoming important at this time in the Northeast, and despite the regions' economic complementarity, wage labor coexisted uneasily with slavery in the South and independent proprietorships in the upper and western Midwest. The contradictions and tensions were most evident in the federal government, where Southerners blocked programs and policies considered crucial by profit-motivated private firms and independent agrarian proprietors. The election of Abraham Lincoln led to several Southern state governments seceding from the Union, and the Confederate States of America eventually numbered eleven slave states. Consequent disputes over the federal property located in the South set off the U.S. Civil War.

Part III (chapters 4–7) includes the fifty years after the Civil War. Chapter 4 begins with the observation that during the Civil War, none of the seceding states was represented in the U.S. Congress. Republican Congresses took the opportunity to raise tariffs and pass the Pacific Railway Act (1862), the Morrill Act (1862), the Homestead Act (1862), the Department of Agriculture (1862), and the National Currency Act (1863). Southern masters had been actively hostile toward these initiatives, including a transcontinental railroad that did not pass through the South. These acts opened the West to white settlement, which required more "clearing" of indigenous peoples onto reservations and was accompanied by virulent anti-Asian sentiments and policies in the Far West. The chapter concludes with the economic problems in the post–Civil War South and the North's attempt to "reconstruct" the social, political, and cultural orders in the South.

Chapter 5 analyzes the robust industrial growth during the last half of the nineteenth century. The industrial expansion was led by large-scale, highly capitalized corporations, producing steel, rubber, petroleum, chemicals, and other inputs for further production. The character of industrial development had changed historically, an understanding that is strengthened by a brief case study of German industrial development at the same time. Nevertheless, the process in the United States was distinctive, because it began to include mass-produced consumer goods. The chapter ends with the massive increase in immigration from eastern and southern Europe, an immigration that brought people very different from the 1840s and 1850s immigrants, making their urban destinations much more complex.

The next two chapters in part III (chapters 6 and 7) cover the same fifty years after the Civil War, and chapter 6 begins with the end of Reconstruction, the return of white control of Southern politics, and the imposition of Jim Crow laws. An irony is that the South was officially to be transformed, and it managed to be the least transformed of U.S. regions in the post–Civil War decades. Turning to the Midwest and North, the chapter details changes in the organization of industrial work, the emergence of combative working-class movements, industrial and financial elites, and an urban middle class. The chapter concludes by discussing the political sources of reform efforts to rein in the power of large corporations up to World War I.

Chapter 7 emphasizes the place of the United States in foreign trade, finance, and diplomacy. Although the United States possessed what amounted to a continent-wide common market, foreign trade and investment by the United States grew significantly at the end of the nineteenth century. Rising tariffs continued to be a contentious political and fiscal issue. Another aspect of international involvement at the end of the nineteenth century and early twentieth century was the vigorous advocacy by some constituencies for creating U.S. colonies in distant lands with nonwhite populations, including the annexation of Hawaii. U.S. commercial and military interests felt threatened by competing nations' potential domination of trade, trade routes, and coaling stations for merchant and military vessels. There was also the conviction that the United States had come of age and as a powerful and mature nation should demonstrate the ability to create an empire similar in scale and reach to the European empires. Despite strong pushback against pursuing such avenues, the United States did become a colonial power.

Part IV (chapters 8–11) begins with the U.S. entry into World War I in 1917, three years after its beginning, but the war did not negate the domestic reform agenda, including woman suffrage. The end of the war in 1918 brought a badly implemented demobilization, industrial recession, agricultural depression, race riots, and heightened persecution of radicals. The three post–World War I U.S. administrations pursued strongly isolationist policies, and the politics of European wartime debt repayments contributed to the rise of fascism. In the 1920s, the instabilities of mass production–mass consumption exploded in the Great Depression of the 1930s, triggered by a bursting stock-market bubble. Innovative New Deal policies and initiatives ameliorated the effects of the Depression but did not solve it. The United States entered World War II in 1941 in response to a terrible miscalculation by the Japanese high command. The speed in mobilizing U.S. industrial, agricultural, and human resources for the war effort was admirable, and forcing 120,000 Japanese Americans in the West into concentration camps was disgraceful.

Chapter 9 shows the manner in which the United States was deeply engaged in reshaping international economic and political structures after World War II. U.S. officials were instrumental in the reconstruction of the international financial system based on the U.S. dollar, and U.S. aid helped rebuild Europe and Japan. The Cold War lent urgency to the projects. The U.S. economy grew rapidly, along with the birth rate. Political and economic configurations, through design and serendipity, formed a new mass production–mass consumption economy that relied on political regulation and guidance (the "mixed economy"), solving the enduring problem of price wars among large corporations. An implicit compact between capital and labor in these dominant firms conceded decisions about production and work organization to management, and the Public Sector monitored and prodded the Private Sector, expanded some safety-net programs, and made remarkable progress in African American civil rights. The last achievement further alienated Southern whites who began to become solidly identified with the Republican Party.

Chapter 10 shows that the international trade and investment system was so successful that foreign competition weakened confidence in the U.S. dollar, the key currency. In 1971, the U.S. government unilaterally abrogated the entire arrangement by breaking the connection between gold and the U.S. dollar. The Organization of Petroleum Exporting Countries (OPEC) quadrupled the price of oil in 1973, and banks took such risks in lending these petrodollar deposits that defaults proclaimed the arrival of the 1982 debt crisis, which was especially severe in Latin America. The IMF imposed such draconian conditions on debtor nations that the 1980s are known in Latin America as "the lost decade." The continuing rise of foreign competition undercut U.S. mixed-economy arrangements, and price competition became paramount. At the same time, outsourcing production to foreign sites grew, which meant U.S. labor was thrown into direct competition with world labor. U.S. workers' wages, protections, and the safety net are imperiled.

Chapter 11 traces the genesis of the Great Recession in the United States and then critically analyzes the policy responses to it. The following section discusses the spread of the Great Recession to Europe and the difficulty of combatting it in the eurozone, where countries have no control over their currency and exchange rates. In both Europe and the United States, monetary policy is not adequate for achieving prerecession levels of growth and employment. The fear of national debts and of using fiscal policy is mistaken, even when it is not a cover for reducing safety nets, regulations, and other social policies that benefit the less prosperous portions of the population. The chapter (and book) concludes with three short essays that deal with the distribution of income, the service economy, and climate change.

After the last chapter, there is a list of U.S. presidents and a short glossary and index. I know; it sounds like high school civics class. Nevertheless, presidential administrations are handy benchmarks that express and shape different eras; ergo, the list.

PART I

COLONIAL ROOTS

1

—⟶ⵣ⟵—

Mercantilism, British Colonialism, and Independence

After a number of disastrous attempts, English settlers established permanent communities in North America in the early seventeenth century. This was a relatively late and minor step in the era of Europe's commercial expansion throughout the world. That expansion began with Portuguese sailors working down the west coast of Africa in the fifteenth century and exploded with the Spanish and Portuguese conquests of the New World from Mexico through South America in the sixteenth century. This commercial expansion had some specific features that need to be appreciated in order to situate the English colonization of North America in a historically productive manner.

MERCANTILISM AND EUROPEAN COMMERCIAL EXPANSION, 1450–1750

Earlier forms of empire were land-based organizations designed to appropriate goods and services from conquered regions for the benefit of the imperial center. Chinese, Egyptian, Mayan, Ottoman, Aztec, and Incan empires all succeeded in these terms, but none of these empires contained the internal tensions that created the capitalism of western Europe. The fifteenth- and sixteenth-century Eurasian Ottoman and Chinese empires had much greater levels of commercial activity, urbanization, centralized political control, scientific and cultural achievements, and concentrated wealth than were found in western Europe in the same period. But the institutions required to operate a successful tribute system—a powerful

3

standing army, a centralized political organization, and elaborate bureaucracies—impeded the emergence of private ownership of the means of
production and a wage-labor system, that is, the development of capitalist
relations.[1]

It was the more primitive and decentralized feudalism of western
Europe that borrowed and adopted such technical and organizational
changes as the water mill and new ways to rotate crops, design plows,
and utilize draught animals. The most critical theme for our story is the
western European struggle to establish coherent nation-states. Although
this protracted process was not independent of the formation of domestic capitalism, there was no direct, linear link with it. For example, the
Iberian nations of Portugal and Spain were successful in their national
political projects by the end of the fifteenth century, although they lagged
behind other regions in the domestic development of private ownership
and wage labor. On the other hand, Germany and Italy contained regions
with well-developed capitalist relations before becoming unified nation-
states in the late nineteenth century.

It was the process of national political consolidation combined with
rising productivity in agriculture and the growth of cities and commerce
that underlay western Europeans' foreign expansion in the fifteenth and
sixteenth centuries that began to integrate the Americas, Africa, and Asia
into a web of mercantile relationships that spanned the world. While commercial profits were the primary motive behind the European expansion,
this was not anything new for merchants, who as an occupational group
throughout the world and for centuries had sought commercial profits.

What distinguished this type of mercantile activity from other commercial endeavors was the alliance between merchants and monarchs that offered merchants monopolies and protection and offered monarchs fiscal
revenue derived from taxing and directly investing in foreign mercantile
ventures. This revenue did not come from an activity that strengthened
local barons—remnants of feudal decentralization—nor did it require
their consent. Therefore, the revenue could be used to strengthen central
authority at the barons' expense.

The resulting western European merchant-monarch alliances varied
in their mix of relative power between merchants and monarchs, and by
the seventeenth century, Holland with its mercantile oligarchy and Spain
with its powerful monarchy defined the range of the western European
continuum. This combination had a unique logic that warrants its being
called Mercantilism with a capital *M*.

The nations that led Mercantilist expansion—Portugal, Spain, Holland,
France, and England—were not the principal markets for their merchants'
trade; western Europe in general was the most important market.[2] Nor
were these nations seeking markets for domestic production. Not until

centuries later would European imperialism seek raw materials, food supplies, investment outlets, and markets for domestically produced goods.

The Mercantilist ideal was to take over an established, lucrative trade and extract profits through a monopoly protected by military force. Western European consumers coveted Chinese silks, porcelain, exotic woods, medicines and drugs such as rhubarb and opium, Indian cotton textiles ("calicoes"), and precious stones, but spices—especially the nutmeg, mace, and cloves from the Spice Islands of present-day Indonesia—were the major prize of the East-West commerce. They created more imaginative and exotic flavorings for elites, who were beginning to eat differently from, not just more than, the poor. In addition, preserving meat through winter was necessary and difficult for all Europeans, and even some peasants bought Eastern spices to complement the use of other, less satisfactory preservatives such as salt and West African pepper.

The Portuguese showed western Europe the way to avoid the Venetian and Ottoman monopolies of the trade in Asian goods by going around Africa and the Cape of Good Hope, to India, and through the Straits of Malacca to the Spice Islands. This meant that they did not have to encounter the Venetian and Ottoman galleys that policed the Mediterranean Sea's calm waters. By the third quarter of the sixteenth century, a high proportion of spices bound for Europe went around Africa in Portuguese ships, and foreign sources constituted 65 to 70 percent of the Portuguese king's fiscal revenues.

In the late sixteenth and early seventeenth centuries, the Portuguese suffered severe reverses. With help and competition from the English and French, the Dutch wrested the Asian trade away from the Portuguese, and between 1630 and 1654, the Dutch also took over Portuguese sugar-producing regions in northeast Brazil. By the eighteenth century, however, the English and French had taken commercial leadership away from the Dutch. These shifts in commercial leadership during the Mercantilist era had little to do with lower prices for superior goods; it was military power rather than market competition that determined winners and losers among the western Europeans' quest for commercial profits.

The Spaniards also sought the spice trade, and persuaded by Columbus's underestimation of the size of the globe, they financed a three-boat flotilla to sail west. They bumped into the New World on the way, and although it was initially a Mercantile endeavor, the discovery of large gold and especially silver deposits changed the Spanish king's mind, and he hobbled Mercantile activity to focus on the extraction of gold and silver.

Cacao and tobacco in the Americas demonstrate that Mercantile forces were willing and able to market brand-new products. Moreover, where local people could not or would not produce desired commodities in sufficient quantities and on agreeable terms, European Mercantilism's potent combination of merchant capital and political backing was capable of organizing the production of commodities by mobilizing labor in whatever mode was expedient to realize the market potential. African slaves themselves became Mercantile commodities.

These examples illustrate a further point: the opportunism of Mercantilist forces in organizing colonial production meant that there was no clear relationship between colonies' being plugged into expanding circuits of Mercantile trade and the colonies' prospects for developing the dynamism of capitalism. The sugar plantations of northeastern Brazil were the colonies of a weak Mercantilist power, while those of the English Caribbean belonged to a Mercantilist power that was becoming the world's leading capitalist economy. Nevertheless, the similar organization of production in the two colonial regions meant that the colonies' futures would be more alike than those of Portugal and England. Production in both colonial regions was for markets, and the comparative vigor of those commodity markets was much less important in influencing future possibilities of these colonies than the ways in which their production was organized. As in the southern United States, plantation slavery indelibly stamped the social formations of northeastern Brazil and the Caribbean in ways that impeded the development of a dynamic capitalism.

THE ESTABLISHMENT OF ENGLISH
COLONIES IN NORTH AMERICA

Mercantilism was the context in which the British established colonies along the Atlantic coast of North America. England of the sixteenth and seventeenth centuries conformed to the Mercantile model that I outlined above in several key dimensions, including monarchs' sponsorship and investment in overseas commercial adventures and in chartering **corporations** with regional monopoly trading privileges, such as the East India Company, the Hudson's Bay Company, the South Sea Company, the Royal African Company, and so on. In addition, there were corresponding monopolies chartered for a number of domestically produced commodities such as soap, bricks, coal, and iron and steel.

The Navigation Acts controlling colonial trade is another illustration of England's adherence to Mercantile principles. This series of acts, passed during the seventeenth century, stipulated that all colonial trade had to be done by English and English colonial ships and crews and that a wide range of enumerated colonial exports, including tobacco, sugar, cotton, indigo, and ginger, had to be sent first to England. In 1663, all colonial imports were to go through England, where duties were collected.

In North America, also consistent with Mercantilist principles, French, British, and Dutch trappers and traders in North America pursued the precious skins of a variety of animals to sell to elite consumers in European-wide markets. The British took over the North American Dutch trading posts in the mid-seventeenth century, and the French and British continued to compete in enlisting Indian allies to trap animals and transport the furs to ports. There were constant conflicts between the French and British over which trapping areas were open to whom and which tribes of Native Americans worked with which nationalities of Europeans.

Unlike the French or Spaniards, however, most of the British who came to North America were interested in agricultural pursuits, and by the eighteenth century, there were twenty times as many British colonists as their French counterparts. So despite the Mercantile character of Great Britain's economic policies, the fur trade, and initial hopes for gold and silver, Britain's North American colonies did not adhere to Mercantile patterns. British North America was predominantly a settler colony, and despite U.S. history textbooks, those colonies were initially a minor and rather uninteresting venture for the British, unlike the more commercially successful Caribbean islands.

Most of the early English colonies in North America began with the British king granting millions of acres to one of his favorites or to a private chartered company to encourage the migration of new settlers. After all, the king "owned" this stretch of seaboard in eastern North America by right of conquest. A corollary to the right of conquest was that the European colonists did not consider Native Americans to be legitimate owners of the land; after all, they had no European land titles and rarely stayed at one site.

Royal grants to friends, family, and private companies included immense leeway for the grantees to set up their own governance systems and to organize the colonies as they saw fit. Grantees such as the Virginia Company (Virginia), the Duke of York (New York and New Jersey), Lord Baltimore (Maryland), or a consortium of Barbadian planters (South Carolina) were profit-motivated speculators. New England, Pennsylvania, and Georgia were exceptions to this general rule.

In New England, religious dissidents ("Puritans") established the Massachusetts Bay Company in 1628, and the English king granted most of the region to the company. Unlike most other colonization patterns, the company's leaders and major investors migrated to New England and supervised the organization and operation of the colony, turning the Massachusetts Bay Company into the Massachusetts Bay Colony. The immigrants' shared religious commitment led to greater coherence than experienced in other colonies, and the durability of central control meant that groups were granted land if they established new congregations and organized land distributions in an acceptable manner.

Religious unity in Massachusetts thus had the advantage of reducing a wide dispersal of its population that plagued other colonies, but it also produced a rigid intolerance of religious dissent, although the colony leaders were called dissenters by the Church of England. Although the Massachusetts Bay Colony eventually absorbed the small, faltering settlement of theological radicals ("Pilgrims") in Plymouth, this was not the colony leaders' usual response to other faiths and practices. The standard responses to people calling for religious toleration, espousing a different kind of Protestantism, or being suspected of witchcraft were expulsion, whippings, and hangings.

Pennsylvania was the second important exception to the general pattern of colony formation. William Penn hoped to create a religious utopia, and his successful advertising campaign drew immigrants to Pennsylvania from all over Europe. Nevertheless, Penn's top-down governance plan was not much different from those of other grantees, and the plan fell victim to the same forces that undercut similar authoritarian ambitions in other colonies. Chronic labor shortages gave agricultural workers political leverage, and plentiful and productive land enabled a large portion of immigrants to acquire substantial economic resources independent from distant grantees. A last line of defense for settlers, although risky, was for individuals, families, and small groups to leave the colony and strike out beyond the frontier on their own. These factors gave immigrants, who in most colonies quickly became geographically dispersed, the means and the will to block the formation of autocratic societies dominated by hereditary elites to whom common folks owed both money and deference with no voice in governance.

Georgia was the third major exception to the general pattern of settlement. It was the last of the formal colonies, established in 1732, and its initial purpose was charitable and, for the British crown, a buffer against the Spaniards in Florida. It was to be a place for debtors, who had often been imprisoned in England, to become upright citizens by working the land granted to them by the grantee corporation. The grantee corporation prohibited slavery and the importation of rum and regulated the size of land holdings through restrictive, conditional land titles. Within two decades, Georgia's leaders rescinded all three of these constraints, and large, slave-worked plantations soon dominated the landscape, and presumably rum flowed freely.

A final point about the seventeenth century is that the most stripped-down, simple form of English land tenure became the norm in the colonies, and land soon became commoditized, bought and sold on unregulated markets like shirts, shoes, and other goods. Colonists readily applied other English values and practices in the colonies. In addition to respecting literacy and numeracy, the white colonial population shared the conviction that contracts freely entered into should be seen as inviolable. And there were other examples. A distinguished economic historian, J. R. T. Hughes (1976: 120), described the seventeenth-century colonists with a sense of wonder:

> People who for long decades were forced to maintain a commercial life only barely above the level of barter . . . [and] having no banks and using corn, tobacco, beaver skins, and wampum for currency, passed laws controlling interest rates, carefully arranged the amortization of their own instruments of credit, and rigorously enforced the transfer of negotiable instruments and the rules for payment of debt.

While many seventeenth-century colonists were poor, they were sophisticated about the practices and institutions of the then-modern commercial society back home in England, and they accepted its tenets and prescribed behaviors as natural. Early colonial society was rudimentary and full of hardships, but it was not economically backward, nor did it contain attitudes, practices, and hierarchies unfavorable to the development of a vigorous capitalism in the northern colonies.

Who Came to the Thirteen Colonies?

Native American populations experienced serious health problems before the Europeans arrived; they suffered from chronic malnutrition, tuberculosis, syphilis, various parasites, and violence, and their life expectancies at birth were lower than in Europe. Nevertheless, it was different when Europeans took over the Americas: wars of conquest, starvation, overwork, and displacement reduced fertility and softened the populations for the principal killers: smallpox, measles, bubonic plague, and various other diseases that had been circulating for centuries among European, Asian, and African peoples but were unknown to the indigenous inhabitants of the Americas.

In North America, sharp declines in Indian populations began with contacts between European fishermen and coastal tribes years before permanent European settlements. For example, the French recorded a pestilence that swept through the Massachusetts Bay region in 1616 and 1617, and the Pilgrims and Puritans agreed that God had emptied so much of the area in preparation for their arrival. This was also the settlers' joyous reading of the smallpox epidemic among Native Americans that began in 1633, an epidemic they fostered with gifts of contaminated blankets.

The indigenous populations in the Americas experienced the worst demographic disaster in history, and it was not until the middle of the seventeenth century that the indigenous populations in Spanish America began to grow again but from a base of around 10 percent of what it had been at the time of Columbus's voyage.

The similarity between the massive depopulations of indigenous peoples in the thirteen British North American colonies and in Spanish America should not obscure the different implications for the two sets of European settlers. Spaniards exploring Mexico, Guatemala, and Peru (including present-day Bolivia and Ecuador) found three sets of well-organized Indian communities that were accustomed to systematic, sustained, and compulsory work and to paying taxes in one form or another.[3] Indigenous people became the principal workforce in Spanish American mines and fields, and their importance to the colonial enterprise is illustrated by the fact that initial grants (*encomiendas*) to those Spaniards who fought and conquered were not of land; they were of villages required to pay tribute to the *encomendero* in goods and labor. The Spaniards brought in African slaves where Indian labor was scarce, especially on the Caribbean islands and along the Caribbean coasts.

In sharp contrast, Native Americans in the east coast of North America were not useful as a source of labor for the European colonists, despite several brutal attempts to turn them into agricultural slave labor. The European immigrants to the thirteen North American colonies by and large came because of the availability of good farmland. For agricultural immigrants, the Native Americans were at least a nuisance and occasionally a threat.

Early missionaries and French and English fur trappers and traders had a more benign view of Native Americans, but by the eighteenth century, failed attempts to "civilize" the Native Americans buttressed by land hunger produced a racial pessimism that became the hallmark of colonists' attitude toward the Native Americans. These colonists saw Native Americans as practically identical to forests and boulders: all three had to be cleared to allow European immigrants to till the land.[4] Since Native Americans were not incorporated into U.S. settler societies in large numbers, census takers did not include them in their population counts. In Spanish America, Native Americans were integral components of colonial society, albeit incorporated at the bottom along with African slaves.

North American Native Americans' depopulation caused severe social and economic disruptions among the tribes, leading to "mourning wars"—raids on other Indian tribes in order to procure captives that could either be enslaved or adopted to increase the raiding group's population. The Iroquois—the Six Nations League of Mohawks, Oneidas, Onondagas, Cayugas, Senecas, and Tuscaroras—in northern New York and New England became dominant through these raids. A major illustration of this power was the Iroquois' 1737 sale of land belonging to Delaware, Shawnee, and other Indian tribes to European settlers in Pennsylvania. They then forced the tribes whose land had been sold out from under them to move west to the Ohio River Valley.

European Settlers

New European immigration to New England all but ceased by the end of the seventeenth century. There was better land and fewer social and political controls in the mid-Atlantic colonies from New York to Virginia, where most of the eighteenth-century voluntary immigrants went. Even in those areas, however, it is easy to overestimate the influence of migration. By the beginning of the United States as an independent republic, one in ten whites had been born abroad. The corresponding number for blacks was two in ten. This heavy reliance on natural increase accounts for the even sex ratios among whites that the first national census found in 1790—50.9 percent men and 49.1 percent women—despite the predominance of men among white immigrants, especially in Pennsylvania. U.S. censuses did not report sex of blacks until 1820, at which time the ratio was virtually identical to that of whites in 1790: 50.8 percent men and 49.2 percent women.

Table 1.1 presents the populations of the thirteen original states plus Vermont (the fourteenth state, 1791) and some outlying areas according to the second U.S. census in 1800. The last two sets of entries are population estimates for Spanish America and Brazil from around the same time, which for Spanish America was one to four decades prior to independence. The most obvious difference between the fourteen newly independent states and the Latin American colonies is the matter of scale: when Europeans arrived in what became the thirteen colonies, there were fewer than two million indigenous inhabitants, while Mexico and Central America had between ten and twenty million and the Andean region had five to ten million. By 1800, the independent United States contained little more than one-quarter the number of people in the American colonies of Spain and Portugal.

In addition to the differences in starting points, some of these regional differences in 1800 are attributable to the Spanish and Portuguese colonies being a full century older, and the *mestizos* (European and Indian mixed race) in Spanish America by themselves were about as numerous as people of European descent in the United States. But another source of disparity is due to the almost seven million Native Americans in 1800 Spanish America, for which there is no corresponding entry in the U.S. census for the perhaps three hundred thousand Native Americans east of the Mississippi.

Table 1.1.   Estimates of U.S. and Latin American Populations, Around 1800

	Population (Thousands)	Percentages
The United States[a]		
New England Total	1,233	100
European descent	1,215	99
African descent	—	1
Middle States Total	1,493	100
European descent	1,409	94
African descent	84	6
Upper South Total	1,229	100
European descent	737	57
African descent	492	43
Lower South Total	987	100
European descent	638	65
African descent	349	35
Newly Settled Areas Total	547	100
European descent	486	86
African descent	61	14
Total United States	5,252	100
European descent	4,254	81
African descent	998	19
Spanish America	**16,820**	**100**
European descent	3,276	19
Indians	7,530	45
Mestizos	5,238	32
African descent	776	4
Brazil[b]	**2,052**	**100**
European descent	577	28
African descent	1,351	66
Indians	124	6

[a] New England includes New Hampshire, Vermont (statehood in 1791), Massachusetts, Rhode Island, and Connecticut. The Middle Colonies were New York, New Jersey, Pennsylvania, and Delaware. The Upper South comprised Maryland and Virginia, and the Lower South was made up of North Carolina, South Carolina, and Georgia. Almost 90 percent of the population in Newly Settled Areas were in regions that became the states of Maine, Kentucky, and Tennessee.
[b] Not including perhaps 300,000 "unpacified" Indians.

Sources: For the United States, data are derived from U.S. Census Bureau, *Historical Statistics of the United States: Colonial Times to 1970*, Part 1 (Washington, DC: Government Printing Office, 1975), 24–37. For Spanish America, data are derived from John Lynch, *The Spanish American Revolutions, 1808–1826*, 2nd ed. (New York: Norton, 1986), 19–20, 360n. For Brazil, data are derived from Dauril Alden, *Colonial Roots of Modern Brazil* (Berkeley: University of California Press, 1984), 604, 607.

The promise of cheap or even free land offered by those with royal grants was a great lure, and thousands from the British Isles paid for their passage to the colonies, but not enough to populate and secure the area, so alternative strategies were employed. Indentured servitude was one of the most successful. Indentured servants were people who were unable to pay for their passage to the colonies and pledged their labor for a certain number of years, usually three to seven, in exchange for the trip.[5] Becoming indentured was voluntary, and a person could shop around and bargain for the best deal. When the ship arrived at its North American destination, an agent auctioned off immigrants' contracts to obtain the highest price. During the indenture, the holder of the contract was to provide food, clothes, shelter, occasionally training, and sometimes tools and land at the end of the contract, although indentured servants' actual experiences varied widely.

By the middle of the eighteenth century, half or more of the white immigrants to the British North American colonies outside New England came as indentured servants. Thus they made up a large portion of the eventual owners and operators of family farms in New York, New Jersey, Pennsylvania, and the western portions of the southern colonies. Many were the children of poor but "respectable" parents who signed the contracts.

Perhaps thirty-five thousand involuntary indentured servants—prisoners who were "transported" to the colonies—supplemented the supply of voluntary indentured servants. These immigrants had longer contracts, usually seven to fourteen years, and they included all sorts of convicted criminals, debtors, women "of abandoned character" rounded up in raids of London brothels, and Irish and Scottish rebels captured in the course of suppressing uprisings. Colonists resisted having large batches of prisoners sent to the colonies, but the British were so fond of getting rid of convicts in this manner that they continued to transport prisoners even after the colonies became the independent United States. The U.S. government prohibited the practice in 1788, and the British had to turn to Australia to relocate those not wanted in the British Isles.

African Slaves

African slaves constituted the largest group of involuntary immigrants, and they were the principal source of labor in producing tobacco, indigo, and rice on the larger plantations in the eastern and central portions of the southern colonies. With the eighteenth-century decline in indentured servants going to the colonies, the importation of Africans accelerated. Half of all African slaves brought to the thirteen colonies were brought between 1700 and 1750.

Between 1619 and 1807, slave traders forcibly brought around five hundred thousand Africans to what became the United States. This was about 5 percent of the ten million or so Africans brought to the Americas as slaves. Almost 40 percent of the total went to Brazil, and roughly the same number went to the Caribbean, mostly to the British West Indies. At the time of U.S. independence, African slaves made up around 20 percent of the colonies' populations. African slaves constituted 46 percent of the Lower South's population, and African slaves constituted 91 percent of the British West Indies' populations. Issues of social control were paramount for whites in these situations.

It is important to emphasize one other demographic aspect of the thirteen colonies: they were a very rural population. In 1790, 4 percent of the population lived in towns and cities of more than five thousand people, all of which were either seaports or located on navigable rivers. The colonies possessed one city (Philadelphia) with a population of more than thirty thousand. The population of Mexico City at this time was around 150,000, roughly the same number of people in all twelve of the cities and towns in the thirteen colonies with populations of five thousand or more.

A Colonial Backwater

Britain was late to begin its colonial venture in the Americas, and the Spaniards and Portuguese had acquired the most desirable areas a century before the British established permanent settlements on the Atlantic coast of North America. British migration policy is one of the key indicators that the British government considered the thirteen British colonies in North America to be a backwater. Before and after the mid-seventeenth-century English civil war and the expansion of Parliament's powers, British kings granted millions of acres of North America to Pilgrims, Puritans, Catholics, and Quakers, all of whom were persecuted in England. Political prisoners, convicted criminals, paupers, and foreigners made up other substantial bases of the thirteen colonies' white populations.[6] English authorities were pleased to have many of these folks disappear into the American wilderness and were indifferent to others.

Contrast this settlement policy with that of the Spanish authorities, who tried hard to prevent Jews and Muslims (even when converted to Christianity), Protestants, Gypsies, foreigners, and even Spaniards from some regions within Spain from immigrating to Spanish America. Some immigrants of prohibited categories did manage to get to Spanish America, but the point is that the American colonies were too important to the Spaniards to risk having large numbers of dubious folks in the mix of colonial populations.

Another striking difference between Spanish and British American colonial projects was in how loosely London governed the British North American colonies compared to how tightly Madrid and Seville bound its American colonies to Spain. There was still no unified, central governance in the thirteen colonies by the mid-eighteenth century, and each colony's assembly set policies about taxes, relations with the Native Americans, and distribution of western lands and had considerable authority over choosing officials. There were few English officials on the ground, and the English government exercised little in the way of coercive power in the colonies, consistent with Britain's principle of empire on the cheap. Moreover, by working with colleagues, allies, and paid agents in London, colonial interest groups enjoyed substantial influence in shaping specific British colonial policies and appointments, acquiring exceptions to disagreeable policies, and even conspiring to evade laws.

The jewels of England's American colonies were the Caribbean islands of Barbados, Trinidad, Jamaica, and some smaller islands. These West Indian colonies were sugar factories worked by African slaves, and the islands conformed to the outline of Mercantilism described earlier. The markets for the islands' sugar exports were worldwide, and they were not significant markets for British goods. The thirteen colonies' economies complemented the monocrop sugar islands and helped to provision these islands. So one might say that the North American colonies' principal importance to England was to make the West Indies more profitable Mercantilist colonies.

COLONIAL UNREST AND REVOLUTION

After the ascension of George I in 1714, British politics became more stable, and there were important changes going on in the British economy. I will describe these changes more fully in the next chapter, but for now, the main point is that Great Britain was moving out of the Mercantile phase into the Industrial Revolution by the middle of the eighteenth century, and the nation's trade patterns reflected those changes. Although selling sugar and furs throughout Europe was still important to Great Britain through the eighteenth century, exports of Britain's domestic manufactures—principally cotton textiles and iron products—and its imports such as cotton, iron, naval supplies, and foodstuffs to supply domestic production suggested that something new was going on.

In the new scheme of things, the thirteen colonies had become more important to Great Britain, outgrowing their status as a home for undesirables. First of all, the populations of the North American colonies had so expanded that the imperial government had to pay closer attention to them. But beyond the demographic change, colonial commercial production was oriented toward exports in a way that complemented the new British patterns. New England colonies exported fish, whale products, and forest products (ships, barrels, timber, and naval stores); the Middle Colonies exported wheat, live animals, and preserved meat; and the South exported tobacco, rice, indigo, and long-staple cotton. The principal destination of the exports was Great Britain and the West Indies, and by mid-century, the colonies were exporting foodstuffs to urbanized Great Britain. And no less important, the thirteen colonies were substantial markets for British-manufactured exports. For example, the North American colonies imported half of Britain's output of nails.

Therefore, the British government began trying to monitor and regulate its North American colonies, and Parliament became much more prominent in colonial affairs at the expense of the king and councils and ministers. This reduced colonists' access and influence in London, because it was easier to work on thirty or forty key players in royal councils than on the Parliament's difficult procedures and fractious membership.

While relations between Britain and the thirteen colonies were changing, social relations within the colonies were also changing. In the colonies that raised and exported tobacco in Virginia and Maryland and rice in South Carolina, large plantations worked by slaves dominated the landscape. The plantation organization became even more prevalent at the turn of the nineteenth century with the invention and manufacture of cotton gins that easily and efficiently separated seeds from cotton, making short-staple cotton cultivation in the Lower South highly profitable. Cotton became the crop of choice and slave-based plantations the organization of choice.

In contrast, family farms were prominent in New England, upstate New York, New Jersey, and Pennsylvania, and conditions on the western frontiers of every colony were fairly egalitarian among the farming families, even if not within the families. There was a lot of work for everyone, and it was imperative that the organization of production be able to employ women efficiently while abiding by a gendered division of labor. In the mixed farming in the north and frontier regions, men produced raw materials (crops, game, and forestry products), and women processed the first two (food and clothing) and were responsible for dairy, poultry, and local marketing.

As the frontiers continued to move west, subsistence-oriented frontier regions became less egalitarian as commercial farming developed. In the 1750s, small yeoman farmers revolted against colonial governments and large landowners in New Jersey, New York's Hudson River Valley and northeastern district (now Vermont), and North and South Carolina. In addition, elites perceived the high emotional pitch of worship in the eighteenth-century Great Awakening as a potential threat to their control over both whites and blacks.

Cherokees attacked western colonists' communities in Virginia, North Carolina, and South Carolina between 1759 and 1761 in an effort to reverse the tide of settlement that was encroaching on their lands. And the economic expansion of the eighteenth century and the decline of indentured servants increased the number of African slaves brought into the colonies. As a direct result, slave unrest became more common, with notable episodes in New York City, South Carolina, and New Jersey. Crackdowns on free blacks and even harsher treatment of slaves were the results.

The French and Indian War (1754–1763), known as the Seven Years' War in Europe, diverted settlers' attention from some of these tensions, but ultimately, it exacerbated them. The scale of the French and Indian War dwarfed the preceding British-French wars, which were European wars that spilled over into North America. In contrast, the French and Indian War began in North America and traveled, as it were, to Europe and beyond.

Tensions among French traders and trappers, British-sponsored farmers, and Native Americans in the Ohio River valley erupted into armed conflict involving regular soldiers and colonial militia two years before the British and French declared war in 1756. Although the indigenous people preferred British trade goods and prices, fears about losing their land to British settlers meant that they favored the French. In the middle of the eighteenth century, the French population of North America was 5 percent of the white population in Britain's thirteen colonies. The French simply were not perceived as the threat to Indian communities that the British agrarian colonies clearly were.

The war in North America ended in 1760, when the British conquered New France (Canada), but the fighting continued in and around Europe, Africa, the Caribbean, India, and Manila in the Spanish Philippines—the first genuine world war of the modern era. In the final 1763 treaty, Great Britain acquired all of Canada except a couple of small islands that gave the French access to the Newfoundland fishing banks, all the lands east of the Mississippi River except for the city of New Orleans, and no French contestation of the British East India Company's domination of India.

The British Empire was the clear winner, confirming its suzerainty over a much-enlarged empire at the expense of its European competitors. This did not mean that the colonized were all at peace. As already noted, there was still frequent fighting between the Cherokee and settlers in western portions of the South, and in 1763, an alliance of Ohio River valley Native Americans fought and lost Pontiac's War in an attempt to prevent further loss of their land.

Pontiac's War prompted the British government to issue the Proclamation of 1763, which reserved all lands west of the Allegheny Mountains for Native Americans and prohibited colonists from settling there. Although the Proclamation of 1763 was more an irritant than an effective ban on new settlements, it was worrisome for speculators such as George Washington, Thomas Jefferson, Patrick Henry, Richard Henry Lee, and other Virginia notables who had bought up impoverished veterans' land grant certificates—given to veterans for their service—at discounted prices. But it was the first of a series of British policies and actions that threatened the financial interests of the prosperous and politically prominent as well as ordinary families' chances to acquire farms.

It made perfect sense to the British Parliament and king that the colonists should pay for a part of the French and Indian War and continuing military and administrative costs in the colonies. Since white settlers in British North America were already among the most lightly taxed in the European world, the British government raised colonial taxes on specific goods and services. The two taxes that caused the strongest reactions in the colonies were the Stamp Act of 1765, which required the purchase of tax stamps for legal documents, diplomas, newspapers, and other missives, and the Townshend Acts of 1767, which raised import duties in the colonies and established a permanent Board of Customs Commissioners there with stronger enforcement capabilities. The effects were substantial; higher rates and better enforcement increased customs duty revenues by a factor of fifteen and increased seizures of ships and smuggled cargoes by six times.

In response to colonial agitation and an effective boycott of British products that colonial women organized and policed, Parliament rescinded the Stamp Act in 1766 but in the same year declared its right to regulate internal colonial affairs, including colonial currency and the levy of taxes. Since North American colonials were not represented in Parliament, the maxim "no taxation without representation" expressed a real grievance. In the face of violent resistance in the colonies, Parliament again backed down and abrogated the higher import duties on all goods but tea, a largely symbolic measure that declared Parliament's right to govern the colonies. At the end of 1773, around one hundred Bostonian whites dressed as Native Americans raided British ships and threw three hundred chests of tea into the harbor.

The Parliament and king responded to the Boston Tea Party with a series of acts in 1774 that colonials called the "Intolerable Acts." The British closed the port of Boston until reparations were made, strengthened the power of the governor at the expense of the Massachusetts assembly, and joined the Ohio River valley to the Canadian province of Quebec, closing the valley to settlers from the thirteen colonies.

Another important British event, although not directed against the North American colonies, also alienated an important segment of colonial society. A unanimous 1772 ruling by the judges of the English Court of King's Bench declared that James Somerset, a slave who came to England from Virginia with his master in 1769, was free. The judges declared that since there were no laws legalizing slavery in Great Britain, it was illegal in Great Britain. This was a major triumph for the abolitionist movement that was gaining momentum in Britain, and it sent shock waves through the slaveholding British colonies in the Caribbean and North American mainland.

These British legislative acts, royal policies, and judicial decisions managed to offend and inconvenience broad swaths of the colonial population. It was an exciting time, with mob demonstrations, protest marches, destruction of British officials' houses, and exaggerated rhetoric. The prewar activities helped rally the colonials to the colonial leadership's narrow version of the independence movement, but there were some important problems raised by their tactics.

The first is that the revolutionary leaders occasionally lost control of the crowds that they had encouraged, allowing the emergence of leaders whose goals included an unrestricted franchise, a more egalitarian society, abolition of slavery, the disestablishment of state religions, and other radical proposals aimed at the colonial elites who were in favor of independence. The genteel leaders of independence—the Sons of Liberty (or "Patriots")—struggled to get as many people into the streets as possible but limit their focus to the narrower purpose of political independence from Great Britain. In their view, this was to be a political revolution and not a social revolution.

The second problem was the inflamed rhetoric of many of the Patriots. They craved "liberty for all"; the British were "enslaving" them; they were fighting for their "natural rights of freedom." Many contemporaries, including slaves, recognized the contradiction with African slavery that made whites nervous. Although the development of a women's rights movement could take several decades, the wives and daughters of male Patriots could see the political potential for their interests in this language.

Colonial leaders recognized the risks of breaking from Great Britain, especially the ability to keep the lid on the aspiration and agitation of slaves and poor whites, but the Intolerable Acts impelled those leaders to form the Continental Congress—the first central political body in the thirteen colonies. The Continental Congress met in Philadelphia in 1774 and called for the British to reestablish colonial political authority along earlier lines, declared a boycott on British goods until that authority was restored (again, organized and led by women), and scheduled a meeting in the following May if deemed necessary.

The British ignored the congress, and British soldiers and Massachusetts militiamen fired at each other at Lexington and Concord in April 1775. Representatives of the thirteen colonies convened the Second Continental Congress in May 1775, and they began the effort to unite the colonies in order to raise an army. By July 1775, the independence movement was becoming a military matter, although the Continental Congress did not approve the Declaration of Independence until July 4, 1776. The members then drew up the Articles of Confederation in 1777, and the colonies/states ratified them by 1781.

But the War of Independence was long and difficult. The Continental army and local militias were a collection of small property owners willing to fight a short war. After one or two years, they went home to plant, reap, and protect their homesteads, often deserting to do so. They were increasingly replaced by anyone who could be convinced or forcibly pressed into service. Criminals, vagabonds, black freedmen, indentures, the unemployed, recent immigrants, and even slaves made up much of the ranks of the revolutionary forces.

These down-and-out men from the margins of society, ironically, might have been better soldiers than those who fit the Minutemen ideal. Soldiers from the least prosperous segments of society were used to physical hardship, including erratic availabilities of food, warm clothing, and decent shelter, no medical services, and no pay for months at a time. Civil society supported the troops poorly, despite the strenuous efforts of women who formed volunteer organizations that supplied food, clothing, and blankets. In addition, thousands of women left without male breadwinners followed the troops, washing and repairing clothing, cooking, rendering medical aid and solace, and occasionally handling weapons. These "camp followers" have often been maligned as prostitutes, but they provided invaluable services to the troops. Some women disguised themselves as men and helped to win the war.

Settlers often used the Revolutionary War as an excuse to terrorize the Indian population, and Native Americans tended to support the British, who were less of a threat than land-hungry colonial settlers. Moreover, the entire Continental Congress approved this charge against George III in the Declaration of Independence: "He [George III] has excited domestic insurrections amongst us, and has endeavored to bring on the inhabitants of our frontiers, the merciless Indian Savages, whose known rule of warfare, is an undistinguished destruction of all ages, sexes and conditions."

African American slaves also were apt to favor the British, who often offered manumission in exchange for military service and sometimes only for deserting plantations. Although the British had to be careful not to alienate slave-owning pro-British Loyalists, tens of thousands of slaves flocked to British-held areas and camps, where disease killed perhaps half. Still, four thousand former slaves accompanied Cornwallis to York-town, and at the end of the war, the British transported thousands out of the colonies as free people. On the other hand, they also returned some slaves to Loyalist masters and sent others to the Caribbean and Florida as slaves.

An estimated 20 to 30 percent of white residents remained loyal to the British crown. Many of them were among the privileged, including the Anglican clergy and New York City merchants. On the other hand, most Loyalists were commoners unwilling to follow the elite Sons of Liberty into war. These poor and middling farmers, artisans, small shopkeep-ers, sailors, and others from similar social strata knew that the Patriot leadership held them in contempt and were an unlikely source of social reforms that would move society in more egalitarian directions. Around 10 percent of the Loyalists left the United States after the war, but most of them stayed behind and moved to another area within the new United States. Local governments confiscated around 2,200 of their farms and other property.

France's and Spain's entry into the war on the colonists' side helped militarily and boosted morale, and after Cornwallis's 1781 defeat at York-town, Virginia, the war began to wind down. In the 1783 Treaty of Paris, Britain recognized the United States' independence and ownership of all lands east of the Mississippi except Florida. No one consulted Native Americans about the treaty, nor did it mention Indian lands, which came as a shock to Britain's Indian allies.

This last point underscores an important aspect of the War of Indepen-dence: It was *not* like the wars of national liberation fought in Africa and Asia after World War II. Local people fought those wars against coloniz-ers, while in the U.S. War of Independence, colonizers fought against the colonizing nation, just as those in mainland Spanish America did forty years later. U.S. and Spanish American leaders shared a common goal: the domination of indigenous peoples. The Spanish American creole leadership wanted to tighten its grip on the indigenous workforce, and the North American colonial leadership together with agrarian settlers wanted to remove the indigenous from the land. Although their proj-ects were divergent, the common ground was the desire to pursue these projects without European interference. One real divergence between the independence movements of Spanish America and British America is that Spanish American independence generally was accompanied by the abo-lition of African slavery, while in the North American colonies, political independence helped to preserve slavery.

PART II

THE NEW NATION: FROM REVOLUTION TO CIVIL WAR

2

—⚏—

Defining the New Nation

Industrial development in the northeastern United States from independence to the Civil War was similar to the British experience with
its "First Industrial Revolution." As important as it was, industrialization
was only part of the era's story, and this chapter also emphasizes the
creation of key federal foundation-building legislation, the agrarian economy, and defining the nation in terms of geography and international
politics. Advocates for continuing geographical expansion christened the
campaign "Manifest Destiny" in order to make the hunger for new territory seem inevitable, proper, and even sacred.

NEW POLITICAL INSTITUTIONS IN A NEW NATION

Three early innovative institution-building efforts laid the political foundation for the United States of America as an independent nation. After
the revolution, the physical destruction and financial chaos of the conflict
and the loss of a privileged position in British markets and British colonial
markets made for difficult economic times. Nevertheless, conventional
wisdom continued to advise that the United States was "a good place
for a poor man to settle," and access to arable land was one of the main
reasons.

Creating procedures for distributing land not yet settled by whites east
of the Mississippi River, south of Canada, and north of Florida was one
of the most pressing pieces of business for the political leadership of the
newborn United States. These were the lands that Great Britain had ceded

to the United States in the Treaty of Paris (1783) and that individual states had ceded to the national confederation. Needless to say, indigenous peoples and slaves were not part of the deliberations.

The Northwest Ordinances

Thomas Jefferson was the principal architect of the Northwest Ordinances of 1785 and 1787, which initially pertained to the lands east of the Mississippi River and north of the Ohio River—the future states of Ohio, Indiana, Illinois, Michigan, Wisconsin, and eastern Minnesota, or the "Upper Midwest." The ordinances drew on the systematic manner in which the Massachusetts colony had distributed land. National officials were to survey standard-sized parcels and sell them, reserving some for civic functions and education. The ordinances also reflected Jefferson's commitment to small farms and a yeomanry-based society; this goal lay behind his desire to set low prices for land so that it would be available to a broad cross section of the population. Alexander Hamilton, soon to be the first U.S. secretary of treasury, disagreed and argued that the land should be sold at high prices in order to finance the indebted national confederation that had no powers of taxation. He lost that argument.

While the ordinances' prescribed procedures were orderly, the actual process was chaotic due to logistical and bureaucratic difficulties, squatting, bounty land warrants issued to veterans of the War of Independence, and an orgy of speculation aggravated by below-market land prices. One parcel might be sold and resold several times within days of its initial purchase ("flipping," in modern parlance).

Native Americans in the way of white settlement were decimated. After an initial setback in the Ohio River valley, U.S. troops defeated the Miami, the Sauk, and allied tribes in a military push culminating in the Battle of Tippecanoe (1811), led by William Henry Harrison, a future U.S. president. By 1830, most of the Native Americans in the Ohio River valley had been pushed west of the Mississippi River.

For white settlers, the cost of buying land was a small part of the expense in starting a farm. Clearing trees from forested land, breaking up the hard, thick sod of the plains, digging wells, and acquiring buildings, wagons, tools, and equipment could cost three times the price of the land, without even counting several months of provisions before the farm began producing. Renting land was less attractive than buying, but for families unable to afford the expense, tenancy was available in areas where speculators had acquired large amounts of land in anticipation of profiting from rising land prices and were willing to rent in the interim.

The ordinances contained important policies that went beyond the distribution of land. The 1787 version provided the procedure and criteria for admitting territories as new states with the same rights and powers of the original states. It specified the governance structure of those territories, set ownership of fifty or more acres of land as the minimum needed to vote, and guaranteed residents in those territories such rights as religious freedom, habeas corpus, and trial by jury. The Articles of Confederation had not guaranteed these rights, but the Bill of Rights of the U.S. Constitution would soon include them. Finally, the ordinances outlawed slavery in the northwest territories but not in territories south of the Ohio River.

Despite procedural difficulties and problematic distribution patterns, the Northwest Ordinances, with minor adjustments, remained the guiding framework for the admission of thirty-one future states into the Union. The first half of the nineteenth century saw an immense expansion of the geographical reach of the United States, including President Jefferson's Louisiana Purchase from Napoleon Bonaparte in 1803.[1] Table 2.1 records the acquisition of territory in these years. We will see how fraught was the process of admitting new states and balancing the U.S. Senate between free and slave states in the next chapter.

The End to the Articles of Confederation and a New U.S. Constitution

Important segments of the political leadership became convinced that the Articles of Confederation were an inadequate framework for governance. Financing the war had demonstrated the need for a more robust central government and one with taxing authority. States implemented **tariffs** on goods traded across state lines and issued money that immediately declined in purchasing power. On the international level, small semiautonomous states had little bargaining power with powerful European nations and were vulnerable to being picked off one state at a time.

These were real concerns, but elites were also haunted by what state legislatures were capable of doing with their considerable authority. While some of the new state constitutions, drawn up after the Declaration of Independence, widened the franchise, the frightening tendency was that even when the franchises were unchanged, common people began voting for common people as their representatives. This was different from the elections to colonial assemblies, dominated by the well-to-do, and the change expressed the empowerment promoted by the mobilizations to support the War of Independence. As ordinary yeomen and artisans were elected to the governing bodies and more delegates came from the western portions of states, traditions of deference to one's "betters" weakened, and a strong populist strain ran through the state legislatures.

Table 2.1. U.S. Land Acquisitions between 1790 and 1853

Year	Location and Source	Estimated Size (mi^2)	Cost
1783	Original thirteen colonies plus the land east of the Mississippi River included in treaty with Great Britain recognizing U.S. independence	889,000	War of Independence
1803	Louisiana Purchase from France, an area that now includes parts or all of fifteen states from Louisiana on the Gulf to the Canadian border, where it stretched from the Mississippi River to the Rocky Mountains	827,000	$15,000,000
1819	Spain ceded Florida and the Gulf Coast to the Mississippi River after the area was handed back and forth between Spain and Great Britain	72,000	U.S. government assumed $5,000,000 of U.S. citizens' claims against Spain
1845	Texas, seceded from Mexico as an independent republic in 1836, became a state of the United States	390,000	
1846	Treaty with Great Britain settled conflicting claims over the Oregon Territory	286,000	
1848	United States took from Mexico all the land from Texas to California	529,000	The Mexican War (1846–1848) plus $15,000,000
1853	The Gadsden Purchase of now southern Arizona and New Mexico	30,000	$10,000,000
1867	Broke from the Crimean War (1853–1856), Russia wanted to sell Alaska	591,004	$7,200,000
Total		**3,614,004**	

The astonishing legislation in New Jersey that briefly enfranchised women (1776–1807) might have been seen as solid proof of the need to rein in state powers. But threatening economic policies were more salient for the elites. State legislatures implemented such disturbing policies as giving debtors relief through moratoria on debt payments and foreclosures and by allowing payment on public and private debt with discounted state-printed money. The states had conceded to the national government control over the distribution of public (Native American) lands, but once that land was distributed, state governments could regulate its subsequent sales. Although indebted tobacco planters benefited from pro-debtor policies, the policies still jolted the immediate interests of creditors, land speculators, and other propertied elites and posed a long-run threat to the inviolability of contracts and private property on which their prosperity and status depended.

These worries led to the Constitutional Convention that convened in 1787 to amend the Articles of Confederation. Instead, this body produced a new document, much different from the Articles of Confederation, in four months of sessions for which no official record was kept.

Joyce Appleby (1987: 799, 804) writes:

> The emphasis that the authors of the *Federalist Papers* put on the weakness of the Articles of Confederation has obscured the fact that it was the strength and vigor of state governments that had created the sense of crisis among the old revolutionary elite. . . . Article 1, Section 10, of the Constitution indicates just how much was taken away from the states. Listed there are the disallowed powers that had wreaked such havoc in post-revolutionary politics: the power to coin money, to emit bills of credit, to make anything but gold and silver coin **legal tender**, to pass laws impairing the obligation of contracts, or to lay any import or export duties.

In addition, Article I, Section 8 reserved the right to establish "uniform Laws on the subject of Bankruptcies throughout the United States" to the U.S. Congress, thus prohibiting states from helping the indebted to escape the hold of creditors.

The Constitution put in place a new system of national governance. The U.S. House of Representatives was to be elected by free male voters, and a state's representation in the House was to be proportional to its population, as determined by a census taken every decade. Although free women were counted for representation, they could not vote (except briefly in New Jersey). There was no reference to women or gender in the Constitution because it was taken for granted that voters and elected officials would all be male.

Article I, Section 2 of the Constitution stated that the number of a state's U.S. representatives "shall be determined by adding to the whole

Number of free Persons, including those bound to Service for a Term of Years, and excluding Native Americans not taxed, three-fifths of all other Persons." (As with the whole class of women, neither the words "slave" nor "slavery" appeared in the U.S. Constitution or Bill of Rights.) At the eve of the Civil War, the three-fifths formula boosted the size of slave-state populations—and therefore the size of state delegations to the U.S. House of Representatives—by an average of 25 percent. In South Carolina and Mississippi, with more slaves than whites, the increase was 90 percent and 74 percent, respectively.[2] In addition to inflating slave-state representation in the House, Article II, Section 1 carried this effect over to presidential elections by declaring that the number of presidential electors will equal the number of U.S. representatives and senators.

The importation of African slaves was to end in 1808, but the internal slave trade was not regulated in any way. Native Americans were to be dealt with as "nations." Among the new document's striking features was its unambiguously secular nature, but its principal thrust was to strengthen the federal government at the expense of the states.[3]

Each state legislature was to elect two U.S. senators, a compromise that made the Constitution more palatable to small states in the same way that the three-fifths rule made it more attractive to slave states. Even with these compromises, ratification of the Constitution was not automatic. The Continental-Confederation Congress, the national legislature that governed under the Articles of Confederation (1774–1789), did not endorse the new Constitution but allowed it to be sent to the specially constituted state conventions to debate ratification. Nine states had to ratify the Constitution before it became the law for all thirteen states.

During the ratification process, Alexander Hamilton, James Madison, and John Jay published eighty-five letters in newspapers urging the adoption of the Constitution by the states. These letters, known collectively as *The Federalist Papers*, touched on most of the shortcomings of the Articles of Confederation except the unruliness of state legislatures. Anti-federalists were also active and articulate in their efforts to influence the state conventions.

Shays's Rebellion helped the arguments of the federalists. Many farmers returned from the Revolutionary War to find that they were deeply in debt, and soon after the war, creditors began to foreclose on the farms and jail the farmers as debtors. Eastern Massachusetts merchants and bankers had not been infected with the populist plague evident elsewhere, and western Massachusetts farmers' anger boiled over in late 1786. Farmers organized armed groups that disrupted official proceedings in Worcester, Springfield, Concord, and several other towns, and in January 1786, the farmers attacked the Springfield Armory.

Members of the Continental Congress found themselves unable to mobilize troops against the farmers, and eastern Massachusetts elite themselves had to do the mobilizing of a contingent of troops that defeated Shays's Rebellion in February 1787. Similar outbreaks occurred in New Jersey, South Carolina, Virginia, and Pennsylvania, shaking the propertied classes by demonstrating that the Confederation government, with no taxing powers and no standing army, was powerless to put down such threats to privilege. This helped the federalists to prevail, especially after the federalists promised to attach to the Constitution a Bill of Rights modeled on the Virginia Constitution, restraining federal power and protecting individual rights.

The New Hampshire state convention became the ninth to ratify the Constitution, and when James Madison presented the Bill of Rights as the first ten amendments to the new Constitution, Virginia and New York also ratified the Constitution. The U.S. Congress set March 4, 1789, as the date on which the new Constitution became the nation's fundamental law. Soon after, North Carolina and Rhode Island ratified the document. On March 4, 1789, the U.S. Congress declared it to be ratified and the law of the land, and by 1791, the Bill of Rights became a permanent part of the new Constitution.

It is remarkable that the Constitution allowed only the House of Representatives to be directly elected by voters. Electors, selected by whatever manner a state decided, elected the president, state legislators elected U.S. senators, and the president appointed the federal judiciary, although Senate confirmation is necessary. It was this distancing of the federal government from popular participation that animated the anti-federalists, who argued the Constitution would promote increasing economic and political inequalities.

While the Bill of Rights enshrined freedom of speech, assembly, and religion, the early years of judicial review—the ability of courts to void laws that they determined to be unconstitutional—further diluted popular rule. In *Marbury v. Madison* (1803), the Supreme Court under Chief Justice John Marshall affirmed this principle, which had already been practiced in both state and federal courts. Its formal articulation in 1803 meant that appointed judges rather than elected legislators decided some of the nation's most important issues.

The power of judicial review enabled the Supreme Court to clarify the status of contracts and property rights in the postrevolutionary era and secure the continuance of the prewar social order. In *Dartmouth College v. Woodward* (1819), the court confirmed that contracts and titles to property from before the revolution, even those issued by the British king, were still valid after the revolution, thus strengthening the social status quo.

This ruling, needless to say, did not include treaties made by Native Americans with the British.

The U.S. Constitution did not put an end to state- and community-level activism in the economy, and both were significant sources of economic policy making until the Civil War. In addition to taking a major role in transportation improvements, state legislatures lessened the long-run concentration of wealth by abolishing the inheritance restrictions of primogeniture (all to the oldest son) and entail (only directly related family members eligible to inherit). Many states also established women's legal right to hold property protected from their husband's creditors, conduct commerce, marry without religious ritual, and divorce. Finally, a number of states provided a homestead exemption that protected certain portions of a debtor's assets from creditors' claims.

The Vagaries of Central Banking

In the first decade of independence, the political leadership made impressive progress in forming durable political institutions and procedures that worked for them. On the other hand, the federal leadership's creativity did not result in the invention of a resilient institution capable of regulating and stabilizing the financial system.

Alexander Hamilton was adamant about the need for a central bank that would service the financial needs of the federal government and impose some order on the financial system dominated by casually monitored state-chartered banks. The U.S. Congress issued a twenty-year charter for such an institution, and Hamilton talked a reluctant President George Washington into signing it.

The First Bank of the United States opened in 1791. It kept the deposits of the federal government, was a source of credit for the government, and through its branches competed with state-chartered banks for private deposits and borrowers. The First Bank also had a regulatory function, performed by turning in state-chartered bank notes and redeeming them for the species (silver or gold) that banks were supposed to hold in order to back the notes. The policy of redeeming notes reduced state-chartered banks' ability to extend credit through the issuance of paper notes without silver or gold backing, and state-chartered banks resented the discipline and limitations imposed by the First Bank's policy. State-chartered banks also objected to being closed out of the federal government's financial business and to the competition from a large and powerful branch bank in their own locales.

Farmers throughout the nation who were convinced that the First Bank reduced their access to inexpensive credit were another source of hostility to the First Bank, and the opposition succeeded in blocking the renewal of the First Bank's charter in 1811. The War of 1812 began the next year, and the financial chaos that ensued changed many people's minds. Congress issued a twenty-year charter to the Second Bank of the United States in 1817. The same resentments against the central bank soon resurfaced, and in the twenty years of the Second Bank, the agrarian interests in the South and Upper Midwest became more influential. Although renewal of the charter passed both House and Senate in 1837, President Andrew Jackson vetoed it on behalf of rural voters. That same year, the Panic of 1837—one of the most severe financial reverses before the Civil War—caused the collapse of overextended banks, taking many well-run banks with them.

From 1837 until 1863, bank regulation devolved to the states, whose rules and enforcement varied widely. In this era of free banking, the farther a transaction using bank-issued notes occurred from the issuing institution, the more the notes were discounted. The need to fix the unstable financial system would plague the economy for decades.

FINDING THEIR PLACE IN THE WORLD

The French Revolution (1789) and subsequent war between Britain and France (1793–1815) partially offset the economic effects from the physical destruction of the War of Independence and from losing preferred access to British markets. Exporters from the United States—a neutral nation—had access to belligerents' markets, and since much of British manufacturing capacity was devoted to the war effort, U.S. manufacturing gained some protection from British imports.

Neutral or not, British and French navies constantly harassed U.S. shipping. Between 1803 and 1807, the British seized over five hundred U.S. ships and cargoes, and always in need of sailors, pressed U.S. sailors into the British navy. In retaliation, the United States passed the Embargo Act in 1807, which closed U.S. ports to *all* shipping, U.S. and foreign—an exaggerated reaction. The embargo lasted fourteen months, and in spite of some smuggling, it damaged U.S. exporters, merchants, and shippers, although it did encourage U.S. textile and iron goods manufacturing.

The next step was to declare war against Great Britain in 1812, sinking any claim of United States neutrality. U.S. troops invaded Canada, won a couple of major battles on the Great Lakes, captured York (now Toronto, then the capital of Canada), and burned some public buildings. A year later, British troops took Washington, DC, and burned the Capitol, the White House, and the Library of Congress. At the end of 1814, the British (still at war with France) and U.S. representatives signed a peace treaty, and two weeks later, U.S. troops won the Battle of New Orleans—the largest battle of the war. News of the war's end traveled slowly.

Another series of major events in the Americas, ones in which the United States was a bystander, were the wars of independence in Spanish America. Brazil and Central America became independent through diplomacy, supported by Great Britain, but most Spanish American colonies had to wage bloody and ruinous wars. By 1825, all mainland Spanish colonies had become independent nations, and the United States was the first nation to extend formal diplomatic recognition to them. Continental European powers were uneasy about the new nations' republican and antimonarchical inclinations, and they encouraged Spain to reconquer its former colonies. These machinations, along with the southern expansion of Russian territory in Alaska, triggered President James Monroe's declaration that the United States would not tolerate European territorial ambitions in the Americas.

The Monroe Doctrine was a bold but not particularly frightening assertion by a small nation, but Great Britain did not challenge it directly; it was interested in the expanded investment and trade opportunities in newly independent Latin America. Northern U.S. producers and merchants also were interested in the new market possibilities, but they were constrained by U.S. southern planters' nervousness about Spanish America, both because of Spanish America's antislavery tendencies and its nations' potential to be competitive producers of cotton, rice, and sugar.

The difficulty of establishing close relations with Latin American nations irritated northern U.S. manufacturers, but they also had a more severe constraint. After the end of the Napoleonic Wars in 1815, manufactured imports from Great Britain again flowed into the United States, damaging local manufactures. But in considering this, it is important to understand that for all practical purposes, there was no national U.S. market in the early nineteenth century. The vast majority of the U.S. population was dispersed; in the countryside, average population densities in 1790 were around nine people per square mile, while in England, the corresponding figure was around one hundred. The urbanization figures underscore the emptiness of the new nation: 5 percent of the U.S. population lived in communities that could be counted as cities and towns, and 30 percent of the English population resided in cities and towns.

Since transportation costs were prohibitively expensive except for those living along the Atlantic coast and navigable rivers, many if not most of the rural population were involved in markets by only occasionally selling surplus produce, buying marketed commodities, and exchanging labor, products, and equipment at local levels.

A TRANSPORTATION TRANSFORMATION

State and local governments were sources of most initiatives to improve transportation, although private entrepreneurs were the principal builders of turnpikes in the early nineteenth century. Few toll roads were profitable, and improvements in water transportation made greater contributions to commerce and economy. The use of steamships on rivers from the second and third decades of the nineteenth century reduced the cost and increased the speed of transporting goods up such major rivers as the Hudson, Ohio, Mississippi, and Missouri and contributed to the growth of Albany, St. Louis, Cincinnati, Louisville, and Pittsburgh. Since there were over twenty thousand miles of navigable rivers in the antebellum United States, the fuller use of natural inland waterways was a major step in integrating the new nation. Steamships soon lowered transport rates on large lakes, along the sea coasts, and in international trade.

Failing to obtain federal aid, New York State, with help from British investors, financed the 363-mile Erie Canal. The canal opened in 1825 and linked Buffalo on Lake Erie with Troy and Albany on the Hudson River and thus with the Atlantic Ocean. The Erie Canal lowered per-ton transportation costs from Buffalo to New York City by 90 percent and established New York City as the premier U.S. port. The canal that linked the Ohio River with Lake Erie in 1833 was another example of connecting major waterways and large regions with each other. Nearly four thousand miles of canals were operating by the 1850s, with three-quarters of the financing coming from state and local governments, borrowed mostly from British investors.

The principal canal networks connected the Northeastern Seaboard with the Upper Midwest. The low cost of canal and steamboat shipping made it feasible to convey even bulky, low-priced goods long distances. This put northeastern and mid-Atlantic grain farmers at a competitive disadvantage in respect to grain from the rich soils of the Ohio River valley and beyond. The beleaguered farmers had to switch to dairying or vegetable and fruit crops to remain viable, but instead they often left farming or migrated west. New England farmers were most likely to migrate, and recurrent sightings of stone walls in deep New England forests are modern-day reminders of those abandoned farms.

The canals were successful, but then came the railroads. The first railroad in the United States—the Baltimore and Ohio—opened in 1830 with a locomotive imported from Great Britain. Thirty years later, the United States boasted over thirty thousand miles of tracks with a total expenditure five times greater than that invested in canal construction. Like the canals, most railroad lines were located in the northern regions of the nation and facilitated east-west transport, and Chicago, with four thousand miles of track converging there by 1860, became one of the major transportation hubs. Rail competition led to the closure of many transportation canals and the cancellation of new canal projects. [4]

Railroads were more flexible than canals because they could move goods and people over a variety of terrains with fewer problems posed by mountains, water levels, freezing weather, and transshipments. They reduced overland travel time on the order of thirty times, and it was the greater speed that made rail travel attractive to people. But railroad freight revenue exceeded passenger revenue by the end of the 1850s, also the point when the volume of freight sent by rail surpassed that of canals. River transport continued to be widely used.

The development of transportation facilities enabled the U.S. Post Office to expand mail service to new areas and to reduce delivery times, and every town and village wanted a post office. When the federal government granted a post office to a village, its residents knew that there would either be a railroad stop at their village or at least regular, subsidized stagecoach service along a post road.[5] The number of post offices grew from 903 in 1800 to 28,496 in 1860, a growth that accommodated wider and faster distribution of the exploding numbers of newspapers, magazines, and books made possible by technical advances and lower costs in papermaking and printing.

The telegraph was a spectacular change in communication. It complemented the expansion of the railroads by enabling railroads to coordinate and monitor schedules. The railroad companies often allowed a telegraph company to string lines along railroads' rights of way in exchange for discounted service fees.

There were over fifty telegraph companies in the early 1850s, when a group of Rochester, New York, businessmen began consolidating small companies into what became Western Union. This consolidation led to better efficiencies and improved service, facilitating the increased use of telegraph service for money orders, business news, newspaper reporting, personal messages, and conduct of war. Western Union completed the first coast-to-coast line across the nation in 1861, leading the U.S. Post Office to cancel the Pony Express.

The availability of relatively inexpensive and reliable transportation of goods and information made it feasible and desirable for regions to become more specialized and rely on products no longer produced within the region. These great strides in transportation and communication between the Northeast and the Upper Midwest supported a trade that surpassed either region's trade with the South in the 1850s. By that time, the U.S. economy was generating more autonomous rhythms in northern regions, and cotton price changes were no longer such an important influence on the business cycle, which continued to fluctuate between prosperity and recession. There were seven business cycles between 1812 and 1861, and three (1819, 1837, and 1857) were severe enough to be labeled depressions.

COMPETITIVE CAPITALIST INDUSTRIAL DEVELOPMENT

The initial process of U.S. industrial development occurred in an era in which industrial growth was led by large numbers of small firms producing wage goods—inexpensive products for working-class families—and buying and selling in competitive markets.[6] This form of industrial development, which I call Competitive Capitalism, lasted from around the middle of the eighteenth century to the middle of the nineteenth century, when another type of industrial development became predominant.

England's "First Industrial Revolution" was the template for Competitive Capitalist industrial growth. The Industrial Revolution in England was an epoch-making process that affected the entire world. Although that development occurred in a context that generated species differences between English and U.S. industrial development, the processes' patterns and textures were of the same genus and make it worthwhile to look briefly at the English experience.

England: 1750–1850

One of the first things to notice is that the First Industrial Revolution did not occur in Portugal, with its successful colonial commerce in spices and sugar, or in Spain, which in terms of total revenues profited immensely from its colonies. Rather, it occurred in England, where colonial trade yielded some benefits but on a modest scale.

The principal contributions that captive, monopolistic colonial trade with the American colonies and India made to English industrialization were in creating mercantile and planter fortunes, expanding commodity and credit markets, stimulating English shipbuilding and auxiliary industries, and aiding in the dissolution of precapitalist social relations. These changes enhanced the relative openness of preindustrial English society and allowed (and forced) greater social, geographical, and occupational mobility. Factors such as these, rather than England's possession of lucrative colonies, enabled a capitalist dynamic to evolve within England and propel it into world industrial leadership.

Changes in the organization of English agriculture were critical. The English Civil War of the seventeenth century confirmed the power of capitalist agriculture by destroying vestiges of feudal bondage and enabling greater mobility. Subsequent agricultural growth increased agricultural employment, and the eighteenth-century consolidation of small plots into larger holdings through enclosure meant this increased employment was typically wage work.

In his inimitable style, Marx ([1857–1858] 1974: 507) described the process of creating "free" wage labor in English capitalism:

> [Workers were] a mass that was free in a double sense, free from the old relations of clientship, bondage and servitude, and secondly free of all belonging and possessions, and of every objective, material form of being, *free of all property*; dependent on the sale of its labor capacity or on begging, vagabondage

and robbery as its only sources of income. It is a matter of historic record that they tried the latter first, but were driven off this road by gallows, stocks and whippings, onto the narrow path to the labor market.

These changes also permitted a merchant-dominated putting-out system to flourish in the countryside. In the putting-out system, merchants contracted with individual rural households to work with, say, yarn supplied by merchants to produce cloth, or cloth supplied by merchants to produce apparel. Although this allowed merchant-entrepreneurs to avoid urban guild restrictions, it limited merchants' supervision of workers and materials.

Some entrepreneurs responded to this lack of control with an organizational innovation that brought workers together into sheds where they and the materials could be more closely monitored. Even though the eighteenth-century factory organization of production increased technical efficiency little, bringing people together for the purposes of production did encourage rearranging the ways in which work was done. The resulting divisions of labor facilitated supervision and the introduction of water-powered machinery and equipment.

These organizational innovations discouraged household production, and the countryside became a growing market for cheap consumer goods flowing from the factories. And it was goods consumed by working-class families that were the leading branches of production in the English Industrial Revolution. But after the Napoleonic Wars ended in 1815, cotton textile firms had the confidence to rely heavily on exporting, and cotton textile exports soon made up more than half of cotton textile production and more than half of English exports.

Factory-made cotton textiles were crude and inexpensive, and the more expensive consumer goods for upper-class markets continued to be hand made by artisans, local and foreign. Competitive markets were also evident in the early iron goods industry, which produced pots and pans, stoves, and other wage goods.[7]

The English countryside also served as a source of the large numbers of factory workers required for producing manufactures in the eighteenth century. Relative prosperity in eighteenth-century agriculture also supported a population growth greater than agriculture's own labor requirements. The wage-labor system in the countryside both allowed and compelled people to migrate to the cities where factories were located after the steam engine freed production from dependence on waterpower. In these industrial cities, men, women, and children from the countryside joined the Irish and ruined artisans to supply the voracious labor needs of this form of industrial growth without putting upward pressure on wages. Moreover, these urban workers also purchased cheap consumer goods. The agriculture-to-industry dynamic, then, was a crucial element in English industrial development, supporting industrial growth by supplying food, labor, product markets, foreign exchange, and some capital for the nascent industrial sector.

The factory form of industrial production prevailed, but its control passed from the hands of merchants to a mixed group that became England's industrial bourgeoisie. The most important qualities for successful entrepreneurship seldom included an acceptable family name, wealth, proper dress and accent, and other accouterments of preindustrial social status. The principal requirement for entrepreneurship was the ability to deal with the vagaries of competitive markets and machines and to organize and control a workforce in factory settings.

Since financial barriers to entry in factory production were low, industrial entrepreneurship was a vehicle for social mobility. The size and heterogeneity of the bourgeoisie enabled them, occasionally with working-class allies, to wield formidable political power and to elevate aggressive individualism and materialism into the national ideology.[8] The logic of the Competitive Capitalist phase, the need for foreign industrial **inputs** (for example, cotton and iron) and cheap foodstuffs for an urbanizing population, and the industrial bourgeoisie's strength in domestic politics and international markets led to reducing or dismantling most of England's own tariffs and other restrictions on international trade and investment.

England's decisive superiority in technology and productivity in factory-made manufactures led to an overseas economic expansion in which England pressed nations to sign free-trade treaties and, when they were reluctant, to coerce them with military force. The two Opium Wars (1839–1842, 1856–1860) in China and the resulting unequal treaties exemplify what John Gallagher and Ronald Robinson (1953) dubbed "free-trade imperialism." The English government in these years preferred informal empire with unrestricted commercial access rather than extending its formal empire with the attendant costs, risks, and responsibilities.[9]

English economists and policy makers represented international free trade as beneficial for all participants. But free trade was also a means to maintain and enhance England's industrial preeminence. Foreigners interested in promoting their own nations' industrial growth, such as Alexander Hamilton and Henry Carey in the United States and Friedrich List in Germany, were aware of this side of the policy and advocated national barriers to shelter their own domestic manufactures from British competition.

Competitive Capitalism was not exclusively English, but in continental Europe at the time of the English Industrial Revolution, the path of Competitive Capitalist industrial development was impeded by the social relations of agricultural production (peasantry and serfdom), the organization of political authority, and wars and revolutions. In the northeastern states of the United States, Competitive Capitalism became predominant in the social and economic formation, but on the world stage, England was definitely the workshop of the world.

U.S. Northeast, 1800–1860

The principal story of early nineteenth-century industrialization in the United States was the growth of manufacturing in the Northeast. Over 70 percent of U.S. manufacturing employment in 1850 and 1860 and 75 percent of the national cotton textile output was located in the region. There was considerable manufacturing production in the Upper Midwest oriented around processing raw materials (e.g., flour, lumber, and shingles), but the region became an important industrial center only after the Civil War.

A number of factors favored the Northeast as a locale for the fledgling manufacturing sector. The availability of waterpower throughout the region was an obvious attraction, as were higher rates of urbanization, wage labor, and literacy. The transportation infrastructure (roads, canals, ports, and railroads) built to distribute foreign-produced imports to the rest of the country was ready-made for distributing regionally produced commodities. In addition, the existence of credit institutions developed for international commerce and the Northeast's increasing lead in regional per-capita income were appealing. Finally, a poor regional agriculture facilitated the recruitment of a factory labor force of agrarian men, women, and children, often replacing more skilled craft workers. Women's mastery of spinning and weaving made them ideal—and cheap—employees in the production of textiles.

The region's agriculture went into a steeper decline as a result of the Erie Canal, releasing more potential industrial workers. And the mostly Irish immigrants fleeing famine at home in the late 1840s and 1850s went principally to northeastern cities and augmented the regional labor supply.

In colonial times, manufacturing was limited to shipbuilding, processing raw materials (flour, rum, candles, lumber, beer), and some crude iron products. Early tariffs, the Embargo Act (1807), and the War of 1812 led to limited expansion of domestic manufacturing, but despite these uncertain beginnings, industry accounted for more than one-fifth of total U.S. production by 1860. Cotton textiles were an important leading industry, but as table 2.2 shows, the strength of the industrial sector in 1860 was its wide array of products, processes, and markets. At that time, no one branch of manufacturing represented even 7 percent of total manufacturing **value added**, and the ten largest branches of manufacturing constituted less than half. (The glossary contains a definition and example of "value added.")

Table 2.2. **Principal Lines of U.S. Manufacturing Production, 1860**

	Value Added		Employment	
	$1,000,000	*Percentage*	*1,000*	*Percentage*
Cotton textiles	55	6.7	115	7.8
Lumber	54	6.6	76	5.2
Boots and shoes	49	6.0	123	8.3
Flour and meal	40	4.9	28	1.8
Men's clothing	37	4.5	115	7.8
Iron	36	4.4	50	3.4
Machinery	33	4.0	41	2.8
Woolens	25	3.1	61	4.1
Carriages and wagons	24	2.9	37	2.5
Leather	23	2.8	23	1.6
Total U.S. Manufacturing	815	100.0	1,474	100.0

Source: Stanley L. Engerman and Kenneth L. Sokoloff, "Technology and Industrialization, 1790–1914," in *The Cambridge Economic History of the United States*, Vol. 2: *The Long Nineteenth Century*, ed. Stanley L. Engerman and Robert E. Gallman (New York: Cambridge University Press, 2000), 376.

New York, Pennsylvania, and Massachusetts led in iron castings, such as stoves, steam engines, and nails. Rails for railroads were initially imported, but local rolling mills were beginning to supply the domestic market for rails by the 1850s. The invention and use of sewing machines drew apparel and boots and shoes into factory settings.

Industrial growth in England and the U.S. Northeast was similar in that industrial development in both nations emerged from productive and expanding agricultural sectors that served as markets and supplied foodstuffs and other raw materials for the industrializing region. The agricultural sectors, however, were not organized in similar ways; the predominance of slavery in the U.S. South and family farms in the Northeast and Upper Midwest contrasted with England's more capitalist agriculture.

In both nations, the large numbers of small firms producing wage goods for working-class families were technically uncomplicated by the standards of even fifty or sixty years later. As in England, these early U.S. manufacturing firms required only low levels of capitalization, and often merchants partnered with artisans who possessed technical knowledge and workbench skills to establish a manufacturing facility. They often began by self-financing, grew by reinvesting profits, and experienced high rates of business failure.

At the same time, there were definite differences between English industrialization and U.S. industrialization. Some of the differences stemmed from the fifty-year lag of U.S. industrial beginnings behind England, and others had to do with individual features of the two nations.

Because England was already becoming an industrial nation, U.S. observers like Alexander Hamilton could evaluate the desirability and prospects of U.S. industrialization more clearly than experimenting leaders in mid-eighteenth-century England. At a more concrete level, the innovation of the wage-labor factory system was well established in England, and its use in the United States did not grow out of the putting-out system, which in U.S. rural areas was not as common. The mechanization of cotton textile production, the refinement of steam engines, more efficient production of iron, and the development of precision machinery for working wood and iron were also well along as U.S. industrial development was just beginning. While being able to "borrow" these technologies was advantageous for U.S. industrial entrepreneurs, some aspects of U.S. industrial production in the first half of the nineteenth century appeared to be behind production techniques in England.[10]

Waterpower still accounted for about half of all U.S. industrial power even in 1860, far more than in England, with its many steam engines. This did not reflect backwardness as much as it expressed the abundance and inexpensiveness of New England waterpower, made even more efficient by substituting water-driven turbines for water wheels. Many waterpowered firms stayed in the countryside near their inexpensive energy source and developed a more paternalistic style of employment. An outstanding example was the Lowell Mills, an integrated mill complex in Massachusetts built on the Merrimac River in the second quarter of the nineteenth century. Employers supplied supervised dormitories and wholesome recreation and study opportunities for unmarried women from nearby farms, whom they expected to stay only a few years before leaving the mill to marry.

Even when U.S. mill owners used steam engines, they often used charcoal to fuel them rather than the coal or coke used in England. Like waterpower, wood in the United States was so plentiful and cheap that people used it anytime they could. Lumber and wood products were still the second-largest branch of manufacturing by value added in 1860 (see table 2.2), while England's forests had practically been used up by the turn of the nineteenth century. U.S. mills, therefore, continued to use charcoal for fuel and substitute wood for iron in construction, machine parts, clock movements, and other functions that iron or steel performed in England.

When surveyors found major coal beds in Pennsylvania and the Upper Midwest, manufacturers turned to coal and coke to fuel steam engines as well as provide heat for the production of ceramics, glass, iron, and iron castings. The twenty million tons of U.S. coal mined in 1860 was almost twenty-three times the volume mined in 1830. And again reflecting the availability of natural resources, U.S. operators preferred the dangerous, fuel-hungry, high-pressure steam engines to the less-fuel-using, low-pressure steam engines favored in England.

The ready availability of U.S. natural resources also contributed to making one **factor of production**—labor—relatively scarce. As noted in the previous chapter, rural population density in England at the end of the eighteenth century was around one hundred persons per square mile, while in the new United States, it was around nine per square mile. In rural labor recruitment for rural manufacturing firms, just as in Upper Midwest agriculture, wage labor was expensive because of its scarcity as well as workers' options to move west. These conditions encouraged employers in the Northeast and Upper Midwest to try to replace workers with machines. While there was some movement in this direction in the early nineteenth century, employers in the 1850s made great strides in substituting machines for workers, particularly for skilled workers.

In the Northeast, urban areas were important markets for domestic manufactures. Along with workers in export and related activities, those needed in complex urban settings to supply police, transport, garbage, education, retail, and other services constituted sizable markets for wage goods. But northeastern cities, and especially New York City, possessed dynamics different from the countryside. The cities tended to be labor-surplus economies brimming over with journeymen and masters ruined by inexpensive New England factory products, free blacks, white immigrants who poured into New York as the principal port of entry, and failed agriculturists whose misery forced them into urban migration. These men tried to squeeze a living out of work as day labor on the docks, construction work, and odd jobs.

The degradation and squalor of the majority of the New York City workforce paralleled that of London and Liverpool, and in general, the urban scene in the North was bleak in the 1850s. Massive immigrations from 1848 forced down urban wages, increased unemployment, and caused declining levels of health and life expectancy—cholera and other severe diseases became endemic throughout the urban North. Both the Irish and free African Americans were subject to racism and exclusion, with blacks always at the very bottom.

Single mothers whose male partners/husbands had died, become unemployable due to disease, accident, and alcohol, or deserted the family were a substantial component of the pool of underemployed and unemployed workers. In New York City, expensive rents and the lack of waterpower retarded factory development, but the availability of these desperate women was an incentive for a system of apparel production ("outside work"), which resembled the putting-out system in rural England. The sewing machine, however, did encourage some employers to draw women into centralized sweatshops ("inside work").

Working women's children spent their time in the streets scavenging, pilfering, begging, and playing. City authorities and agents of private charitable organizations rounded up random throngs of children, labeled them orphans, and shipped them west on "orphan trains" to become agricultural laborers in the hinterland. This practice lasted from 1850 through the 1920s.

One bright spot of urban working life was that by the 1840s and 1850s, it was becoming possible for single young women to support themselves in New York City without having to work as domestic servants, the chief occupation of women working outside their homes, or as prostitutes.[11] According to Christine Stansell (1987: 91), the growing sex-segregated occupations included those such as "factory girl [making paper boxes, hoopskirts, shirts and collars, umbrellas and parasols, ladies' cloaks], shopgirl [retail clerk], milliner, dressmaker, book folder, map colorer, [and artificial] flower maker." These opportunities drew voluntary migrants from the countryside to escape oppressive families and narrow horizons, and they contributed to the creation of a lively singles scene centered in the Bowery.

The social mobility experienced by the English industrial bourgeoisie was more disruptive to traditional social and cultural patterns in England than in the more fluid Northeast and Upper Midwest in the United States. On the other hand, the rigid caste system in the U.S. South was more extreme than England's aristocratic order, but the geographic separation embodied in law helped mitigate frictions between regions.[12]

U.S. tariffs did not disappear or even decline with industrialization. The first U.S. tariff was enacted in 1789, the first year of the U.S. Constitution, which granted taxing powers to the federal government. These first duties provided revenue for the indebted federal government, and except for the Civil War and a couple of years of exceptional land sales, tariffs continued to be the source of 80 to 90 percent of federal government revenue up to World War I. Before the Civil War, tariffs also began to offer deliberate protection to domestic cotton textile production, making the tariff tax structure more regressive by targeting wage goods.

Despite differences in tariff policy, the confluence of Anglo American social and political thought was significant. The English Industrial Revolution produced powerful theory and ideology along with cotton textiles and iron products, and the U.S. experience, in appearing to confirm its core ideas, proved to be a fertile ground for the ideas' elaboration, refinement, and ossification. This system of ideas held economic freedom as one of its central themes, and it was a freedom defined negatively in the tradition of classical liberal theory.

Materialism and individualism were elevated into a creed in England, while these convictions were stronger prior to industrialization in the

United States. Stylized versions of the English and U.S. industrial economies suggested that vigorous competition among small units of production created an unrelenting pressure to lower costs and prices. Increased
productive efficiency through technological and organizational innovation increased the productivity of human labor, rather than increasing
workers' output by driving workers harder through physical coercion as
in slavery, extending their workdays, or employing more workers.

Modern Anglo American economics detached an idealized version of
the capitalist market system from its social and political roots, represent-
ing markets as self-equilibrating, universal, fair, authentically natural,
and necessary for individual freedom. This paved the way for liberal
thought to view the economy as a realm of freedom and productivity,
possessing its own laws of motion separate from politics. On the other
hand, government was seen to be a parasitic realm of coercion in which
economic policy had the capacity only to distort and impede markets' efficient operations.

The suspicion of government along with virulent reactions to taxation
were stronger in the United States than in Britain and encouraged narrow
political agendas. Interested parties were eager to regard policies aimed
at reforms in the economy to be outside the scope of legitimate government policy making. This restricted scope of government policy placed a
rigorous burden of proof on those who believed some political controls
and ameliorations of market outcomes were necessary and desirable.[13]

In accordance with these tenets, the English government in the late
eighteenth and early nineteenth centuries was decentralized and non-
professionally administered, and its domestic policy programs were few
and reactive. The U.S. federal government's contributions to industrial
growth in the first half of the nineteenth century were also few: securing
property rights, enforcing contracts, tariffs, patent law, mail service, open
immigration, and a (mostly) stable financial system. Both governments'
most important role in industrialization was consistent with the *laissez-
faire* principles of liberalism already latent in English and U.S. thought.

As a precept of government conduct, *laissez-faire* does not mean general
nonintervention by government. It means that the government was to be
vigorous in enforcing the rules of the game (that is, protecting property
relationships and enforcing contracts) but not to intervene in favor of one
fragment of the possessing class over another. Intraclass competition was
to be worked out in the marketplace; That is, employers were to compete
among themselves in selling products, and workers were to compete
among themselves in selling their labor services to employers. The conditions for that competition required government intervention to suppress
interclass competition involving working-class challenges to property and
to class privilege. Within-class competition was fine among producers and

among workers, but interclass vertical competition between workers and owners had to be contained by government.

The next chapter describes the economic complementarity of the other major regions in the new nation but stresses how tensions arose among the regions over politics and policies.

3

—๛—

Regions, Sections, and Civil War

As interesting and vital as the manufacturing sector is, most people of European and African extraction in the early nineteenth-century United States were rural and worked in agriculture or in activities closely related to agriculture. There was a great variety of how agriculture was organized in the different regions, leading to tensions.

CONTRASTING PATTERNS OF REGIONAL DEVELOPMENT

The contrast between the South's focus on an industrial crop, industrial growth in the Northeast, and the Upper Midwest's emphasis on food crops was, as noted, a source of strength by the regions' complementarity. But the logic of a slave-based economy versus that of an economy dominated by yeoman farmers and wage workers was decisive. Both southern and upper midwestern agrarians bought and sold in markets, but since wage labor was less important in both, they technically were not capitalist. But that does not mean that they were incapable of significant expansion and growth.

It makes little difference within a region whether the products in which the region specializes and therefore sells outside the region ("exports") go to another domestic region or to a foreign country. In either case, the connections between exports and the broader regional economies can be divided into three market linkages.[1] **Backward linkages** are the stimuli to local production of inputs used for export production. That is, tools, fertilizer, and credit are necessary for agricultural production, and if the

47

agricultural sector is large, prosperous, and fast growing, these goods and services are likely to be produced within the region.

Forward linkages are the stimuli to local production from transporting and further processing the export commodity. Flour, meat packing and leather products, and furniture and shingle production are examples of forward linkages derived from exports of grain, cattle, and timber, respectively. The third linkage is the income-multiplier linkage that looks at how consumption expenditures by those receiving income from export production and related activities affect local production.

Although the distinctions among these categories are a bit blurred around the edges, they are useful for tracing disaggregated effects from regional export production and assessing the capacity of that production to be economically progressive.

Early Western Expansion

Although the Far West by 1860 was not yet a major part of the United States, there were two significant pre–Civil War migrations into the region: the establishment of the Mormon community in Utah and the gold rush of prospectors to California and elsewhere.

Vigilantes persecuted the Latter Day Saints' successive efforts to establish permanent settlements in Ohio, Missouri, and Illinois. Despite the settlements' prosperity and the distinctively U.S. roots of the founding and character of the Mormon religion, non-Mormons considered their social and religious practices to be a threat to local mores and to the nation and its principles. After a Missouri massacre and the murder of founder Joseph Smith in Illinois, Brigham Young became the new Mormon leader and in 1847 began leading Mormon migrants to the present site of Salt Lake City, Utah. Between 1840 and 1860, over forty thousand migrants made the trip to Utah in order to isolate Mormons and Mormonism from such appalling hostility.

The new location did indeed insulate the Mormons from the harassment and deadly mob violence they experienced in the Midwest, and the community thrived despite some internal dissension, ugly responses to others' wagon trains passing by, and antagonism from the federal government to territorial autonomy and polygamy. After four decades of back-and-forth assertions and resistance (and the death of Brigham Young), the Mormons renounced polygamy in 1890, and Utah became a state in 1896.

The Mormons' goal of establishing a utopian community set them apart from other early migrants, especially prospectors who constituted the largest segment of pre–Civil War migrations to the West. The California gold rush drew two hundred thousand, mostly men from the eastern United States, Europe, and Asia in the twenty years before the Civil

War, and when California did not work out for most of them, they and additional migrants dashed to the next rumored gold and silver strikes in Colorado and Nevada (1859–1860), Idaho (1862), Montana (1864), the Black Hills of South Dakota (1874), and several locales in the Southwest.

The Upper Midwest

Table 3.1 shows that between 1830 and 1860 the population of the Upper Midwest grew by more than five times, from 12.5 percent of the U.S. population to almost 30 percent. These counts did not include Native Americans because, as noted in the previous chapter, the northern U.S. Native Americans had been militarily defeated and pushed west of the Mississippi by 1830, and the pressure continued as settlers entered territory between the Mississippi and Missouri Rivers that had supposedly been reserved for indigenous peoples.

The decline in transportation costs drew new farms into the market as sellers of produce, buyers of inputs, and more and more, purchasers of consumer goods. In addition to the rapid expansion of Chicago and other regional cities, the growth of small towns was an integral part of the region's vitality. These towns and cities together supplied surrounding farms' backward-linked demand for machines, tools, glass and stone products, leather goods, milled lumber, wagons, shingles, fabricated metal products, and a range of financial, repair, and other services as well as responding to income-multiplier-generated demand for clothing, shoes, carriages, furniture, and other consumer goods for the commercialized farms.

The strength of the income-multiplier and backward linkages reflected both the overall commercial success and prosperity of upper midwestern farming and the relatively evenly distributed income among small farmers. These agrarians relied increasingly on markets for goods and services. In discussing this phenomenon, Jeremy Atack, Fred Bateman, and William N. Parker (2000: 283) observe that "commercialization beyond some critical point is a one-way street; once family self-sufficiency began to unravel, skills were lost, equipment abandoned, values altered, and tastes changed."

The scarcity (and expense) of agricultural labor for hire, especially at planting and harvesting times, limited the size of grain and corn farms in the Midwest. This situation encouraged large families and hiring seasonal workers, but the effect of mechanization was more striking. The potency of backward-linked demand was expressed in the development of the mechanical reaper, patented in the 1830s. At first, reapers were slow to catch on, but by the 1850s, there were around 250,000 of them at work. The reaper along with the mechanical thresher, seed drill, and improved

Table 3.1. Regional Populations, 1830 and 1860

Regions[a]	Population (Thousands)		1860			Per Capita Income,
	1830	1860	African Americans as % of Populations	% Urban[b]	% Foreign Born	% of U.S. Average
Northeast	5,542	10,594	1.5	35.7	19.1	139
Upper Midwest	1,610	9,097	2.0	13.9	17.0	68
South	5,708	11,133	36.8	10.0	3.5	72
Far West	—	619	0.6	16.0	28.9	—
Total U.S. Population	12,860	31,443	14.1	19.8	13.1	100

[a] The regions are defined as follows, and the names of areas with negligible populations in 1830 and 1860 are in italics:
Northeast: Maine, New Hampshire, Vermont, Massachusetts, Rhode Island, Connecticut, New York, New Jersey, and Pennsylvania.
South: Delaware, Maryland, Virginia, North Carolina, South Carolina, Georgia, Florida, Kentucky, Tennessee, Alabama, Mississippi, Louisiana, Arkansas, *Oklahoma*, and *Texas*.
Upper Midwest: Ohio, Indiana, Illinois, Michigan, Wisconsin, Minnesota, Iowa, Missouri, *North Dakota*, *South Dakota*, Nebraska, and Kansas.
Far West: *Montana*, *Idaho*, *Wyoming*, Colorado, New Mexico, *Arizona*, Utah, Nevada, Washington, Oregon, and California.
[b] Urban includes people living in towns with 2,500 or more residents.

Sources: U.S. Census Bureau, *Historical Statistics of the United States: Colonial Times to 1970*, Part 1 (Washington, DC: Government Printing Office, 1975), 22–23; Robert E. Gallman, "Economic Growth and Structural Change in the Long Nineteenth Century," in *The Cambridge Economic History of the United States*, Vol. 2: *The Long Nineteenth Century*, ed. Stanley L. Engerman and Robert E. Gallman (New York: Cambridge University Press, 2000), 53.

plows reduced the number of people-hours necessary to cultivate an acre of grain or corn. Many farmers could not afford to buy these new machines, which had capacities greater than needed on a small farm, but they could rent them for short periods or go in with a group of other farmers to purchase machines jointly. These labor-saving devices began to make larger farms feasible.

The forward linkages of processing farm and forest products, such as flour, meat packing, and shingles, augmented the mix, and it added up to a dynamic agrarian economy with rapidly expanding auxiliary manufacturing production.

The South

The South was the most specialized region, and cotton was its principal export. The 1793 invention (or improvement) of the cotton gin made short-staple cotton an attractive cash crop, which was well suited to the land and climate of areas south and west of South Carolina. Slave-worked plantations moved into western Georgia, Florida, Alabama, Mississippi, Louisiana, and eventually eastern Texas. Tobacco, rice, and sugar became secondary crops in the region, and sugar was a principal crop only in Louisiana.

This extension of slave-worked plantations required two major steps. The first was to secure the land from the Native Americans, who lived in these areas in much greater numbers than in the Upper Midwest. Andrew Jackson, future president, led U.S. troops in 1813 and 1814 to defeat groups of Creek, who were forced to give up tens of thousands of acres. He then led U.S. troops in the First Seminole War—in southern Georgia and Florida in 1818 and 1819— that forced the Seminole to evacuate northern Florida and convinced Spain to cede Florida to the United States in 1819.

In 1830, Andrew Jackson, then president of the United States, signed the Indian Removal Act, which required all Indian tribes east of the Mississippi River to relocate west of the Mississippi to "Indian Territory" (now Oklahoma). This sparked the Second Seminole War (1835–1842), which resulted in the capture of thousands of Seminoles who were also sent to the new "territory." Some held out in the Everglades until U.S. troops, having lost around 1,500 men at a cost of millions of dollars, gave up in 1842. The Third Seminole War (1855–1858) sealed the fate of the tribe, and U.S. troops sent most of the Seminoles remaining in Florida to Indian Territory, leaving a small group who stayed in the Everglades.

The most notorious episode of the mass Native American removal occurred in 1838 and 1839, when U.S. troops gathered the Cherokee together in northwest Georgia and adjacent areas and forced them to trek the thousand miles to Indian Territory. Thousands of men, women, and children died along the way of what became known as the "Trail of Tears," a name that came to include similar travails by other tribes, such as the Seminole, Creek, Choctaw, and Chickasaw, whom the U.S. military forced to relocate from the Southeast.

The second major step in expanding the plantation system in southern and western directions was procuring an adequate supply of slaves to work the land cleared of Native Americans. Article I, Section 9 of the U.S. Constitution used opaque and euphemistic language to forbid Congress from abolishing the slave trade before 1808, and Congress did indeed act to prohibit the international slave trade on January 1, 1808. By that time, the number of slaves brought to English-speaking North America far exceeded the number of European immigrants who had crossed the Atlantic. Britain banned the slave trade to its colonies in the same year, but its significance was different: the slave population in the United States, unlike in any other slave society in the Americas, grew by natural increase. Abolishing the international slave trade, therefore, did not mean the end of slavery in the United States.

Although the international slave trade was illegal, there was still an active slave trade within the United States, and the geographical expansions invigorated domestic slave markets. Between 1830 and 1860, around one million slaves were relocated from Old South states on the Atlantic Seaboard to new plantations in southern and western states and territories. Some slaves went west with their masters' families, some were sold to new masters, and speculators bought and transported others south and southwest. Thousands of slave families were broken up, and many parents never saw their children again. As with Native Americans, transport for slaves, by and large, meant walking. Ira Berlin (2010), evoking the horrors of the "Middle Passage"—the shipping of slaves between Africa and North America—called this forcible relocation that broke apart families the "Second Middle Passage."

Virginia and Maryland were predominant sources of slaves for the internal traffic because soil exhaustion and competition from Kentucky and North Carolina tobacco reduced the profitability of tobacco farming. These former tobacco planters turned to mixed farming that did not require extensive slave labor and sold off many of their slaves.[2] Virginian slaveholders were four out of the first five U.S. presidents, but by the end of the period, much of their political influence in national affairs had been eclipsed by more dynamic states and regions.

Thus, two forced population movements—clearing Native Americans from their land and relocating black slaves—allowed the western movement of southern white planters and lay behind the stunning increase in cotton production, which doubled every decade between 1800 and 1860.

Three-quarters of the harvest was exported, comprising half of U.S. export earnings, and two-thirds of those exports went to Great Britain. The United States dominated the world market in cotton, and slave-produced cotton and its commerce were central to the U.S. economy in this period. Slaves, not farmers or industrial workers, fueled the economic engine of the new "republic" of the United States.

In the South, cotton was king, but the benefits flowed in narrow channels. One-third of southern whites owned slaves, and the 10 percent who owned twenty or more owned half of all the slaves. The wealthiest 1 percent in the South were about twice as wealthy as the wealthiest 1 percent in the North, and two-thirds of U.S. men with incomes of $100,000 or more (the *very* rich) lived in the South.

Research published over the past three or four decades has demonstrated that southern slavery was both productive and profitable, flying in the face of earlier, more romantic assumptions. By the middle of the nineteenth century, 75 percent of the slaves in the United States worked in cotton fields, mostly organized in labor gangs. Many scholars, notably Robert Fogel (2003: 36) are convinced slaves in smaller plantations produced at about the same levels as free northern farmers, and "those who toiled in the gangs of the intermediate and large plantations were on average over 70 percent more productive than either free farmers or slaves on small plantations." Physical coercion made workers highly productive and profitable.

Being economically viable is not the same thing as being economically progressive. The self-sufficiency of large plantations that used slaves as blacksmiths, mechanics, carpenters, seamstresses, and so on weakened backward linkages. In addition, the ready availability of manufactured inputs and financial and other services from the Northeast contributed to the debility of backward linkages. Table 3.1 shows that the proportions of southerners recorded as living in urban settings were not much different from those of the Upper Midwest, but the similarity is misleading. In the Upper Midwest, myriads of small towns with fewer than 2,500 residents produced goods and services for the surrounding farms, while there were many fewer such small towns in the South's countryside, reflecting the lack of robust backward linkages.

Forward-linked activities were apparent in the first stages of processing cotton, tobacco, sugar, and rice, but they did not compete with northeastern industries in the more complex stages of processing these crops into, say, cotton textiles, cigarettes, candy, and liquor. The South's highly concentrated distribution of income muted the effects of income-multiplier linkages, and European producers of luxury goods probably felt the income-multiplier linkages from cotton more than did local manufacturers. Altogether, the productive and growing agrarian economy did not produce linkages strong enough to generate significant economic diversification.

The economic formation of the South was also the foundation of a rigid, conservative society. Most whites were poor, only sporadically involved in market activity, and the rich held them in profound contempt, referring to them as "poor white trash." The middling sectors of craftsmen, shopkeepers, and professionals were thin, even in the few cities, where occupational ladders for upward mobility were limited in number and size. As recorded in table 3.1, immigrants therefore avoided the Deep South even as they were pouring into the Northeast during the 1850s.

The planter aristocracy was politically dominant, and the "southern way of life" was, by and large, limited to whites on large plantations, where a fascination with the European Middle Ages led to medieval fairs, jousts, and a stylized courtliness toward women of the "proper" class and race. While the members of this thin upper crust were often cultured and well traveled and educated, they had little interest in public education. North Carolina was the only Confederate state to have had a statewide public school system before the Civil War. Lower expenditures on education and higher rates of illiteracy among even native whites compared with other regions again reduced chances of upward mobility in the South.

Despite the findings that southern slavery was a productive and viable economic organization, there is little indication it would have evolved into anything like a dynamic capitalism. The strength of caste and class shut the majority out of economic opportunity and severely curtailed the possibility of broadly based initiative and social mobility. The U.S. South in the first half of the nineteenth century was more prosperous than northeastern Brazil and the British West Indies, but plantation slavery in all three regions indelibly stamped the social formations in ways that impeded the development of a vigorous capitalist industrialization or a democratic politics.

SECTIONAL CONFLICT AND WAR

In mid-nineteenth-century United States, the main struggle that erupted was not among races or classes but rather between regions (or sections)—the slave South versus the Northeast and Upper Midwest. The most divisive conflicts played out at the level of the federal government, where divergent needs, interests, and aspirations of the sections' leaderships directly confronted each other over policies.

Tariff policy was one source of sectional contestation. Since the South produced mostly agricultural exports and bought manufactured products from the Northeast and abroad, tariffs caused southern purchasers to pay higher prices that subsidized Northeast manufacturers. Tariffs continued to rise until 1828—the "tariff of abominations." In response to antitariff forces, the Compromise Tariff of 1833 assuaged southern anger by including a plan to reduce tariffs over the next decade. Despite occasional backsliding, there was some gradual lowering of tariffs up to 1861.

The most serious collisions, however, were not over a particular bill or policy area, where compromise was always possible; they were over the existence of slavery. The abolition movement had gathered substantial momentum in the northern states over the six decades since ratifying the Constitution, and its roots were varied and deep. In the early nineteenth century, the second Great Awakening rejuvenated the Protestant revivalist tradition and contributed to a growing conviction among northern church members that slavery was not only immoral but a national sin. The strength of this belief led to the division of the Baptist, Methodist, and Presbyterian churches into northern and southern denominations.

Abolitionists were also active in other reform movements such as woman suffrage and temperance. The two organizers of the famous 1848 women's rights meeting in Seneca Falls, New York, were responding to the humiliation of their (and all women's) exclusion from an abolitionist conference in England, and Frederick Douglass (former slave and leading antislavery activist) participated in the Seneca Falls assembly. The first sentence in the "Declaration of Sentiments" from the Seneca Fall meeting, borrowed from the founding document of the United States, reads:

> When, in the course of human events, it becomes necessary for one portion of the family of man to assume among the people of the earth a position different from that which they have hitherto occupied, but one to which the laws of nature and of nature's God entitle them, a decent respect to the opinions of mankind requires that they should declare the causes that impel them to such a course.

Most northerners had little interest in slaves' welfare or divine opinions about slavery; much more mundane reasons informed their opposition to the "peculiar institution." Craftsmen and wage workers feared that if they had to compete with slave labor, the result would be a devastating decline in their earnings. Yeomen in the Upper Midwest did not want to compete with slaveholders for product markets and land in territories and new states. On the other hand, northern industrialists were divided on slavery, although the merchant community, especially in New York City, was strongly interested in avoiding any disruption of the lucrative cotton trade.

Immediate economic interests played a role in some northerners' attitudes toward slavery, but probably the most pervasive reasons for northerners' hostility toward a vibrant slave-based economy in fifteen states were not the system in the abstract. Despite the economic complementarity of the three sections and the insulation of northerners from the everyday practices of slavery, the differences in the systems collided in federal politics. The issue was about the influence of the slave states (i.e., slaveholders) and who would control future directions of the nation.

Northern politicians saw the slaveholders' wealth and power and the aggressiveness with which they wielded them as the greatest threat. Existing as a cohesive oligarchy within the South, slaveholders' representatives confronted a much less unified set of northern interests in federal politics, and southern politicians were formidable opponents, capable of even physical attacks on the floor of Congress. The southern bloc succeeded in blocking a range of northern-sponsored legislation considered to be imperative for the continuing development of the northern industrial and agrarian economy. Such legislative initiatives as infrastructure investments ("internal improvements"), banking regulation, and public higher education could not overcome southern resistance. Northern abolitionist opinions were informed at least as importantly by political distrust and hostility toward masters as they were by concerns about the welfare of slaves.

Political conflicts between the sections were bitter and wearing at the national level. One indication of the tumultuous national politics of the second third of the nineteenth century was that not one of the eight presidents between Andrew Jackson and Abraham Lincoln was reelected to a second term (two—William Henry Harrison and Zachary Taylor—died in office, and their vice presidents—John Tyler and Millard Fillmore—were never elected president). In contrast, five of the seven presidents from Washington through Jackson served two terms; only John Adams and his son, John Quincy Adams, did not. Sectional politics took a heavy toll.

One of the most highly fraught issues between the sections was the admission of new states. As new states were admitted, representatives from the more populous free states dominated the U.S. House of Representatives despite the three-fifths rule of counting slaves for representation. In the U.S. Senate, the balance between free and slave states seesawed temporarily one way and the other, but as table 3.2 shows, the admission of Alabama in 1819 meant there were eleven slave states—six original states and five new states—and eleven free states—seven original states and four new states. This meant that each section had twenty-two senators.

Since voters in free states frequently elected Democratic Party candidates sympathetic to the South, congressional strength was not entirely a matter of sectional representation. Unlike the Methodist, Baptist, and Presbyterian churches, the Democratic Party managed to maintain its national organization up to the brink of the Civil War through its north-

Table 3.2. The Admission of New States between 1787 and 1861

State or Territory	Year Admitted as a State	State or Territory	Year Admitted as a State
Pennsylvania	1787	Louisiana*	1812
New Jersey	1787	Indiana	1816
Delaware	1787	Mississippi*	1817
New Hampshire	1788	Illinois	1818
Massachusetts	1788	Alabama*	1819
Connecticut	1788	Maine	1820
New York	1788	Missouri*	1821
Maryland*	1788	Arkansas*	1836
Virginia*	1788	Michigan	1837
South Carolina*	1788	Florida*	1845
Georgia*	1788	Texas*	1845
North Carolina*	1789	Iowa	1846
Rhode Island*	1790	Wisconsin	1848
Vermont	1791	California	1850
D. of Columbia*	(1791)	Minnesota	1858
Kentucky*	1792	Oregon	1859
Tennessee*	1796	Kansas	1861
Ohio	1803		

* The fifteen (out of thirty-four, not counting D.C.) states with slavery.

ern leadership being, in the words of Joel Silbey (2005: 170), "tolerant of slavery, or indifferent to it, and above all, committed to letting it alone."

But the free state–slave state count still mattered to both sides. When Missouri applied to become a state, its admission would have changed the balance in the U.S. Senate in favor of slave states. The Missouri Compromise of 1820 took care of this by admitting Maine and preserving the balance. The compromise also included a prohibition against slavery in states above the line formed by the southern border of Missouri (except for Missouri itself). There was still another step to the admission of Missouri: its proposed state constitution prohibited free blacks from entering or residing in Missouri. The majority in Congress considered this type of ban inappropriate for U.S. citizens, and Missouri was finally admitted only when Missouri lawmakers struck the clause from the state's constitution.

The next struggle was over whether the United States should annex Texas as a new state. U.S. settlers in Texas, a part of Mexico, had been unhappy about the chaos of Mexico's political affairs in the first half of the nineteenth century, and they were especially unhappy about Mexico's abolition of slavery in 1829. The settlers from the United States, around 80 percent of the Texas population, declared themselves to be an independent republic in 1836. Not only was it to be independent, it was to be more than twice as large as its previously acknowledged borders.

Although there were initial military setbacks (Remember the Alamo?), the settlers prevailed, and Texas became an independent republic with its leaders' promise that it would not join the United States. Nevertheless, Texans immediately began trying to convince the U.S. Congress to annex them as a state of the United States. Although President Andrew Jackson was sympathetic, U.S. public opinion was divided, and Jackson believed it would precipitate war with Mexico.

President John Tyler (1841–1845) was another slaveholding southern Democrat who became a Whig to run as William Henry Harrison's vice president, and he became president when Harrison died after one month in office. As president, Tyler worked with southern legislators and more than once vetoed tariff increases, a new Bank of the United States, and other pieces of the Whig platform. The Whigs threw him out of the party and tried to impeach him.[3] At the end of Tyler's administration, he pushed the annexation of Texas through Congress, and his successor, another southern Democrat named James Polk, provoked the Mexican War (1846–1848) in disputed territory south of Texas. The United States won and acquired Mexico's lands west of the Louisiana Purchase and south of Oregon in 1848.

During the war, the Polk administration negotiated with Britain over the Oregon Territory, agreeing to its northern U.S. border at the forty-ninth parallel north (except Vancouver Island), disappointing those who had vociferously shouted "fifty four forty or fight" (that is, fifty-four degrees, forty minutes north—near what is now the southern point of Alaska). They accused Polk of being aggressively expansionist in acquiring future slave states while quite willing to compromise about new territory of potentially free states.

Up to 1850, the admission of three new slave states and three new free states preserved the balance in the Senate between slave and free states. (See table 3.2.) The admission of California would upset that balance, especially with Minnesota and Oregon waiting in the wings. So the Compromise of 1850 admitted California, and in exchange, Congress awarded $10 million to Texas to drop some of its territorial claims, included a much stricter fugitive slave law mandating severe penalties if escaped slaves were not returned to their former owners, and prohibited buying and selling slaves in the District of Columbia. Millard Fillmore worked hard on this compromise, first as vice president and then as president (1850–1853), again demonstrating that northeastern members of the waning Whig Party could also accommodate southern interests.

The Kansas-Nebraska Act of 1854 was the last major effort to figure out a procedure acceptable to both North and South for admitting new states. The act allowed the territories' residents, rather than Congress, to determine through referenda ("popular sovereignty") whether they would be admitted as free or slave states. This effectively eviscerated the Missouri Compromise, and the result was bloody conflict in Kansas between proslavery Missourians and antislavery settlers that lasted for years. After some fraudulent elections, the Kansas territorial legislature submitted a proslavery state constitution (the "Lecompton Constitution"), which was supported by President Buchanan but rejected by the U.S. Congress. Congress finally admitted Kansas as a free state in 1861, but only after southern states had begun seceding from the union. By that time, the new states of Oregon and Minnesota had already upset the balance in the Senate.

The competition for new states went beyond the U.S. borders. Southerners had for years been interested in wresting Cuba from Spain and annexing it as a slave state. Cuban exiles with southern support attempted several invasions, all of which were disasters. In 1855, some partisans in a Nicaraguan civil war invited a U.S. citizen named William Walker to assist them by bringing some troops. So Walker and a group of Mexican War veterans did make the difference, but Walker then made himself president of Nicaragua. President Franklin Pierce (1853–1857) recognized the Walker regime, which legalized slavery in Nicaragua and petitioned for admission to the United States as a slave state. There was strong support in the U.S. South for Walker and his initiatives, but an alliance of Central American nations soon routed Walker.

Presidents Pierce and James Buchanan (1857–1861) carried on the tradition of northern Democrats by being solicitous of southern interests. The final political milestone before the Civil War was the U.S. Supreme Court's *Dred Scott* decision in 1857. Scott and his wife, Harriet, sued for their freedom based on having lived two years in nonslave states and territories. The seven to two ruling asserted that African American citizenship was inconsistent with the Declaration of Independence and the U.S. Constitution, thus the Scotts did not have the standing necessary to bring a suit in U.S. courts. One might have thought that this was the end of it (so thought the two dissenting justices), but the majority of the court took the opportunity to assert that the federal government could not prohibit slavery anywhere in the United States, since that was an unconstitutional limitation of a person's freedom to use his or her private property. The extraordinary judicial activism therefore vacated all of the compromises crafted to maintain the free state–slave state balance.

The reaction by the Republican Party to the *Dred Scott* decision was mixed.[4] At this time, the Republican Party was a recent upstart political party whose presidential candidate, John C. Fremont, had done surprisingly well in the 1856 election. The party was composed of antislavery remnants of the Whig Party, former Free Soil Party members, and anti-immigrant nativists from the declining American (or Know Nothing) Party.

The growing number of northern states that prohibited blacks from voting illustrates the trend against black suffrage. In 1830, fifteen out of twenty-four states excluded African Americans from the polls, and by 1850, it was twenty-five out of thirty-one states, not including New York State that placed a high property qualification exclusively on African American voters. Some states barred "negroes, mulattos, and colored," but most of them were written to include only whites, thus excluding Native Americans and, in California and Oregon, Chinese. The federal government also denied voting rights to African Americans in territories, a situation buttressed by the *Dred Scott* decision. In this setting, the Republicans knew that coming out in favor of black citizenship would make Republicans more vulnerable to Democrats' racial demagoguery.

Abraham Lincoln was an abolitionist, but not like the firebrands of New England. At the time he was nominated by the Republicans to run for president in 1860, he favored abolition to be gradual, compensated, and probably accompanied by "colonization"—voluntary repatriation of former slaves to Africa or Latin America—thus dodging issues of citizenship and civil liberties. Although northern Democrats worked hard to appease the party's southern wing, the Democrats' presidential nominating convention in 1860 fell apart. The southerners walked out of the convention and nominated their own candidate for president. Despite the cautious nature of his views, when Lincoln won the four-way election of 1860 with less than 40 percent of the popular vote but 60 percent of the electoral vote, South Carolina, Mississippi, Florida, Alabama, Georgia, Louisiana, and Texas seceded from the Union before Lincoln was inaugurated, making good on threats that some of them had been making for decades.[5]

President Buchanan's response was restrained, acting on the belief that if not provoked, the seven might return to the Union under feasible conditions. When South Carolina fired on Fort Sumter a month after Lincoln's inauguration—April 1861—Buchanan strongly and publicly supported Lincoln's decision to go to war. Arkansas, North Carolina, Tennessee, and finally Virginia joined the first seven in seceding from the union, and the Confederate States of America (CSA) was formed from eleven of the fifteen slave states.

Maryland, Delaware, Kentucky, and Missouri—slave "border states"—did not secede. The western portion of the state of Virginia, whose small farmers had decades of conflicts with the eastern slaveholder planters, broke off from Virginia in 1861 and became a state in the Union as West Virginia.

Both sides anticipated a short and victorious war, but it lasted four long years and caused the deaths of 620,000 soldiers—360,000 Union soldiers (one in six) and 260,000 Confederate soldiers (one in three), more than half by disease. Internal dissensions within each side complicated the prosecution of the war. The CSA was riven by the divide between whites and blacks (nearly of equal numbers) as well as between planters and poor whites. Potential conflicts between urban residents and rural settlers, employees and employers, and nativists and immigrants plagued the Union side.

An important watershed of the war occurred when President Lincoln, in September 1862, risked alienating the four slave states that had stayed in the Union by issuing the Emancipation Proclamation, scheduled to go into effect on January 1, 1863. The proclamation declared all slaves in Confederate-held areas to be free, and there were no provisions to compensate either former slaves or slaveholders.[6] The proclamation was an act of a commander in chief during wartime and could be seen as a tactic to weaken the South militarily.

The proclamation did not affect the bondage of almost half a million slaves in Delaware, Maryland, Kentucky, and Missouri or of the three hundred thousand in Louisiana, occupied by Union troops since 1862. In early 1865, Lincoln pushed hard to get the Thirteenth Amendment, which outlawed slavery everywhere in the United States, through the two-thirds vote needed in the House of Representatives. (The Senate had passed it easily.) The amendment was then sent to the states, and in the absence of the eleven seceding states, three-quarters of the state legislatures had ratified it by December 1865 when it became a permanent part of the U.S. Constitution. It contains the first use of the words "slave" or "slavery" in the Constitution.

While the Emancipation Proclamation did not free one slave, it had important effects. First, it reduced the ambiguity of the status of slaves on the increasing numbers of plantations captured by Union troops as they moved deeper into the South. Union officers often had considered these people to be a Southerner's private property or confiscated property ("contraband") rather than freed prisoners or refugees. Second, the proclamation encouraged slaves to leave their plantations and cross Union lines. Altogether, around five hundred thousand did and contributed to the Union effort in various capacities by building fortifications, transporting materiel, preparing food, and performing other nonmilitary functions. In addition, the Emancipation Proclamation had declared that African Americans "will be received into the armed service of the United States," and two hundred thousand African American men, including recently freed slaves, served as Union soldiers and sailors. Third, the proclamation reduced the likelihood of British support for the Confederacy because of the strength of the British abolitionist movement that had ended slavery in its Caribbean colonies thirty years earlier.

Fourth, when word of the Emancipation Proclamation reached the slaves, it increased their restiveness and worried Southern whites already concerned about controlling the slave population. One notorious measure to maintain slave discipline was contained in the CSA conscription laws passed in early 1862, when it was becoming clear that soldiers were not reenlisting after completing their one-year enlistments. In addition to involuntary extensions of soldiers' enlistments, the laws exempted from conscription one able-bodied man for every twenty slaves on a plantation. The system also exempted certain occupational categories from the draft and allowed draftees to purchase substitutes. Altogether, these legislative decisions provided wealthy slaveholders and their sons and overseers multiple avenues to avoid conscription.

This angered poor whites, who spoke of "a rich man's war and a poor man's fight." After a year, poor whites' initial enthusiasm for the war dissolved; they desperately needed to return to their farms and families, which were going through hard times. Poor whites became resentful of the unequal apportioning of the war's burden, an unfairness that included the conscription laws as well as the tax system and inflation that financed the war. Poor whites, especially those from the hill country of western Georgia and the Carolinas, northern Alabama, and eastern Tennessee, registered this discontent in armed resistance to the draft and massive desertions from the Confederate armies, which declined in strength from early 1863. The guerrilla campaigns rural whites waged against the Confederacy during the Civil War were the most extreme expression of what has been called the South's "inner Civil War."

The North also had troubles with conscription. State quotas did not produce the quantity of troops needed to prosecute the war, and the U.S. government began national conscription in 1863. A draftee could pay the federal government three hundred dollars to avoid the draft, and similar to the South, a draftee could hire a substitute. Again similar to the South, the expression "a rich man's war and a poor man's fight" began to be heard. Poor immigrants, primarily Irish, were among those least able to buy themselves off the draft lists, and almost a quarter of Union troops were recent immigrants.

When a drawing of the New York City draft lottery was held in July 1863, a riot broke out with significant participation by Irish immigrants. The rioters looted public buildings and targeted some municipal and draft officials, but the mob's principal effort was to beat, lynch, and otherwise murder African Americans and to burn homes and buildings identified with them, including an orphanage. The "draft riot" was second only to the Civil War as the most serious insurrection in U.S. history; it lasted five days until troops drawn from the Union victory at Gettysburg restored order, and not gently.

On July 4, 1863, the fall of Vicksburg, Mississippi, and the withdrawal of the Confederate army after defeat at Gettysburg, Pennsylvania, marked the beginning of the end of the war. But the war, which both sides believed would be short and victorious, did not end until April 1865. While the effects of the Civil War on the nation as a whole continue to be debated, one of those effects is incontrovertible: the end of slavery in the United States, with ramifications throughout the nation that are still being felt.

PART III

FIFTY YEARS AFTER
THE CIVIL WAR

4

—⚶—

Wartime Legislation,
Western Expansion,
and Reconstruction

There were many important themes unfolding in the fifty years after the end of the Civil War, themes that deeply influenced the twentieth century and continue to reverberate in the twenty-first. In this chapter, we examine the large-scale demographic relocations involved in the westward movement of the U.S. population from east of the Mississippi River, enabled and encouraged by wartime legislation passed while Confederate states were absent from U.S. governance. The second theme of this chapter concerns the federal government's struggle to reform and reconstruct the South against white Southerners' resistance.

SIX WARTIME POLICY INITIATIVES

During the Civil War, the senators and representatives of the seceding states withdrew from the U.S. Congress, but this did not paralyze Congress. On the contrary, the withdrawal of the seceding states' senators and representatives gave northern and western legislators the opportunity to pass laws benefiting their states and regions without southern resistance. Congress would have had trouble passing the Thirteenth, Fourteenth, and Fifteenth Amendments and achieving the necessary ratifications by three-fourths of the states if most of the slave states had not seceded, and Lincoln successfully rushed through Republican-leaning Nevada's statehood in 1864 to clinch the deal about the amendments (and to help his reelection). In addition to the amendments, Congress passed six sets of legislation that significantly influenced the shape of the post–Civil War

United States. Unlike the three amendments, they were not directed at the South but for different reasons had been or would have been opposed by southern legislators. And the U.S. government wasted no time in taking advantage of the withdrawal of the southern states.

1) Tariffs

There were sharp increases in tariffs. The initial hikes were in good part to help pay for the war, but the federal government continued to raise tariffs until the McKinley Tariff of 1890, which made U.S. tariffs the highest among those of the world's industrialized nations. Southern politicians believed, probably correctly, that tariffs on imported manufactured products disproportionately burdened the South.

2) The Pacific Railway Act (1862)

Although the Illinois Central Railroad had received federal land as a subsidy in 1851, it was not until the Pacific Railway Act that land grants and cash subsidies became large and systematic with the goal of forging a transcontinental rail system. States-rights Southerners did not agree with such heavy federal involvement or with creating a northern route to the West. With little Southern participation in Congress, the program could proceed, and by 1871, when Congress terminated the subsidies, the federal government had granted two hundred million acres—around 10 percent of the public domain—to railroad companies that could be sold to homesteaders and land speculators.

Union Pacific Railroad began laying track westward from Omaha, Nebraska, employing mostly Irish workers, and the Central Pacific Railroad (later the Southern Pacific) began building eastward from Sacramento, California, with mostly Chinese workers. They met at Promontory in northern Utah in 1869—remember the golden spike? This transcontinental achievement did not immediately connect the Atlantic and Pacific Oceans; it took several more years to build a railway bridge over the Missouri River between Omaha and Council Bluffs, Iowa, and to extend tracks from Sacramento to the San Francisco Bay.

3) The Morrill Act (1862)

This act granted thirty thousand acres of federal land to state governments for each senator and U.S. representative, and the revenues from investing the money from their sale was to be used to establish the so-called land-grant public colleges and universities with agriculture and mechanic arts curricula.[1] The second Morrill Act (1890) extended the grants, which became the bases of African American technical colleges in the South and public colleges in western states that had recently become states. Again, Southerners would have fought such federal activism, and planters tended to be indifferent, if not hostile, to public education.

4) The Homestead Act (1862)

Under its provisions, the federal government granted 160 acres to anyone who was a citizen or intended to become a citizen. The government would issue a final deed to the homesteaders after they made some modest improvements and resided on the land for five years. Giving away public land was the final step in U.S. land policy, and Southerners had opposed it for decades. Such a policy designed to produce a yeoman-dominated agriculture would close off any possibility of spreading slavery into the territories, and Southerners wanted public lands to be a source of federal revenue in order to reduce tariffs. Responding to this pressure, President James Buchanan had vetoed a similar measure during his administration, but without the Southern bloc in Congress and with a Republican president, it became law.

→ Lincoln

5) The Department of Agriculture (1862)

President Lincoln created an independent Department of Agriculture in the executive branch to promote and support agricultural improvement. Earlier proposals to do so had become bogged down in debates over slavery. The department did not achieve cabinet status until 1887.

6) National Currency Act (1863)

The Currency Act (later known as the National Bank Act) offered federal charters to banks as an alternative to state charters and was the final noteworthy piece of Civil War legislation. Two years later, Congress imposed a tax on the issue of notes by the 1,600 private banks, an action that essentially precluded the practice. The purpose was to establish a national, uniform banknote currency free of the vagaries of local banks' locations, durability, and honesty.

Larger banks found the national charter to be attractive, even with the accompanying regulation and reserve requirements, but state banks continued to be a vigorous part of what became a dual banking system. Although this act could be seen as a step toward the Federal Reserve System (FRS) of 1914, it did not set up a central bank like the First or Second Bank of the United States. Nevertheless, it was an assertion of federal authority that reduced state governments' prerogatives and constrained banks' ability to create credit. Southern legislators historically had opposed such acts on both grounds.

FEDERAL GOVERNMENT FINANCES

When compared to the German/Prussian state, the decentralized U.S. government was not very powerful. The U.S. federal government had been created by the states, and state governments retained significant areas of authority, often bolstered by U.S. Supreme Court decisions. In the late nineteenth century, federal civilian employees, most of whom were in the Postal Service, made up less than 20 percent of the number of state and local government employees. State and local governments consistently outspent the federal government and with few exceptions did so through 1940. But the consolidation of federal authority during the Civil War, postwar popular pressure, and increasing national economic integration launched a vigorous federal government that began to fashion national policy on a scale inconceivable before 1860.

The Civil War severely strained federal finances. Correcting for inflation, the U.S. government increased its expenditures by over twelve times between 1860 and 1865, and at its height, the war absorbed about a quarter of total Northern production. The U.S. federal government financed the war using a combination of the three sources of revenue available to central governments: taxation, printing money, and borrowing.

Taxation is the most straightforward: a government takes money (purchasing power) away from the Private Sector, including individuals, and uses those resources for government priorities. Tax revenues paid for around 20 percent of the war's financial costs to the North. The federal government raised tariffs and a host of other taxes, and a slightly **progressive income tax** was one of the most radical innovations, somewhat offsetting the **regressiveness** of other taxes, but it still yielded less revenue than tariffs.

A government's creation of new money is the most inflationary means of financing; the government uses the new money to bid products and services away from private purchasers and, in the process, raises those prices. Ten percent of Northern war financing came from printing money. The U.S. government suspended **convertibility** (that is, the ability to convert paper currency into specie—gold and silver) and then issued a currency that came to be called "greenbacks" that was not convertible but was legal tender—by law, greenbacks had to be accepted in payment "for all debts public or private." (Look for that phrase on any denomination of our current paper money.) In order to encourage foreign investors, interest payments on the national debt were an exception that required payments in specie-backed money rather than greenbacks.

The North did experience inflation, mostly due to the issuance of greenbacks. Table 4.1 shows that the average prices almost doubled in the North between 1860 and 1864. Also recorded in table 4.1, wages of Northern workers lagged behind prices, causing real wages to decline nearly 30 percent during the war. But Northern farmers benefited, experiencing rises in agricultural prices and declines in the real value (corrected for inflation) of their mortgage burdens. But this pattern was quickly reversed after the war, when **deflation** became the norm into the 1890s. Real wages rose a bit, while farmers faced declining crop prices (although manufactured goods' prices fell even faster) and rising real mortgage burdens. The Confederacy relied more than the North on printing money to finance the Civil War, and over the four-year period, prices in the South in 1865 were ninety-one times higher than before the war.

In the North, borrowing by selling interest-bearing U.S. government bonds (IOUs) financed 70 percent of the financial cost of the war. The **national debt**—the value of federal government bonds outstanding—went from $65 million in 1860 to $2.3 billion in 1866. The need to sell bonds led to banking reforms and the development of a network of financial markets. These markets contributed substantially to postwar economic growth by expanding credit and creating new financial institutions that facilitated corporations' expansion through borrowing and issuing **stock**. After the Civil War, the federal budget was in surplus every year from 1866 to 1893, and the U.S. government managed to return its currency to convertibility in 1879; by 1893, successive administrations had reduced the national debt to $600 million.

Table 4.1. Average Real Earnings of Nonfarm Employees and the Consumer Price Index, 1860–1920

Year	Avg. Annual Real Earnings (1914 prices)	Consumer Price Index (1914 = 100)
1860	457	79.5
1865	328	155.9
1875	403	105.0
1880	395	97.8
1885	492	90.7
1890	519	91.5
1895	520	84.3
1900	573	84.3
1905	592	88.5
1910	649	94.7
1914	683	100.0
1920	718	199.7

after 1880 country experienced deflation

Source: Derived from U.S. Census Bureau, *Historical Statistics of the United States: Colonial Times to 1970*, Part 1 (Washington, DC: Government Printing Office, 1975), 164–65.

How did the federal government reduce its postwar indebtedness while subsidizing the movement of large numbers of people into areas with few people of European descent? One piece of the puzzle was the government's use of its huge holdings of public land. Three pieces of bold congressional legislation passed during the Civil War—the Homestead Act, the Pacific Railway Act, and the Morrill Act—were expensive but were primarily funded by grants of land to homesteaders, railroad companies, and state governments. That is, the federal government made substantial progress toward such ambitious goals by spending its largest resource—land—with the effects on the federal budget limited to administrative and military costs.

THE CONQUEST OF THE WESTERN FRONTIER

The movement of people west has been a major theme in U.S. history since the seventeenth century, but as table 4.2 indicates, the sheer magnitude and complexity of the movements between 1865 and the end of World War I set the era apart. The U.S. population tripled between 1860 and 1920, its spatial compositions shifted drastically among and within regions, and eleven new states—Colorado (1876), North Dakota (1889), South Dakota (1889), Montana (1889), Washington (1889), Idaho (1890), Wyoming (1890), Utah (1896), Oklahoma (1907), New Mexico (1912), and Arizona (1912)—completed the contiguous forty-eight states.

The legislation that Congress passed without Southern participation during the Civil War was vital to the pattern and pace of westward population movements. The Homestead Act gave between four hundred thousand and six hundred thousand families access to land ownership, but the Homestead Act's limit of 160 acres did not make the free land attractive in arid and semiarid regions of the West, where more land was needed to support a family, and ranching often replaced farming. As a result, the railroads and the state governments sold far more and often better land from their generous federal grants through the Pacific Railway Act and the Morrill Act. These sales were without the Homestead Act acreage and domicile restrictions, therefore enabling that enduring, endemic theme in U.S. history: land speculation.

An example of how valuable the federal land grants were for the railroads occurred in the early 1870s. Financing the construction of the Northern Pacific Railway ran into difficulties with the collapse of the railroad's principal financial institution, Jay Cooke & Co. The Philadelphia banking house had been instrumental in financing the Union side of the Civil War, and it was so important to the national financial system that its collapse contributed to the Panic of 1873 and subsequent recession.

Table 4.2. U.S. Population, 1860–1920

Regions[a]	Population (Thousands)	African Americans as % of Population	% Urban[b]	% Foreign Born	Per Capita Income, % of U.S. Average
1860					
Northeast	10,594	1.5	36	19	139
Upper Midwest	9,097	2.0	14	17	68
South	11,113	36.8	11	4	72
Far West	619	0.6	16	29	—
Total	31,423	14.1	20	13.2	100
1920					
Northeast	29,662	2	60	33	132
Upper Midwest	34,020	—	52	12	100
South	33,126	27	28	5	62
Far West	9,214	1	52	16	122
Total	106,022	10	51	13	100

[a] The regions are defined as follows, and the names of areas with negligible populations in 1860 are in italics.
Northeast: Maine, New Hampshire, Vermont, Massachusetts, Rhode Island, Connecticut, New York, New Jersey, and Pennsylvania.
South: Delaware, Maryland, Virginia, North Carolina, South Carolina, Georgia, Florida, Kentucky, Tennessee, Alabama, Mississippi, Louisiana, Arkansas, *Oklahoma*, and Texas.
Upper Midwest: Ohio, Indiana, Illinois, Michigan, Wisconsin, Minnesota, Iowa, Missouri, North Dakota, *South Dakota*, Nebraska, and Kansas.
Far West: *Montana, Idaho, Wyoming,* Colorado, New Mexico, *Arizona*, Utah, Nevada, Washington, Oregon, and California.
[b] Urban includes people living in towns with 2,500 or more inhabitants.

Sources: U.S. Census Bureau, *Historical Statistics of the United States: Colonial Times to 1970*, Part 1 (Washington, DC: Government Printing Office, 1975), 12, 14–18, 24–38; Robert E. Gallman, "Economic Growth and Structural Change in the Long Nineteenth Century," in *The Cambridge Economic History of the United States*, Vol. 2: *The Long Nineteenth Century*, ed. Stanley L. Engerman and Robert E. Gallman (New York: Cambridge University Press, 2000), 53.

Small farmers had already demonstrated the fertility of the land that the federal government had granted to the Northern Pacific Railway, especially around the Red River for growing wheat. Northern Pacific, therefore, traded thousands of square miles of that land in exchange for its investors' bonds—that is, it paid off its debts with land, reestablished its creditworthiness, borrowed more money, and completed the rail line to the Pacific.

The investors, now absentee landlords, created "bonanza farms" of between three thousand and thirty thousand acres using migrant labor, including Mexicans and Mexican Americans, and utilizing the most modern technologies, such as steam-powered plows and harvesters. The Northern Pacific transported grain across Minnesota (for a price) to huge Minneapolis flour mills established on the banks of the Mississippi River where the highest waterfalls on the river powered the mills. This was a very profitable arrangement for landowners, the railroad, and mill owners for about twenty-five years, but early in the twentieth century, the landowners faced reduced land fertility and declining wheat prices. Over the next decade, they broke up the bonanza farms and sold the land in smaller plots. The flour mills began to relocate eastward.

The economy as a whole slowed during the Civil War, and railroad construction was no exception. After the war, however, rail expansion exploded: from 30,000 miles in 1860 to 140,000 miles in 1890 and to 250,000 in 1914, not counting mileage in rail yards. It was a lot easier to travel in heretofore isolated places.

Generalized Conflict and Violence

In her reflections on the diversity and struggles among variously defined groups in the U.S. West, Patricia Nelson Limmerick (1987: 291) writes:

> Whether in Indian removal or Mormon migration, the theory was the same: the West is remote and vast; its isolation and distance will release us from conflict; this is where we can get away from each other. But the workings of history carried an opposite lesson. The West was not where we escaped each other, but where we all met.

The suddenness with which thousands of Euro American aspiring farmers, ranchers, and miners could show up in areas that the United States had promised to Native Americans destabilized Native American–U.S. relations, and conflicts were frequent. The wars between Native Americans and U.S. troops expanded considerably after the Civil War, when the availability of rail transportation and of land through the Homestead Act, state governments, and railroad companies encouraged migration by people intent on securing large tracts of land for farming and ranching. In addition to white–Native American conflicts, the Sioux (or Lakota) and Cheyenne of the northern plains often raided Pawnee villages, and the Apache and Navajo regularly raided Pueblo settlements. The new white settlers simply offered a wider scope of animals and goods for these traditional forays, which occurred on land that Native Americans held by treaty with the federal government.

There were repeated atrocities and massacres initiated by both whites and Native Americans, and although U.S. troops lost many of the battles, they won the war through attrition. Soldiers, along with commercial buffalo-hide hunters, reduced the herds of bison and disrupted and pursued Native American villages during the periods in which winter provisions and shelter had to be prepared. The U.S. Army's strategy succeeded, and large numbers of starving Native Americans surrendered at U.S. forts and agencies in winter. While conflicts continued, total conquest was not in doubt after the early 1880s.

The goal of putting Native Americans in reservations had evolved after U.S. officials abandoned the short-lived idea of a permanent Native American territory in Oklahoma. Whites told themselves that forcing Native Americans onto reservations was to protect them from white invaders that the U.S. government could not control. While developing the reservation system, the idea of Native American autonomy and sovereignty changed into Native Americans as dependent wards. Native Americans received food and some money, but corruption and indifference cut deeply into what they actually received. The conditions on the reservations were ghastly, and people routinely died of disease, hunger, and cold. Deserters were tracked down, returned to the reservation, and punished.

White Californians were especially hard on indigenous populations. They initially coerced work from the Native Americans through the formerly Mexican method of debt peonage as well as vagrancy laws and outright kidnapping and sale of Native Americans as slaves. When these practices became illegal in 1863, Californians turned to deliberate genocide as the preferred policy, and high rates of diseases such as measles and influenza added tens of thousands to these deaths. Native Americans practically disappeared in California.

Reformers, frequently connected to northeastern religious denominations and optimistic about the capacities of Native Americans, became influential in the policies to drag Native Americans into the U.S. mainstream. Officials suppressed traditional Native American practices, rites, and languages and forced the young into English-language schools, often in boarding schools far from parents. The Dawes Act of 1887 divided reservation lands and allotted 160-acre plots to individual families in an attempt to imbue a sense of individualism among Native Americans by dissolving communal landholding. There was usually land left over after the allotments, enabling officials to declare large portions of tribal lands to be "surplus" and thereby sold to whites. Whites also acquired Native American lands from Native Americans who rejected "farms" that could not sustain a subsistence living. Reservation lands thus diminished from 155,600 acres in 1881 to 77,900—one-half—in 1900, and acreage of tribal lands continued to decline into the 1930s.

Despite these assaults, Native American culture, in all its diversity, proved far more durable than the reformers had expected, discouraging the proponents of assimilation. In the early twentieth century, federal Native American policy dropped its activist agenda in favor of neglecting the Native Americans (but not their natural resources).

Two additional populations were actors in the drama of the U.S. West. Spain had colonized what became the U.S. Southwest and California in the eighteenth century, and these lands became parts of Mexico after its independence from Spain in the 1820s. After the Mexican War, in which the United States appropriated what is now the U.S. Southwest, Rocky Mountain region, and California, there were substantial numbers of former Mexican citizens who, according to the Treaty of Guadalupe Hidalgo (1848), suddenly became U.S. citizens guaranteed full civil liberties and property rights, at least in theory.

The largest group of instant U.S. citizens lived in New Mexico: in 1850, there were fifty thousand former Mexicans and one thousand U.S. "Anglos." The New Mexico colonial society had developed to the point that there was a powerful landowning elite who cooperated with the Anglos and retained much of their lands. Some smaller landholders also hung onto their lands, but many others lost out through Anglo purchases, fraud, armed squatters, and other machinations.

Texans, who became independent of Mexico in 1836, had already dealt with an existing population of Mexicans (Tejanos) within their borders, and the Tejanos' experience was uneven. Some kept their lands; some were unable to do so. On the other hand, Anglos in California often did not distinguish between the former Mexicans (Californios) and Native Americans, and they immediately discriminated against them in the mines by a special tax. Over the years, Californios generally became unskilled agriculture laborers.

The Chinese were the fourth important ethnic group, and they, like those from the eastern United States and Europe, initially came to the U.S. West in response to the opportunity to search for gold and silver. The tax on Californio miners soon was applied to the Chinese, who turned to wage labor or occasionally to opening small retail and service shops. The financial successes of some Chinese did not mitigate Anglos' hatred; it simply produced fear of competition.

At the behest of California labor organizations and other anti-Asian groups, the U.S. Congress passed the 1882 Chinese Exclusion Act that exempted only merchants and students. The Act was renewed in 1892 and made permanent in 1902. Subsequent changes included a definition of "Chinese" that held for all people of Chinese descent irrespective of nations of birth and residence. Although two hundred thousand Chinese immigrants had followed the initial groups of Chinese immigrants in the 1850s, the lack of many Chinese women immigrants, Anglos' putative abhorrence of race mixing, and continued hostility led to a steady decline in the number of Chinese Americans.

The Japanese who immigrated around the turn of the twentieth century met with opposition in the West similar to that of the Chinese, but Japan, unlike China, was a politically coherent and militarily strong state. President Theodore Roosevelt negotiated with Japanese officials and came up with an informal "gentleman's agreement." It was never written down, but the Japanese government promised to reduce Japanese immigration to the United States. Roosevelt, in turn, promised to shield Japanese residents in the United States from discriminatory laws. That was a difficult promise to keep.

Congress followed the exclusion of Chinese and Japanese with an omnibus act of exclusion. The Immigration Act of 1917 created the Asiatic Barred Zone, prohibiting immigration from the rest of East Asia, all of Southeast Asia and South Asia, large parts of Russia, Mongolia, the Middle East, and Turkey through the eastern coast of the Mediterranean Sea and the Arabian Peninsula.

The violence among Anglos, Native Americans, Mexican Americans, and Chinese took place in a context in which violence was a general phenomenon and not just limited to racial hostility; white-on-white violence was widespread. In camps for miners, lumberjacks, and cowboys, single young men made up large proportions of residents, and they were turbulent communities with frequent brawls and chaos and where vigilante justice often prevailed over the law. Moreover, many of the mining communities were founded on fraudulent information, and even when there was gold or silver, swarms of miners quickly exhausted the placer deposits accessible for individual miners. When that happened, most of the mining camps disappeared almost overnight, reemerging a century later as tourist sites. In areas with promise, large mining companies, usually financed in the Northeast, took over operations. These were companies with the capital to invest in the machinery and infrastructure needed for tunneling, hydraulic mining, and mills and smelters for low-grade ore.

When these mining communities survived, they became more orderly company towns populated by wage workers and salaried managers, but conflicts between miners and mine owners' agents frequently led to open warfare. Hiring armed thugs was a common labor-management tactic that also was used in interfirm competitions over railroad routes and copper veins.

In addition, there were violent struggles between small ranchers and large ranchers, who were trying to monopolize public-domain grazing rights, between cattlemen and sheep herdsmen, and between herdsmen and farmers. The introduction of barbed wire in the 1870s and 1880s did not always ameliorate these conflicts. And among practically every economic and social category, including urban dwellers versus rural residents, there were chronically fierce battles over access to water.

The regions populated by homesteaders were not as tumultuous as others, but in thinking about the family farm, it is important not to romanticize the coziness of these communities. Women's lives, for example, were often full of hard physical labor, little access to medical care during their child-bearing years, and weeks of being snowbound on tiny homesteads. As Stuart Blumin (2000: 838) reminds us, "Emptiness and loneliness, not community, are the dominant themes of the literature of the Great Plains, from Hamlin Garland and Ole Rolvaag to Willa Cather."

PRESIDENTIAL AND CONGRESSIONAL RECONSTRUCTIONS IN THE SOUTH

Southern whites struggled to regain political control of the South in the years following the Civil War. The principal threat to white political dominance was neither Union troops nor African American violence but rather African American electoral potential. In 1870, African Americans were majorities in the states of Mississippi, South Carolina, and Louisiana and only slightly fewer than half in Florida, Georgia, and Alabama. Although the ratio of black men to white men twenty-one years old or older varied, it was clear that black participation in elections in most former Confederate states would be fraught with dangers for whites' control of state and local governments and U.S. congressional delegations.

Under the terms of presidential Reconstruction implemented in 1865 and 1866 by President Lincoln's successor, Andrew Johnson, black voting blocs were not a problem because whites could prevent African Americans from registering and voting. Andrew Johnson of Virginia and Tennessee became president when Confederate supporters assassinated Abraham Lincoln five days after General Robert E. Lee surrendered at Appomattox. Although President Johnson was strongly pro-Union, he had been a proslavery slave owner and a Democrat until he switched parties to run as Lincoln's vice president in the 1864 election.

Presidential Reconstruction required the states in the Confederacy to convene constitutional conventions to declare secession proclamations null and void and to outlaw slavery as a condition of being readmitted to the Union and having their congressional delegations seated in the U.S. Senate and House of Representatives. The 1865 ratification of the Thirteenth Amendment, which outlawed slavery, rendered the last condition moot.[2] Nevertheless, the U.S. Congress continued to deny seats to the representatives of the former Confederate states between 1865 and 1868, except Tennessee, which quickly satisfied all of the conditions for readmission to the Union and was readmitted in July 1866.

President Johnson encouraged the state constitutional conventions to enfranchise blacks with steep and essentially exclusionary property qualifications along the lines of the New York state constitution, but in the months after the war, the whites-only conventions were so terrified by any hint of enfranchising black men that they ignored Johnson's cynical ploy. White voters then elected state legislators, governors, and U.S. representatives and senators. In 1865 and 1866, Southern state legislatures passed a series of laws about contracts, apprenticeships, debt, and vagrancy that severely restricted African Americans' freedoms. These laws, collectively known as the Black Codes, demonstrated that local whites were resuming control over state affairs with the approval of the president.

The November 1866 national elections, however, were a serious setback for white Southerners by bringing strong, veto-proof Republican majorities to both the U.S. House of Representatives and the U.S. Senate. The new Congress supplanted the mild nature of presidential Reconstruction with a harsher congressional Reconstruction in March and July of 1867. Overriding successive presidential vetoes, Congress declared martial law in ten Southern states, enfranchised black men in former Confederate states (but not in Northern states), established the Freedman's Bureau to protect the welfare of newly freed slaves, and laid the groundwork for abolishing the Black Codes by dissolving the all-white state legislatures and executives that had created them.

The Republican Congress and the nominally Republican president fought each other throughout the almost four years of the Johnson administration, and the nature and control of Reconstruction in the South was the central issue. The chasm between the president and legislature grew so large and acrimonious that in 1868, the House of Representatives impeached President Johnson, but the Senate failed by one vote to convict and remove him from office.

The new congressional Reconstruction acts required additional constitutional conventions in the former Confederate states, and high rates of black voter registration and the temporary disenfranchisement of some categories of former Confederates made African Americans a serious threat at the polls. By boycotting the elections for the second constitutional conventions, whites in several states believed that they could stall the conventions and the entire process of congressional Reconstruction. This strategy enabled black constituencies to elect their own representatives to the conventions without challenge, and although blacks were majorities in only two of the delegations, the white delegates were "**carpetbaggers**" and "**scalawags**" (see the glossary) generally committed to Reconstruction. The prewar white political class was being eclipsed.

In a further step, Congress proposed the Fourteenth Amendment to the states in June 1866. Its first section defines "citizen" as "All persons born or naturalized in the United States," thus overturning the assertion by Chief Justice Roger Taney of the Supreme Court in the 1857 *Dred Scott* case that African Americans were not eligible for U.S. citizenship. In addition, U.S. citizens are citizens of the nation first and foremost, and states cannot abridge national constitutional guarantees (for example, the Bill of Rights). The amendment, along with the Civil Rights Act of 1866, therefore sought to guarantee former slaves full civil rights and "equal protection of the laws." Although it took almost a century, the amendment significantly endorsed gains in civil rights.[3]

The Fourteenth Amendment is the first time in the Constitution that "male" or "man" was used. Radical women's rights leaders felt betrayed, and the amendment served to divide women's rights activists over Reconstruction. By July 1868, the twenty-eighth state had ratified the amendment, thus achieving the necessary approval by three-quarters of states for the amendment to become a permanent part of the Constitution.

Economic Doldrums

A few Southerners did well from the war, but the war was an economic disaster for the majority of the region's whites, including rich and powerful planters, whether they fought in the Confederate army or stayed on their plantations. All through the war, their highly visible estates were vulnerable to looting and destruction by passing Union and Confederate armies, black and white refugees, and Confederate deserters and demobilized soldiers on their way home.

Cotton was no longer a reliable source of income. The war, including the Union blockade, had led to a "cotton famine" for textile mills in Europe and the northern United States, a shortage that had stimulated new sources of cotton production in Egypt, India, Guatemala, and elsewhere. When the U.S. South could again engage in large-scale cotton exporting after the war, oversupply drove cotton prices down. And storms, floods, and the **army worm** (see the glossary) further impeded agricultural recovery in 1866 and 1867.

In this unpropitious market situation, planters had few financial resources with which to bring their properties back to previous levels of production. In addition to the physical destruction of the plantations and to what they lost from the uncompensated manumission of 3,500,000 slaves, planters' holdings of Confederate dollars and bonds were worthless. During the last years of the war, desperate Confederate state governments squeezed all resources within reach, and the congressional Reconstruction constitutions established statewide property taxes for the first time, adding to planters' financial difficulties.

There were a few examples of Union forces expropriating and redistributing large estates during the war. The best-known examples were in the Georgia Sea Islands and Missouri, but it was General William Tecumseh Sherman who instituted the most extensive redistribution of land. He granted twenty thousand freed slaves an average of fifty acres apiece of former plantations between Jacksonville, Florida, and Charleston, South Carolina. Federal authorities, however, quickly reversed the reforms, and antebellum landowning patterns changed little after the war. While large landholdings survived, there was some turnover of ownership.

The principal reason for the insecurity of planter property was more mundane than redistributive land reform. Like most agriculturists, Southern planters depended heavily on credit; they borrowed to prepare for the next crop cycle and repaid the loans when the crop was sold. During the war, however, the Union blockade of Southern shipping and the lack of security made it difficult and more expensive for planters to sell their cotton and roll over their debt. As a result, the accumulation of debt principal and unpaid interest created large debts for the planters when the war ended in 1865, and as slaves had frequently been used as collateral, manumission meant that the plantations were exposed to foreclosure.

Regional banks and cotton brokers were in crisis, which forced them to sell planters' debts to people and institutions outside the South in order to remain solvent. Northern institutions and opportunists as well as local debt holders foreclosed on plantations, forcing changes in the personnel in the planter class and adding to the weakness of the post–Civil War planter aristocracy.

The new property taxes were hard on all farmers, large and small, and small farms that had lost their young male workforce to the army during the war were also deeply in debt. Some states' new constitutions provided some form of debt protection through homestead provisions that exempted a certain value of personal and real property from creditors' reach, but these measures were not enough to alleviate what were hard times for most whites.

The freeing of slaves was an enormous blow to the very foundation of plantations' productive organization and the region's social system. Although slaves had rejected the Confederate cause *en masse* by crossing battle lines and serving as laborers and soldiers for the Union army, planters often expressed deep disappointment when former slaves left their plantations as soon as they could. Efforts to employ an agricultural wage-labor force of freedmen after the war were seldom successful in cotton. Without physical coercion, freedmen would not acquiesce to the rigors of the gang-labor system along with subsistence wages, long hours, and overseers' humiliations.

Mixed with tenancy, wage labor was widespread in coastal South Carolina and Georgia rice production, and wage labor was common in Louisiana sugar production, encouraged by the occupying U.S. Army since 1862. Rice and sugar were crops less well suited than cotton for production in small units, but tobacco did lend itself better to small farms. As a result, there were wide variations in the modes of labor organization in Virginia, North Carolina, and Kentucky.

Most slaves had worked in cotton production, and it took a few years after the war for the sharecropping system to become dominant as a sort of workable compromise between workers without land and landlords without capital. A landowner supplied a family with a plot of land, tools, seed, and provisions; the family supplied the labor. When the crop was harvested, it generally was divided evenly between the family and landowner. Part-time wage labor is not inconsistent with being a sharecropper, and wage labor did play some role in the Cotton Belt. In addition, although most sharecroppers were black, many poor whites had to enter into sharecropping agreements as well.

The disadvantage of the system for workers was that it allowed less independence to freed men and women than owning or even renting land. At the same time, sharecropping gave landowners less direct control over black labor than they desired. As James L. Roark (1977) observes, planters had to make the transition from lord to landlord and from master to employer, and although slavery bound the planter class together, competition among planters for free labor divided them. It was a new world.

White Political Resurgence

Slavery was more than an organization of production, and its abolition weakened the structure of social control that underlay white supremacy. Anxiety about personal security permeated the white Southern elite after the Civil War; the debility of the formerly powerful and the restlessness of the formerly enslaved seemed a terrible menace. Secession itself had triggered fears of slave revolts, fears enhanced by the Emancipation Proclamation, and congressional Reconstruction nullified the Black Codes designed to reconstitute white control of newly freed blacks.

Southern elites' focus on race was a common strategy to control non-slaveholding whites, whom they held in profound contempt but needed to contain. For example, Daniel Robinson Hundley (1860: 254–58) describes poor whites as "untutored, uncultivated, and servile creatures." The white leadership's recognition of poor whites' dislike for Southern elites was clearly expressed from Mexico by the former governor of Missouri, Thomas C. Reynolds. Reported by Rolle (1965: 150), Reynolds characterized President Andrew Johnson as the embodiment of the poor-white spirit of the South, and it was this background that made the president "side against secession, because the wealthier classes supported it." The white Southern leadership was hostile to universal white male suffrage, and its termination was to be on the agenda after the South achieved independence as the Confederate States of America.

The bleakness of the postwar period caused many white Southerners to entertain the idea of emigrating out of the South. Despite appeals from such Confederate luminaries as Robert E. Lee, Jefferson Davis, and P. T. Beauregard for loyal Southerners to stay in the South and fight to reestablish former conditions and values, thousands not only moved into the West and North, thousands more went to Latin America to create permanent expatriate communities that would reflect the "Southern way of life." The vast majority of such community-building efforts were ultimately unsuccessful.

Most antebellum white leaders did not leave the South but in staying believed that they could not count on federal authorities to protect them and their property from the anger of former slaves, the resentment of poor whites over the war that cost them so dearly, the avarice of Northern carpetbaggers, and the perfidy of Southern scalawags. Southern whites, then, were intent on regaining political control of state and local governments.

Their initial political strategy had been to boycott the elections for state constitutional conventions in 1867, and it had backfired. White Democrats then founded a movement called New Departure, which hypocritically declared acceptance of Reconstruction, stressed clean government and economic issues (for example, lower taxes), allied with dissident Republicans, and occasionally tried to attract black voters. The moderate rhetoric was aimed at the U.S. Congress as well as local constituencies, and it enjoyed some success in the border states and Upper South where whites were clear majorities. Where it did manage to control state politics, the New Departure governments restricted the franchise, tightened labor control measures, and reduced support for public education, especially but not exclusively for African American children.

Black voters never went for New Departure candidates in significant numbers, and in the Deep South states with large numbers of blacks, New Departure was not a winning strategy. For these states, the strategy of choice to reduce black political participation was to systematically terrorize the black population. A common pretext for murdering and intimidating blacks was whites' need to defend themselves from (nonexistent but supposedly imminent) "Negro uprisings"—a strategy known throughout the South as the Mississippi Plan.

There had been postwar incidents of terrible white violence against blacks, such as the 1866 race riots in Memphis and New Orleans, but chaos fueled by fear and hatred was not a viable long-run strategy. Both riots did, however, encourage more systematic use of white violence, because they demonstrated how often federal troops and their officers were unwilling to come to the aid of black citizens and to prosecute white-perpetrated crimes against blacks. The violence against blacks was not a regionally coordinated effort, but it did yield tangible results in strengthening white dominance, contributing to the spread of violence. The most infamous organization in this line of endeavor was the Ku Klux Klan (KKK), formed shortly after the end of the war as a social club by former Confederate officers. It grew quickly and turned into a decentralized terrorist organization that connected elite whites and poor whites in a common cause.

Instead of attacking armed federal troops, they were classic bullies, riding in large numbers at night, garbed in bizarre costumes, and intimidating mostly black families by threats, beatings, and killings. The KKK, like the Knights of Camellia, the White League, the White Line, and similar organizations, also targeted carpetbaggers and scalawags prominent in state and local governments and blamed for corruption, extravagance, and high taxes. In Mississippi, terrorists especially favored victimizing blacks and whites involved in new statewide public school systems, even though the schools were racially segregated.

In the national presidential election of 1868, Democrats, and especially the nominee for vice president, Francis Blair Jr., campaigned on virulently racist themes, criticizing the Fourteenth Amendment and Reconstruction as obstructing the return of the South's only qualified people (that is, local whites) to political leadership. While President Ulysses Grant won the national popular vote by a small margin, voters returned a strong Republican majority to Congress despite significant gains by Democrats. Republicans generally prevailed in the South, although the elections were marked by pervasive and vicious violence against blacks who wished to vote, particularly in Louisiana and Georgia—the two formerly Confederate states where Democratic candidates won.

The Republicans' confidence was bolstered by the election, and in response to the violence against blacks around the election, Congress proposed the Fifteenth Amendment to the states early in 1869. It was ratified by the requisite three-quarters of states in early 1870, and the prose is quite clear: "The right of citizens of the United States to vote shall not be denied or abridged by the United States or by any State on account of race, color, or previous condition of servitude."[4] It did not contain the sweeping language—and complexities—of the Fourteenth Amendment, but it had some ambiguity as to who would vote.

One of the Republicans' motives for passing the amendment was to garner blacks' votes in the border states and the South. But along with the Fourteenth Amendment, the Fifteenth split the woman suffrage movement. The division was between those who believed that the betrayal of women's aspirations justified opposing the amendment (National Woman Suffrage Association) and those who believed, like the black leader Frederick Douglass, that this should be "the Negro's hour" and who formed the American Woman Suffrage Association. This was a tragic end to what had been a close collaboration between advocates of black equality and women's rights. The two organizations did not merge until 1890.

With white Southerners becoming politically stronger at the state and local levels in the 1870s, secret societies like the KKK receded. Some of white strength in elections, of course, was predicated on terrorism. Nevertheless, when whites became local and state officials, they were able to violate blacks' rights in a more official and open manner, such as through sheriffs' offices and, later, public lynchings. As a result, there was less need to depend on secret, difficult-to-control gangs of costumed men who rode at night.

While whites were making a political comeback in the South through a combination of the ballot, intimidation, and forcibly taking over local governments from elected officials, reconciliation between whites in the North and South was the next step. Defections from the congressional coalition that had backed Reconstruction rose sharply due to frustration, its expense, and increasing interest in other, more pressing (or rewarding) projects. At the same time, the post–Civil War flood of soldiers' memoirs, especially those by generals from both sides, emphasized the experience of battle and the bravery and principled loyalties of both Southern and Northern soldiers. This literature helped to recast the reasons for the Civil War—that is, it was about preserving the union or states' rights and definitely *not* about slavery and race. The conveniently selective understanding of the war, essentially the white South's claim, helped set the stage for reunion and reconciliation between whites in the North and South at the expense of black rights and opportunities.

In 1870, Congress readmitted to the Union the last four of the former Confederate states—Virginia, Mississippi, Texas, and Georgia—in addition to ratifying the Fifteenth Amendment. In the early 1870s, the U.S. Congress also passed a series of acts that dispatched special units of U.S. cavalry to protect southern blacks from white violence. These acts, which for the first time made violence a federal crime, further reduced KKK activities. At the same time, the acts sharply increased the split within the Republican Party between those who supported enforcing Reconstruction and those who denounced its expense and increased centralization of government power.

Three Responses to Racial Oppression

Despite laws and amendments, life for African Americans in the South continued to be very difficult, and one response to segregation, discrimination, and violence was for blacks to emigrate from the region. The American Colonization Society, formed in 1816, transported eleven thousand free black men and women to Liberia in the forty years before the

Civil War. In the 1870s, responding to rising violence by whites against blacks, disenfranchisement, and heightening economic oppression, African Americans began to consider leaving in large numbers. Liberia was one of the most sought-after destinations, but Kansas was more feasible.[5]

Abolitionist and temperance Republicans controlled Kansas, and although they did not make special provisions for southern black migrants, they did not severely discriminate against them. The 1880 census in Kansas found over twenty-eight thousand African Americans who had been born in former slave states. Many more tried to go, but the lack of resources together with white resistance frustrated their attempts.

*[An alternative to emigration was to accept segregation and disenfranchisement (but not lynching) while founding industrial and agricultural schools for African Americans with the goal of enhancing skills and enhancing middle-class proprieties among former slaves. The Hampton Normal and Agricultural Institute (1866; currently Hampton University) in Virginia was the model for schools training teachers but with strong emphases on practical work skills. The Tuskegee Institute (1881; currently Tuskegee University) in Alabama was almost as famous as Hampton, and its first principal, Booker T. Washington (1856–1915), born a slave, became the leading national spokesman for African Americans. He was an adviser to Presidents Theodore Roosevelt and William Howard Taft and advised northern charities interested in contributing to African American causes in the South. George Washington Carver was a member of the Institute's faculty all his professional life, earning an international reputation in scientific circles.]

Booker T. Washington was adamant that African Americans should develop the "Christian character" and work habits and skills that would enable them to be materially successful. With property and standing, political and civil rights would be a natural consequence. Washington was always a bit vague, even ambiguous, about these political goals in public, which allowed his gospel of self-help through industrial and agricultural training for semiskilled occupations to be acceptable to white southerners and attractive to northern philanthropists. Although he secretly supported some activist political efforts to reduce segregation and obstacles to the vote, he publicly condemned political activism on behalf of African Americans, insisting that blacks had to "earn" their rights. His public message was accommodating, even conciliatory, with respect to white southerners. It probably had to be; he and the institute were in rural Alabama.

A third response to the difficulties of southern African Americans was to speak out against the racial injustices and work politically to obtain federal protections for southern African Americans. Ida B. Wells (1862–1931), also born into slavery, was a teacher, investigative reporter, newspaper editor, speaker, and lifelong activist against lynching. She studied at Shaw University (currently Rust University), LeMoyne Institute (now LeMoyne-Owen College), and Fisk University, and her writings were searing indictments of the way southern whites abused southern blacks. Her researches on lynching were cogently documented from contemporary newspaper accounts and supplied information generally unavailable to both black and white readers.

There are several clues as to her personality and convictions. Seventy years before Rosa Parks's refusal to give up her seat in a Montgomery, Alabama, bus, Wells declined to give up her first-class train seat to a white man, and it took three men to get her out of the seat and off the train. She then sued the railroad but lost on appeal. In her pamphlet *Southern Horrors: Lynch Law in All Its Phases* (1892) she writes, "The lesson this [lynching] teaches and which every Afro-American should ponder well, is that a Winchester rifle should have a place of honor in every black home, and it should be used for that protection which law refuses to give." She shocked northern and southern whites when she wrote that white men rape black women more frequently than black men rape white women and that most sex between black men and white women was consensual. In Washington, DC, for a woman suffrage demonstration, she met with President William McKinley about a lynching in South Carolina.

Wells founded the first black woman suffrage organization, several African American women's clubs, and antilynching organizations. She was an instrumental figure in the Niagara Movement, which became the National Association for the Advancement of Colored People (NAACP), although W. E. B. Du Bois (1868–1963) maliciously always downplayed her role. She spent much of the last two decades of her life in community organizing to improve life in Chicago's ghetto, which had expanded greatly during World War I.

The U.S. South, which was to be officially transformed, turned out to be the major region that experienced the least in the way of transformation. The South increasingly became a backwater while rapid and renovating changes in industrial development created new opportunities and social actors in other regions.

5

—⚍—

Changing Forms of Industrial Development

In this era, a new pattern of industrial growth emerged, different in form and rhythm from the first fifty years of industrial development. We use a short study of German industrialization to highlight the new features of U.S. industrial development in the second half of the nineteenth century. Complementing the westward shift of the U.S. population and rapid industrialization, this era saw a massive increase in immigration from Europe and rising rates of U.S. urbanization.

FINANCE-CAPITALIST
INDUSTRIALIZATION: NEW PATTERNS

Economic activity in the nineteenth-century West centered on exploitation of natural resources through mining, lumbering, cattle raising, and farming. Processing these products, such as crushing and smelting minerals, milling flour and lumber, and refining beet sugar, were technically manufacturing activities, but the principal regions of the era's manufacturing development were the Northeast and Upper Midwest. And in the late nineteenth century, the character of industrial production changed in ways that profoundly altered the social and political implications of industrial growth. The new and distinctive features of this second phase of industrial development were evident in all industrialized nations at the end of the nineteenth century, but an analysis of German industrial growth between 1850 and World War I highlights these new patterns in the United States— and the industrialized world. This form of industrialization in which large corporations dominated much of the industrial landscape also developed new social formations, which in turn fomented reform efforts that brought the national government into monitoring and regulating economic affairs in unprecedented ways and with unprecedented reach.

Germany, 1860–1914

Germany became a unified nation in 1871, when Prussian leadership consolidated the German principalities into imperial Germany. Prussia dominated the new nation and encouraged industrial growth based on products important to reasserting its military superiority on the continent, severely challenged during the Napoleonic Wars, and resisting the British threat. Therefore, it was not market demand for wage (consumer) goods that propelled German industrial growth; rather, **producer goods**—sold to firms, the military, and other government purchasers rather than individuals—became the leading branches of German industrial development.

Capital goods (for example, machinery) were one of the major components of producer goods. During the initial phases of English and U.S. industrial growth, there was no distinct capital goods sector; it was not unusual in both settings for workers recruited to work in a new factory to build the plant and construct the machinery before operating it. The second major category of producer goods central to Germany's industrial drive were intermediate products such as steel, chemicals, fuel, glass, and eventually rubber and electrical equipment, all inputs for further production. These intermediary products, important early in German industrialization, either were not produced at all in the early years of English and U.S. industrialization or else were ancillary production from small workshops.[1]

In addition to the contrasting compositions of leading products, German industry from the beginnings of its mid-nineteenth-century industrialization utilized modern nineteenth-century technology that built upon a century of English and U.S. advances. As a result of both product mix and technology, a few large-scale, capital-intensive industrial enterprises made up the dynamic heart of German industrialization. The size and capitalization of German producer goods firms meant that German industrial development did not diffuse economic power among a large number of owner-operators of diverse backgrounds. Instead, industrial growth constituted the basis for new concentrations of economic power controlled by those who had access to the considerable financial resources necessary for establishing an enterprise on an economically viable scale.

This did not mean that family fortunes, the Public Sector, and foreign investors were the exclusive founders of new firms; from the beginnings of rapid industrial growth of the 1850s, joint-stock investment banks increasingly supplied the financial capital. These banks did not operate as just financial intermediaries. By the later 1840s, external sources of funds were not important for the largest banks, which financed, directed, and even established industrial enterprises through their own retained profits. Hence the label "Finance Capital."

Instead of open, competitive determination of market prices, centralization of industrial production and mutual recognition of interdependence led to coordinated decisions, often directed by banks, concerning production, prices, and mergers. Formal, legally enforceable **cartels**—the contractual agreement among competing firms to reduce competition, adapted from an organizational form with a long history in Germany—embraced most of the firms that constituted the dynamic core of German industrial growth. This managed capital-capital relationship did not completely suspend market forces, especially for exporters, but cartels did reduce competition among producers of the leading branches of manufacturing. Tariffs that protected domestic markets from foreign products also helped insulate German firms from market competition. Finance Capitalism was not friendly to free trade.

The product composition, technology, and industrial structure of Germany's late nineteenth-century rapid manufacturing growth meant that the formation of a German industrial labor force was a more modest endeavor compared to eighteenth-century English wage-goods production. Labor needs for German industry required neither abolishing legal barriers to geographical mobility for semiserfs on eastern *latifundia*—the economic base of the Prussian aristocracy (*Junkers*)—nor dispossessing the freeholding peasantry in the south and west. And population growth did not make a vital contribution to German industrial development.

The relatively few industrial workers, the early strength of their large-firm unions, and their high productivity compared to agricultural and consumer-goods production set them apart from the general working population in income as well as work-life experience. Thus, although modern sector workers achieved political influence early in Germany's industrial growth, it was difficult for them to speak for the interests of the majority of German workers. Factions of the industrial working class had radical moments, but Otto von Bismarck, the Prussian prince who led the unification of Germany and became its first chancellor, was creative in managing capital-labor relations by mixing repression with social insurance and welfare legislation for industrial workers. The segmented character of the workforce rendered the privileged stratum of workers vulnerable to the combination of carrots and sticks and increased their susceptibility to nationalist appeals in times of crisis, such as World War I.

German agriculture was commercialized in that large proportions of its products were sold in domestic and foreign markets, but agricultural output and productivity growth in Germany lagged far behind that of industry. During the first decade of the twentieth century, average labor productivity in German manufacturing was 50 percent greater than in agriculture, while average labor productivity in English manufacturing was still a bit lower than in agriculture as late as the 1850s. German agriculture did not have to be a source of labor supply or product demand for industrial growth, and the agricultural sector could deliver additional goods to domestic markets by switching from exports without transforming its organization or labor relations. German agriculture did experience some productivity growth at the end of the nineteenth century, but agricultural progress was the *result* of an industrial development that supplied agriculture with farm machinery and chemical fertilizers rather than a source of that development.

Finance-Capitalist industrial growth was led by giant, capital-intensive plants with no need to develop strong consumer-goods markets or to transform the countryside. The result was not liberal industrial capitalism. Militaristic nationalism rather than individualistic liberalism was the predominant ideology of industrial development, and the economic theory produced in the period of Germany industrialization was deliberately framed in opposition to the individualism of the free-market "Manchesterian economics" of Britain.

The few industrial leaders, the acceptability of industrialists' backgrounds and values to the preindustrial aristocracy, and occasional revolutionary agitation among the best-organized workers enabled the German imperial government to convince the *Junkers* and the agents of industrial growth that nationalist aspirations transcended or were compatible with their interests. Thus the "marriage of iron and rye" was consummated in the 1870s.

German industrial development demonstrated that industrialization could come from above, preserving and strengthening precapitalist hierarchies and cultural forms. Finance-Capitalist industrial development did not create conservative societies, but it allowed conservative societies to become industrial societies. In the German case, the *Junkers* and imperial government were in a position to ensure that if German industrialization had not been conservative, there would have been no industrialization.

The idea of a distinctive Finance-Capitalist path to industrialization in the late nineteenth century helps in understanding some striking similarities in the patterns of French industrial development that began during Louis Bonaparte's mid-nineteenth-century reign, the nature of Japanese industrial growth after the Meiji Restoration of 1868, and the incomplete nineteenth-century achievements in capitalist Russia, Bulgaria, and northern Italy. And the twentieth-century "socialist" industrial development of the Soviet Union has some striking parallels with the German-Prussian path that would not have been possible under the product mix and industrial structure prevailing in the era of Competitive Capitalism.

United States, 1860–1914

U.S. manufacturing grew rapidly after the Civil War, and by the 1880s, U.S. manufacturing production surpassed Great Britain's and became the largest in the world. Table 5.1 shows that late nineteenth-century industrial growth in the United States, as in Germany, was oriented toward intermediate and capital goods, in contrast to its earlier emphases on

Table 5.1.   Changes in the Principal Lines of U.S. Manufacturing

	Value Added		Employment	
	$1,000,000	*Percentage*	*1,000*	*Percentage*
1860				
Cotton textiles	55	6.7	115	7.8
Lumber	54	6.6	76	5.2
Boots and shoes	49	6.0	123	8.3
Flour and meal	40	4.9	28	1.8
Men's clothing	37	4.5	115	7.8
Iron	36	4.4	50	3.4
Machinery	33	4.0	41	2.8
Woolens	25	3.1	61	4.1
Carriages and wagons	24	2.9	37	2.5
Leather	23	2.8	23	1.6
Total U.S. Manufacturing	815	100.0	1,474	100.0
1910				
Machinery	690	8.1	530	8.0
Lumber	650	7.6	700	10.6
Printing and publishing	540	6.3	260	3.9
Iron and steel	330	3.9	240	3.6
Malt liquors	280	3.2	55	0.8
Men's clothing	270	3.2	240	3.6
Cotton textiles	260	3.0	380	5.7
Tobacco	240	2.8	170	2.6
Railroad cars	210	2.5	280	4.2
Boots and shoes	180	2.1	200	3.0
Total U.S. Manufacturing	8,529	100.0	6,615	100.0

Source: Derived from Stanley L. Engerman and Kenneth L. Sokoloff, "Technology and Industrialization, 1790–1914," in *The Cambridge Economic History of the United States*, Vol. 2: *The Long Nineteenth Century*, ed. Stanley L. Engerman and Robert E. Gallman (New York: Cambridge University Press, 2000), 376.

consumer wage goods. This composition of manufacturing output was a common feature of Finance-Capitalist industrial growth.

Prices of U.S. manufactures declined from the end of the Civil War through the mid-1890s, especially during the sharp depressions ("panics") of 1873 and 1893 that lasted most of their respective decades. The Panic of 1907, although severe, was not as long lasting due in good part to the leadership of J. P. Morgan, the nation's most powerful banker. He rallied other New York City financial moguls to lend sufficient funds to banks experiencing runs to calm the panic. (The role of leading financiers in the 2008 financial debacle was far different.)

Railroads were important forerunners of some key features of U.S. manufacturing's course of development, and we can use them to introduce U.S. industrial history in these decades. Railroad corporations were the first big U.S. businesses to depend on large-scale external financing. One-third of the financing came from European investors, and the scale of domestic and foreign investing further stimulated the development of financial markets—stock exchanges, bond markets, trust companies, insurance companies, and a multitude of specialized banks—especially in New York City. This interrelated web of financial organizations facilitated the growth of large-scale, publicly owned corporations in many branches of production and distribution by enabling them to tap into large pools of finance.

Railroads also pioneered in using professional managers, clearly demarcated bureaucracies, the telegraph, and new accounting techniques. The proven effectiveness of these innovations led to their adoption in other sectors to enhance the ability of multiplant manufacturing and retail firms to monitor and control production, inventories, and distribution from a central office.

The railroads were also important to the manufacturing sector through its linkages. Andrew Carnegie introduced the Bessemer process for steel production to the United States, a process that made steel faster and cheaper. In 1872, 4 percent of U.S. pig iron output was used to make steel, and in 1913, 93 percent went into steel. The railroads' demand for iron rails became a demand for the more durable steel rails, and more than 80 percent of national steel output went to the railroads for tracks. Locomotive production also stimulated the iron, steel, and machinery sectors. The railroads' use of wood for ties, bridges, stations, and railcars constituted about a full fifth of the total lumber milled between 1870 and 1900, keeping lumber milling near the top in value added among all branches of manufacturing.

One of the most important lessons for the manufacturing sector from the railroads was how to deal with price competition. Competition among the railroad companies was fierce, and it was rife with dangers for the companies. Much of the railroads' costs were **fixed costs** that had to be paid whether or not there were any customers. For example, the purchase of tracks and rolling stock was already committed, and the resulting debts had payment schedules to be met irrespective of the volume of traffic and revenues. The railroads' **variable costs**, like wages and fuel that did depend on the amount of traffic, were much smaller. Thus, maintaining or expanding the volume of traffic was critical in order to cover the costs. As a result, rate wars were frequent and damaging, and the actual operation of the railroads was often not all that profitable. Railroads going through bankruptcy owned 20 percent of rail mileage in 1897, up from 18 percent in 1877.

The immense wealth generated for a few from railroads was principally from real estate and manipulation of railroad stocks and bonds, not from the day-to-day transportation of freight and passengers. Nevertheless, if more railroad companies had been designed for efficient and profitable transportation service rather than for real-estate and financial speculation and peculation, money could have been made from their freight and passenger services. For example, Great Northern proved to be profitable without large federal subsidies through sound construction and financing, good management, and ruthlessly squeezing their workers and customers.

Railroads tried a number of strategies to mitigate the problem of rate wars. Without the force of law, informal agreements in various forms repeatedly broke down because the incentive to cheat by lowering agreed-upon prices in order to increase traffic was so high. Some managers even hoped that state legislation could make the railroads a regulated public utility in order to guard against rate wars. But nothing seemed to work.

Unlike the German imperial government, the U.S. federal government did not have the authority to coordinate capital-capital relationships among independent railroad corporations by enforcing pricing and production agreements. Beyond questions of authority and capacity, the U.S. government, responding to farmers, among others, discouraged such agreements and other anticompetitive practices. U.S. banks, rather than trying to coordinate the activities of competing firms, preferred the strategy of reducing the number of competing firms through mergers and acquisitions, consolidating them into new, larger entities.

As the Panic of 1893 began, railroad companies, working with banks, began to consolidate to protect themselves from the hazards of full competition. They were so successful that by the beginning of the twentieth century, seven financial groups controlled two-thirds of track mileage and 85 percent of earnings, and when one looks at the interlocking connections, it was four groups. This reduced the likelihood of rate wars that benefited no one but customers.

In the manufacturing sector, technological change drove higher levels of capital intensity. The average capital investment per manufacturing firm doubled between 1850 and 1870, and by 1890, it had more than doubled again. Technological advances and increased capitalization usually increased the scale of production necessary to achieve greatest efficiency and lowest per-unit costs. In the terminology of the economics discipline, the economies of scale became greater, increasing plant size. Another incentive to increase size and market share was the ability to influence prices through the exercise of market power.

As the manufacturing sector grew and developed, industrial managers found themselves in a bind similar to that of the railroads' executives. The increased capitalization of manufacturing plants meant that larger proportions of their total costs were fixed and that achieving low per-unit costs required large-scale, near-capacity production. Whether in newsprint or steel nails, the leading branches of manufacturing were **oligopolies**.[2] When a firm with excess productive capacity attempted to lower its price in order to increase its market share at the expense of the two, three, or four other large firms in the industry, the responses and counterresponses of a price war were the likely consequences.

Manufacturing associations, like the railroads, tried a number of tactics to lessen the dangers of price wars, but without the force of law behind such agreements, as in Germany, the pressures to cheat were too great. Consolidation seemed to be the only solution. There had been some systematic consolidation among industrial firms prior to the 1890s, but the prevailing form was to achieve **vertical integration** through merging backward (that is, with suppliers of inputs) or forward to marketing and distribution. When steel firms bought iron ore mines in the Mesabi Iron Range in Minnesota, it was backward-linked vertical integration. Forward-linked vertical integration occurred when firms making complex products such as mechanical reapers and sewing machines established retail outlets in order to provide the necessary training for customers and maintenance and repair services.

The second type of integration is **horizontal integration** and occurs when firms take over competitors engaged in the same lines and stages of production, as in the case of the railroads. This is the type of integration that reduces competition and thus the danger of price wars. Standard Oil led the way for manufacturers in the early 1880s by consolidating allied refineries into a holding company chartered in corporate-friendly New Jersey. The busiest time for mergers was between 1895 and 1903, peaking in 1899. The depression years of the 1890s had touched off price wars among firms producing a wide range of goods from paper to chemical fertilizers, and in those nine years, there were 154 multifirm mergers that dissolved 1,800 firms through consolidation.

The most blatant and successful of bank-led consolidation occurred in 1901, when J. P. Morgan bought Andrew Carnegie's steelworks for $480 million. Morgan convinced a number of other steel producers to combine with the Carnegie steel company to form the United States Steel Corporation, and the world's first billion-dollar corporation produced 70 percent of U.S. steel output. The profitability of such market power is why the value of a consolidated firm can be considerably greater than the sum of its parts.

Nevertheless, through an obsessive focus on stock prices and financial manipulation, the new corporation soon squandered its lead by carrying excessive debt, lagging in adopting new technology, and fiercely, expensively, and often violently opposing labor union activity. Bankers have particular views on how to make money, and efficiently producing quality steel is not one of them.

U.S. banks were engaged in these mergers and acquisitions. It was common practice for participating banks to place representatives on the expanded firms' boards of directors. This encouraged a fusion between manufacturing and finance that had a definite German feel to it. By the 1920s, however, manufacturing firms had mostly freed themselves from monitoring by banks and their representatives.

In the product mix of leading branches of manufacturing production, the rise of the large, highly capitalized corporation, the concomitant formation of oligopolistic markets, and the central role played by banks in industrial mergers and acquisitions, we have four of the most important ingredients identified as Finance Capitalism in Germany and replicated in the United States but with different political and economic consequences.

Mass-Produced Consumer Goods

As in Great Britain, the implications of Finance-Capital industrialization in the United States were tempered by the previous strength of Competitive Capitalism, and the United States was distinctive in its decentralized political organization, the almost universal white male franchise, widespread literacy, and the diffusion of landownership in northern and western U.S. agriculture.

By 1900, the United States was a continent-wide common market of seventy-six million people with, for the times and in most of the world, a high standard of living. This market was knitted together by 250,000 miles of rails, coastal and riverine steamers, and improving and expanding roads, and landowning farmers and ranchers along with the growing urban middle class constituted a market for mass-produced consumer goods. It was a large market, but it was just the beginning of the formation of a mass market with broad swaths of people enjoying substantial discretionary income; a true mass market emerged only after World War II.

In the United States, mass-produced manufactured consumer goods grew up within the leading intermediate and capital goods firms. This was different from Germany, and even from Great Britain, where the average standard of living was close to that of the United States but the less equitable distribution of income constricted the market for mass-produced consumer products. The United States industrial economy, with its unique foundation combining intermediate, capital, and consumer goods, had a different dynamic.

For consumer-goods firms, an important necessary step had to do with trademarks and brands. Manufacturers were interested in distinguishing their consumer products from those of competitors, but to do so, products had to be packaged in a distinctive, identifiable manner. But a firm could advertise heavily, and another company could use the same packaging and brand name in order to fool customers intending to buy the advertiser's brand. The situation called for formally registering trademarks and making it illegal for others to use them without permission. In other words, make trademarks similar to copyrights and patents, a category already sanctioned in the U.S. Constitution and capable of being bought and sold as property.

The U.S. Congress passed the first trademark legislation in 1870, but it was not until 1881 that Congress passed legislation that survived judicial review. While trademarks were similar to copyrights and patents, they were different in that trademarks never expire. Advertising was now on more solid ground, and advertisers got the message out in the rapidly multiplying print media, placards in public transportation, billboards, and, eventually, radio.

The market organization for mass-produced consumer goods began to look like that for capital and intermediate goods, and gigantism and oligopoly began to become evident in agricultural processing and retailing as well. When railroads built into areas where high transportation costs had protected local firms (say, a flour mill) from competition, the resulting market integration meant that the local firm that had had a local monopoly suddenly had to compete with giant firms such as Pillsbury, Gold Medal, Washburn-Crosby, and other large flour-milling neighbors in Minneapolis along the banks of the Mississippi River.

Another example in agricultural processing is meatpacking, in which Gustavus Swift of Swift & Co. was the innovator. The wider availability of rail transportation had already rendered obsolete the massive cattle drives from the plains states to railheads, and Swift took it another step. In the 1870s, instead of shipping live cattle, pigs, and sheep to eastern markets by rail, Swift's crew slaughtered and processed the animals in, for example, the Chicago stockyards and then shipped the meat in refrigerated rail cars to eastern markets. That was cheaper than shipping live animals, and immediate success led to emulation. By the end of the 1880s, Swift and three similarly organized companies produced two-thirds of dressed beef in the United States, replacing hundreds of local slaughterhouses.

More than half the firms created between 1895 and 1903 failed quickly, and firms introducing successful new consumer products, like typewriters (1874), barbed wire (1876), telephones (1876), incandescent electric light bulbs (1879), gasoline-powered automobiles (1885), and Kodak cameras (1888) began small. Often protected by patents, they grew through reinvestment and acquisitions and created familiar patterns of dominant firms. For example, although there were a myriad of small automobile producers early in the twentieth century, half of the automobiles in the United States in 1918 were Model Ts made by Ford, which had grown through reinvestment. Dodge Brothers (growing through reinvestment) and General Motors (growing through acquisitions) were beginning to challenge Ford's lead at this time. Combining new and not-so-new products, the first decade of the twentieth century saw firms producing electrical equipment, farm equipment, dressed meat, wools and silks, and automobiles in plants as large as or larger than steel mills, railroads, and locomotive and rail car manufacturers.

The consumer-goods firms that prospered formed brands and an industrial structure that lasted for decades. Similar to intermediate-product firms such as petroleum products, steel, paper, and lead, agricultural processing firms such as Campbell, Heinz, Borden's, Kellogg's, Quaker Oats, and American Tobacco grew through mergers, acquisitions, reinvesting profits, and selling corporate shares. They joined already consolidated firms in flour, whiskey, sugar, and some vegetable oils. General Electric, Westinghouse, American Telephone and Telegraph, Victor Talking Machine Company (subsequently RCA Victor), United Shoe Machinery, International Harvester, American Steel and (barbed) Wire, Eastman Kodak, Amalgamated Copper, Ford Motor Company, General Motors, Singer Sewing Machine, and Remington Typewriter either dominated or were one of the dominant players in their respective markets.

Distribution was problematic in consumer goods that individual buyers purchased in small volumes. This meant reaching thousands and thousands of current and potential customers. The railroads could deliver goods to fixed points, but it took an even more complex web of transportation and communication for successful advertising and final delivery.

In addition to passengers and freight, railroads, coaches, and wagons carried mail. Towns and villages lobbied strenuously for a post office to ensure regular transportation links to the outside world. The number of post offices grew from 28,498 in 1860 to 76,688 in 1900. The next step in the expansion of postal service was Rural Free Delivery, beginning in 1896, where mail was delivered without extra cost to mailboxes on public roads throughout the countryside. Parcel-post legislation, passed in 1912, enabled post offices to handle parcels over four pounds in weight, and rural routes were included for parcel-post deliveries in 1919.

Reflecting the high literacy rates from what economists call investments in **human capital** through schooling in the United States, post offices handled four billion pieces of mail in 1890, including growing newspaper and magazine subscriptions, books, catalogs, fliers, and letters from friends and families. The paper intensity of the explosion of the printed word was made possible by the sharp decline in the price of paper when papermaking began using wood pulp instead of rags, which continued to be used for high-quality writing paper and paper currency. The large scale of modern pulp-based paper mills created another concentrated industrial structure.

Expanded communications served to reduce cultural differences between urban and rural, and consumer tastes were an important aspect of the general cultural trend. In 1872, Aaron Montgomery Ward and a partner established in the loft of a Chicago stable a mail-order business that targeted people on farms and in small towns. Annual sales had risen to forty million dollars by 1913. Richard W. Sears and Alvah C. Roebuck established a general merchandise catalog in 1893, and by the early twentieth century the company was the largest mail-order retailer. Edna Ferber, in *Fanny Herself* (1917), wrote about a fictional giant mail-order company that was said "to eat a small-town merchant every morning for breakfast."[3] Walmart and e-commerce were not the first retail changes to batter local merchants who had trouble competing in price and product choice.

Both Sears, Roebuck and Montgomery Ward began to establish brick-and-mortar stores in the early twentieth century in competition with J. C. Penney's network of stores. In doing so, they were contributing to the growth of chain stores licensed by manufacturers or by large retailers. As mentioned earlier, International Harvester and Singer Corporation had established this model of chain stores licensed by manufacturers before the Civil War in order to instruct buyers about the use and care of their harvesters and sewing machines and to provide repair services. At the turn of the twentieth century, large retailers and manufacturers were establishing chains of branded stores. A&P and Kroger grocery stores, Woolworth and Kresge variety stores, and American Tobacco Company's United Cigar Store are notable examples, but there were many smaller chains selling clothes, health products, pianos, burial services, and a range of other goods and services.

Adding to mail-order catalogs and the chain stores, the growth and popularity of large department stores in urban areas represented a third type of mass-marketing innovation. Department stores sold a wide range of consumer goods in individual departments within one building and offered attractions such as large outside display windows, lavish decorations, and trained staffs as well as restaurants, music, reading rooms, home delivery, wrapping services, restrooms, and money-back guarantees. Department stores had been a part of the retailing scene in Europe since the early nineteenth century, and in the United States, Marshall Field (1873, Chicago), John Wanamaker (1876, Philadelphia), and Rowland Hussey Macy (1878, New York City) and their department stores were among the most successful and best known. Department stores became a major employer of women. The women clerks were from publicly educated working-class backgrounds and served the upper- and upper-middle-class women customers.

The three types of large retailers—mail-order merchants, chain stores, and department stores—had enough purchasing power to bargain down manufacturers' prices through quantity discounts, easy credit, low-cost shipping, and other advantages wrung from manufacturers. The mass marketers in turn cut prices to stimulate sales, much to the dismay of manufacturers. Small independent retailers did not receive such discounts and were thus unable to cut final prices. In an alliance of convenience, small retailers joined with manufacturers to allow manufacturers to set prices for their packaged, branded, and nationally advertised goods through the entire chain of transactions: wholesalers, retailers, and final purchasers. The manufacturer would refuse to sell their advertised and popular product to a firm that cut prices below that set by the manufacturer.

Not all manufacturers participated in this, but enough did to make it a contentious issue. The advocates of "fair trade laws" (more accurately "retail price maintenance laws"), led by the Kellogg Company, mendaciously presented the scheme as something to protect consumers. The resistance of consumers and mass marketers prevented the U.S. Congress from passing legislation that put the force of federal law behind this practice until 1937, during the Great Depression, when deflation was a real threat. The U.S. Congress repealed that legislation in 1976, and in 1988, the U.S. Supreme Court decided against retail price fixing by manufacturers.

It is ironic that the development of national markets and the rise of giant, centralized enterprises in manufacturing, transportation, and retailing could create greater market competition. But this was not the competition of Adam Smith's "invisible hand," where an impersonal market mediated relationships among atomistic competitors. Alfred D. Chandler (1977) argues that this was a situation in which markets were controlled by the "visible hands" of managers of giant firms who negotiated, col-

luded, and administered price and output decisions while appealing to
the federal government to protect them from competition.

Foreign Mass Immigration

At the time the U.S. population was undergoing a major shift westward,
the Northeast and Great Lakes regions experienced rapid manufacturing growth. So who was left to work in the new factories? The form of
industrialization occurring in the late nineteenth century was more capital intensive and less labor intensive than antebellum industrial growth,
so employers needed fewer additional workers than one might think
from the earlier experience. But employers still did need workers. Table
5.2 shows the massive increases in foreign immigration in the last two
decades of the nineteenth century and the first two decades of the twentieth, listed individually, when World War I affected the size and source
of immigration. These numbers and rates of immigration far surpassed
the 1850s immigrations. Table 5.2 shows that disproportionate numbers
of immigrants settled in the Northeast, although they were important
components of population growth in all areas outside the South. Scandi-
navian immigrants who settled in the northern plains were exceptional,
because two-thirds to three-fourths of the new immigrants went to urban
locations in whichever region they resided. By World War I, one-third of
the U.S. manufacturing labor force was foreign born.

Note the changes in the sources of the immigrants. Northern and
western Europe had been the largest source of immigration to the United
States after outlawing the international slave trade, but toward the end
of the nineteenth century, eastern Europe (including Russia) and southern Europe (mostly Italy) dominated the immigration numbers. While
Catholicism in the earlier wave of Irish immigrants was undesirable to
many U.S. Protestants, many of those immigrants escaping persecution in
eastern Europe were not even Christians. A special animus was reserved
for them, and a general nativism once again animated national politics in
the United States.[4]

The nativism was strong on the West Coast, directed mainly at the
Chinese, and as already noted, the U.S. Congress acceded to westerners'
pressure and passed the first national Chinese Exclusion Act in 1882. The
1790 and 1802 Naturalization Acts stated "that any Alien being a free
white person . . . may be admitted to become a citizen" of the United
States, but the decentralized U.S. naturalization system had often permitted Chinese, Japanese, and South Asians to become naturalized citizens
until an authoritative and unambiguous federal law or ruling. This laxity
ended with the Chinese Exclusion Act.

Table 5.2. Recorded Immigrants to the United States by Region of Origin, 1821–1920

	Total (Thousands)	% From Europe			% from Americas	% from Asia	% of Total
		North & West	East & Central	Southern			
1821–1840	742	74.59	—	1.5	7.06	—	100.0
1841–1860	4,311	93.3	0.1	0.6	3.3	0.8	100.0
1861–1880	5,127	80.7	2.5	1.8	10.8	3.6	100.0
1881–1900	8,935	58.3	22.4	12.7	4.6	1.6	100.0
1901–1910	8,797	21.7	44.5	26.3	4.1	2.8	100.0
1911–1920	5,736	17.4	33.4	25.3	19.9	3.4	100.0

Notes: All together, immigrants from Australia, New Zealand, Africa, and other unlisted areas never added up to as much as 0.5 percent of the total in these years. The last two decades are listed individually. Totals may not be the sum of parts due to rounding errors.

Source: Derived from Michael R. Haines, "The Population of the United States, 1790–1920," in *The Cambridge Economic History of the United States*, Vol. 2: *The Long Nineteenth Century*, ed. Stanley L. Engerman and Robert E. Gallman (New York: Cambridge University Press, 2000), 196.

Over time, there were a number of court cases contesting the definition of "white," and in 1922, the U.S. Supreme Court ruled that Japanese were not white and therefore not eligible for citizenship. The court made a similar ruling in 1923, arguing that the South Asian plaintiff might indeed be Caucasian, but he was not white, and that's what the law said.

In 1868, the Fourteenth Amendment had opened a crack in the racial ineligibilities for naturalization, when its first sentence read: "All persons born or naturalized in the United States, and subject to the jurisdiction thereof, are citizens of the United States and of the State wherein they reside." It took three decades for this sentence to be honored in the courts, however, and in 1898 the U.S. Supreme Court ruled that Asians born in the United States were citizens.

Urbanization

Despite all the westward movement, much of which was to work farms and ranches, the agriculture share of the labor force declined from 55 percent in 1860 to 36 percent in 1900 and to 26 percent in 1920. Only the South had a majority of workers in agriculture. You can see related figures for urbanization in table 4.2, which shows that in 1920, for the first time, urban residents outnumbered rural residents in the nation as a whole.

Cities that were well established in the early nineteenth century, such as New York, Boston, Philadelphia, Baltimore, Charleston, and New Orleans, newer cities like Cincinnati, Memphis, Chicago, Cleveland, and St. Louis, and the newest cities like Minneapolis-St. Paul, Kansas City, Omaha, Des Moines, Dallas, Denver, and San Francisco all grew after the Civil War. The movement west also led to the establishment of myriad small and medium-sized towns. A rail connection was important for the development of the newest cities, which depended on processing activities like flour milling, meat packing, tanning, and lumber milling.

Until the 1920s, urban mortality rates were higher than those in rural areas, and the larger the city, the higher the death rates, especially for infants and young children. Some of the unhealthfulness of cities was due to the large numbers of migrants from rural areas, foreign and domestic, who were not accustomed to living in high-density settings and had no immunities to some of the common pathogens. The rural-urban mortality differential narrowed from the late nineteenth century due in part to increasing filtration and chlorination of public drinking water, inoculations, sewers, and garbage collection. Regional differences in mortality among regions, such as the Northeast, South, and Midwest, converged even more rapidly.

The close association of industrial growth and urbanization stems from the economies available to a firm that locates in an already established urban area. These cost savings are from a firm not having to build an entire transportation infrastructure, worker housing, sanitation systems, schools, parks, hospitals, and supply services such as security and specialized repair firms. Moreover, there was already a pool of labor that may also have been potential markets for its product. The expansion of cities often seemed to have a self-renewing momentum. When a city grows in population, it employs a large number of people to build the additional infrastructure, and since construction is a labor-intensive activity, its growth may require recruiting more people from the countryside to satisfy the need. Municipal services are also labor intensive; workers needed to maintain and repair the infrastructure, teach, police, douse fires, and provide sanitation services grow at least proportionally to a city's population and maybe more than proportionally.

Foreign immigrants, who often came with no capital or property, were stuck in ports of entry, contributing to rising urbanization rates in addition to considerable rural-urban migration by the native born. One major example was the movement of rural southerners, white and black, to northern cities. World War I created 3,000,000 new manufacturing jobs at the very time that European immigration dropped from 1,200,000 in 1914 to 110,000 in 1918. Not only were northern employers forced to drop racial hiring exclusions, they began advertising in southern newspapers to recruit both white and black workers. Of the almost five million southerners who left the South between 1910 and 1920, twice as many whites as blacks migrated to cities in the Northeast and Upper Midwest and (fewer) to the West, which means migration rates of southern blacks and whites were similar. Whites returned to the South in greater rates than blacks, whose motivation to leave the South included escaping Jim Crow laws, racial violence, and employment discrimination. Although northern cities were not racial paradises and several upper midwestern states were experiencing growing KKK membership and activity in the early twentieth century, racial discrimination in the North did not have the rigidity and viciousness of southern racial relations.

As I mentioned in the introduction, major economic changes affect social structure, which in turn affects politics. This is the subject of chapter 6.

6

—ᴍ—

Social Change,
Politics, and Reform

The similarities between German and U.S. industrial growth in the decades before World War I sprang from the common features of industrial growth in the era of Finance Capitalism wherever large-scale industrialization took place. At the same time, however, there were significant
differences between Germany and the United States. Diffusion of U.S.
property ownership, especially among rural majorities outside the South,
led to high rates of literacy and political participation. This created a political dynamic far different from that of Germany, and it enabled strong
protests against big capital by farmers, workers, and other constituencies.

The economic role of the U.S. government evolved significantly due to
the Civil War and postwar developments, adding to the federal government's economic functions during Competitive Capitalism—securing
property rights, tariffs, patent law, mail service, open immigration, and a
mostly functional financial system. The late nineteenth-century U.S. federal government also dealt with the struggle between labor movements
and business elites, directly subsidized selected activities, extended property rights to corporations, supported a larger national military, and created a regulatory system to monitor and stabilize an economy dominated
by giant corporations. Nevertheless, the U.S. government was politically
incapable of coordinating capital-capital relationships and occasionally
blocked industrialists' and bankers' efforts to fashion such coordination.

Another source of difference between the United States and Germany
was the relatively even distribution of U.S. income that created a large
market for standardized consumer goods. These goods were beginning to
be produced and distributed by firms organized like the core intermediate

and capital-goods firms. In a final dimension of difference, U.S. employers' visceral hatred of workers' organizations obstructed the development of anything resembling the welfare-repression mode of capital-labor coexistence mediated by the German state.

This chapter is organized into three main parts. The first records the failure of northern efforts to reconstruct the South. The second describes the emergence in the postwar northern and western United States of new social and political actors: a wage-labor working class, powerful financial and industrial elites, and the urban middle class. The third section shows how the political dynamics among these actors played out in reform-leaning policy.

THE END OF RECONSTRUCTION IN THE U.S. SOUTH

Retreating from Reconstruction was an extremely important federal policy. Despite the split within the Republican Party over continuing to support Reconstruction in the South, Ulysses S. Grant won reelection in 1872, and Republicans increased their majority in the House of Representatives. But more Republicans were becoming convinced they had won despite their identification with Reconstruction, and when Democrats became the majority in the House of Representatives in the election of 1874, it seemed to confirm this reading. This was a time when serious racism was on the rise in northern media, heightening indifference to the plight of African Americans and making it easy and convenient for northerners to believe that southern blacks now had the tools to ensure their civil and political rights: they had the vote in states that were full members of the United States, and they and their supporters were prominent in several state and local governments. The conclusion was that northerners had done what they could, and it was time for southerners to cooperate and run their own affairs.

Federal intervention and supervision of southern conflicts were expensive in time and money, and there were other pressing matters. For example, financial reform to stabilize credit markets suddenly appeared urgent when the financial Panic of 1873 threw the economy into a depression that lasted the rest of the decade.

In addition, blatant political corruption as well as the spoils system, where electoral victors fired all government employees in reach and replaced them with friends, family, and donors, caused prodigious inefficiencies in municipal, state, and federal government as well as popular distrust of politics and politicians. These problems had been obvious for years, but the Grant administration brought them to new heights at the federal level.

Another pressing concern was that the 1870s depression exacerbated labor-capital conflicts, and employers and owners who valued a disciplined labor force and the protection of private property above all else observed with increasing dismay some radical industrial and mine-worker organizations and aggressive organizing and politicking among small farmers through the Grange movement. These were not emphases that encouraged the continuing support of Reconstruction. In addition, Republicans, over northern Democrats' protests, were willing to use federal troops to break strikes as a sign of their growing interest in allying with the financial and manufacturing classes, whom the post–Civil War economic advance had enriched beyond antebellum imagination. And the end of Reconstruction released more military to contain combative workers and intensify the effort to clear most of the Great Plains of Indian communities.

For these reasons, and despite occasional spurts of support, Republicans had been winding down Reconstruction for years when they formally declared it dead in 1877. The bitterly contested and inconclusive presidential election of 1876 required secret backroom negotiations between Republicans and Democrats and northerners and southerners, and the so-called Compromise of 1877 allowed the Republican candidate, Rutherford B. Hayes, to become president by one electoral vote. One clear element of the quid pro quo between parties and sections became evident when Hayes ordered the remaining federal troops in the South to stand down from statehouses and not interfere in local affairs.

When southern whites fought their way back to power in state governments after the Civil War, the so-called Redeemer governments repudiated the debts that Reconstruction-era state governments had incurred. In the process, they managed to include some wartime and prewar debt as well. Although the formal end of Reconstruction also enabled southern state and local governments to sharply reduce public services and taxes, it did not lead immediately to major shifts in racial relations.[1] Blacks still voted, occupied lower-level municipal offices, and even sat in some state legislatures. This changed when the agricultural depression of the 1880s and 1890s contributed to the rise of the Populist Party, which demanded immediate and substantial relief from foreclosure and destitution. The popularity of the Populists among small farmers and their vociferous resentment of upper-class privileges alarmed wealthy white southerners, who viewed the movement as a threat of a magnitude that could not be neutralized by, say, easier credit. It would take a larger and more powerful means to counter it, and racism was the tool of choice.

Although wary of reviving secret, night-riding groups like the KKK over which elite control could be uncertain, white southern leadership rallied poor whites using the language used during the last years of

Reconstruction but opted for officially sanctioned means. And they had some help from the North. The U.S. Supreme Court declared laws requiring racial segregation to be constitutional in its 1896 decision about racially segregated seating in railroad cars (*Plessy v. Ferguson*). The court rhetorically softened the blow by demanding that facilities were to be "separate but equal," and Jim Crow legislation flourished in every former slave state.

Laws segregated public facilities like schools, parks, buses, courtrooms, jails, drinking fountains, and restrooms as well as private hotels, restaurants, workplaces, and lunchrooms in the early twentieth century. There was no reliance on the "invisible hand" of the market; no detail was too minor for state and local governments to regulate. Facilities for blacks were consistently inferior. For example, per-pupil expenditure for blacks' schools had dropped from one-third to between 10 and 20 percent of that for whites by 1890. In the meantime, the "Lost Cause" romanticized the Civil War, celebrated the Klan in fiction, and justified oppressing African Americans.

At the same time, changing laws disenfranchised blacks. The use of literacy tests, property requirements, poll taxes, and wide discretionary authority of local registrars effectively took the ballot away from African Americans. For example, in Louisiana, there were 130,334 blacks registered in 1896, and after the passage of new electoral laws, there were 1,342 registered in 1904. The changed franchise requirements also reduced the number of whites eligible to vote, which was not inconvenient for the white leadership.

The Jim Crow laws were laws, not just conventions, and they were enforced through the police and courts. In addition to official channels and to unsanctioned but unpunished individual white-on-black violence, there was lynching, which by the 1890s had become a semiofficial mechanism for disciplining and terrorizing African Americans in the South. White communities not only condoned lynchings, they actively supported them, often with police participation. The Tuskegee Institute recorded more than 1,200 lynchings in the 1890s, when the Jim Crow laws were new, and the number of lynchings remained at around eight hundred a decade for the first two decades of the twentieth century. While occasionally a white—perhaps a recent immigrant or a Jew, as in the case of Leo Frank in Atlanta—was murdered by a white mob, lynching was principally a weapon against blacks' transgressions, many of them imagined.

Southern whites lost the Civil War and thus lost slavery and the right to secede, but they reserved a crucial aspect of states' rights: the ability to disenfranchise, ostracize, humiliate, beat, and kill African Americans without interference from the federal government. As late as 1933, the U.S. Congress would not pass an antilynching law.

NEW SOCIAL STRUCTURES

While southern whites were squandering time, energy, and resources on repressing African Americans, the dynamism of Finance Capitalist forms of industrial development in the North and the conquest of the West were generating a new social structure that changed the nature of U.S. politics. The industrial working class, the industrial-financial elite, and the urban middle class brought new agendas to national politics in the five decades after the Civil War. And farmers, although certainly not a new social formation, entered national politics in these years as an organized interest group for the first time. We begin with the fastest growing of the new elements, the working class, follow with the economic elite, and then discuss the modern middle class.

The Working Class

Although a wage-earning working class in factories and mines was visible before the Civil War, the growth of both manufacturing and mining after the war transformed the composition, scale, and politics of the class. Table 6.1 shows that the number of manual workers in manufacturing and mining more than quadrupled between 1870 and 1910.

Table 6.1.   Manual Industrial and Mine Workers, 1870 and 1910

Sector	Workers (in Thousands and % of Total)		Index of Increase (1870 Level = 100.0)
	1870	1910	
Construction	795 (22.4)	2,662 (18.7)	334.8
Metalworking	310 (8.7)	1,664 (11.7)	536.8
Garments	276 (7.8)	1,190 (8.4)	431.2
Textiles	253 (7.1)	804 (5.7)	317.8
Mining	186 (5.3)	917 (6.4)	493.0
Shoes	173 (4.9)	209 (1.5)	120.9
Railroads	157 (4.4)	1,158 (8.1)	737.6
Woodworking	129 (3.6)	565 (4.0)	438.0
Teamster	106 (3.0)	558 (3.9)	526.4
Food processing	87 (2.5)	300 (2.1)	344.8
Printing	50 (1.4)	237 (1.7)	474.0
Iron and steel	25 (0.7)	326 (2.3)	1,304.0
Chemical, oil, and rubber	10 (0.3)	200 (1.4)	2,000.0
Total U.S. Manufacturing	3,546 (100)	14,234 (100.0)	401.4

Source: Derived from David Montgomery, *The Fall of the House of Labor: The Workplace, the State, and American Labor Activism, 1865–1925* (New York: Cambridge University Press, 1987), 50.

Labor Organizations

Workers, primarily craftsmen, had formed local associations since colonial times, but as wage labor became the way by which most working people earned incomes, it became obvious that national unions were necessary for influence through elections as well as for supporting local job actions. Table 6.2 shows the rates of union membership growth over a forty-year period ending in 1920. The Knights of Labor, the American Federation of Labor (AFL), and the Industrial Workers of the World (IWW) were the most important national labor unions behind this growth.

The Knights were inclusive, organizing skilled and unskilled workers and white-collar workers. They formed alliances with farmer groups to promote wide-ranging political and social reforms. They denied membership only to bankers, lawyers, stockbrokers, professional gamblers, and those who produced or distributed liquor. Founded in 1869, membership grew sporadically through the 1870s and early 1880s, when the union's leadership accepted strikes as a legitimate tactic. After several successful strikes, the Knights expanded rapidly to a peak in 1886, when the Knights had nearly 750,000 members, including 50,000 African Americans and 10,000 women. On the West Coast, the Knights along with the Workingmen's Party led anti-Chinese efforts in San Francisco, and neither organization supported the somewhat successful 1867 strike by ten thousand Chinese builders of the Central Pacific Railroad or the successful 1884 strike by Chinese cigar makers.

Table 6.2.   Union Membership and Worker Strike Activity, 1881–1920

	Annual Average of Union Membership over Five-year Period (Thousands)	Annual Average of Labor Strikes over Five-Year Period	Annual Average of Workers Participating in Strikes (Thousands)
1881–1885	n.a.	527	148
1886–1890	n.a.	2,223	255
1891–1895	n.a.	1,436	256
1896–1900	608[a]	1,390	386
1901–1905	1,702	2,301	584
1906–1910	2,053	n.a.	n.a.
1911–1915	2,556	1,399[b]	n.a.
1916–1920	3,695	3,727	n.a.

[a] 1897–1900.
[b] 1914–1915.

Source: Derived from U.S. Census Bureau, *Historical Statistics of the United States: Colonial Times to 1970,* Part 1 (Washington, DC: Government Printing Office, 1975), 178–79.

The loss of a couple of large, bitter strikes, the violent 1886 Haymarket Square riot in Chicago, the heightening antiunion sentiment among political leaders and the middle class, and loss of members to more radical as well as more conservative unions led to a precipitous decline. The union was largely irrelevant to the labor movement by 1900.

Several workingmen founded what became the American Federation of Labor (AFL) in 1886. The AFL was organized along craft lines rather than by an entire industry or by individual participation. Skilled workers such as cigar makers, electricians, carpenters, and cutters in the garment industry were the principal targets of the AFL organizing. Women, factory and agricultural workers, miners, and lumberjacks were considered too difficult to organize in an increasingly antilabor environment. Samuel Gompers, one of the founders, was the first president and, with the exception of one year (1895), retained the presidency until his death in 1924.

Gompers and the AFL were not shy about engaging in strikes when they believed that the time was right, but they focused on modest improvements in wages, hours, and working conditions and opposed being more broadly political by lobbying for prolabor legislation. The AFL leadership fought strenuously against even progressive reformers and the nonrevolutionary Socialist Party, fearing that railroad, metal trades, and coal miner unions would take over the AFL and advocate nationalization of key industries and workers' control of workplaces.

The Socialist Party did grow in the early decades of the twentieth century with strong support from miners, machinists, brewers, ladies' garment workers, and tailors. In the United States, unlike in Europe, a near-universal white male franchise and widespread public education was achieved without the need for working-class mobilization, blunting the socialists' message. Moreover, high rates of internal migration as well as the presence of extremely large numbers of farmers, virtually all firmly committed to the importance of private property, also impeded the formation of a strong socialist movement in the United States. The fierce official repression of socialism and socialists during World War I and after the Bolshevik Revolution in 1917 further stunted the growth of a socialist movement.

The building trades, glass workers, and boot and shoe workers adhered to the AFL strategy, which was strengthened by the AFL's effective administrative apparatus and by Protestant and Catholic churches' and the Democratic Party's uneasiness about the growth of the Socialist Party. The AFL's membership grew slowly and rather steadily until it reached about five hundred thousand in 1900 by emphasizing the organization of workers in small and medium-sized businesses, employers without the capability of breaking the union. AFL membership then exploded to around four million members by the end of World War I; in 1920, with about 16 percent of the nonagricultural labor force in unions, 80 percent of them were in locals affiliated with the AFL.

The AFL refused affiliation to any worker's group that excluded blacks, although it softened that stance during the turn of the twentieth century when racism directed against African Americans was becoming especially strong in the North. A telling episode in a different direction occurred in 1903, when eight hundred Japanese and four hundred Latino sugar-beet workers struck in California and asked to be affiliated with the AFL. Gompers personally overrode local affiliates' recommendations when he made the admission of the local Mexican American affiliate conditional on their never including Chinese or Japanese workers.

The Western Federation of Miners, the Socialist Labor Party, and a number of other organizations and individuals founded the Industrial Workers of the World (IWW, or Wobblies) in 1905, and it grew rapidly in the decade before World War I. It organized aggressively and in opposition to the AFL, organized across occupations, skill levels, race, and gender, aspiring through "one big union" to generate general strikes that would paralyze the nation and enable workers to destroy capitalism and reorganize unequal capitalist society. The IWW was particularly strong among miners, dockworkers, northwestern lumberjacks, migrant farm workers in the Midwest and South, and textile workers in the Northeast. Estimates of the decentralized union's membership at its peak, usually thought to be 1912 or soon thereafter, vary greatly—maybe one hundred thousand, maybe thirty thousand.

Employers and those working on their behalf fiercely opposed all union activity. Nevertheless, the forces of repression reserved a special savagery for the IWW, and it was intensified when the United States entered World War I in April 1917 and the Bolshevik Revolution succeeded in Russia. The IWW's antiwar stance, repeatedly broadcast since the European war began in 1914, intensified the campaign against IWW members, a campaign that included executions, lynchings, long prison terms, illegal deportations, injunctions, and frequent violence. This extreme pressure, exacerbated by disagreements within the IWW about the appropriate responses, severely diminished the IWW in size and influence, and it never recovered its prewar stature. Nevertheless, the visions and efforts of organizers such as Joe Hill, Elizabeth Gurley Flynn, Big Bill Haywood, Mother Jones (Mary Harris Jones), and Eugene Debs still intrigue scholars and the popular media.

Strikes

The withdrawal of labor services, or striking, was workers' most potent weapon against employers. One of the earliest was when Philadelphia shoemakers struck for higher wages and were found guilty of criminal conspiracy in 1806. Textile workers and carpenters struck several times in the 1820s and 1830s, but it was not until the industrial growth in the decades after the Civil War that strikes increased in size and frequency. Coal miners, garment makers, iron and steel mill workers, printers, and railcar builders led in combative striking before 1894, after which machinists took the lead.

Strong product market competition among firms and deflationary pressures until the late 1890s compelled employers to cut costs even in times of general economic expansion. Therefore, nineteenth- and early twentieth-century strike activity was aimed at raising wages in good times of economic expansion and protecting wages in times of economic decline. Wage levels were not the only issue, and fighting against **piecework**—an individual worker being paid by the number of units he or she produced—also motivated strikes. Piecework is ancient, but in the United States, it increased significantly after 1860 and was a constant source of contestation. In addition, issues of hours, working conditions, the right to belong to a labor union, and the behavior of particular foremen in levying fines were always present and became more important in the early twentieth century.

At the same time, U.S. Catholic intellectuals introduced a new term into the union lexicon: a family wage. A family wage was defined as a wage sufficient to keep a family in "reasonable and frugal comfort" without the wife's having to engage in paid labor. The idea was more popular among men workers than among women workers.

The Great Railroad Strike (1877); the Port of New York longshoremen's strike (1887); the strike (actually a lockout) at Andrew Carnegie's Homestead steel mill in Pennsylvania (1892); the Massachusetts cotton textile strikes in Lawrence (1894) and the "Bread and Roses" Strike (1912), Lowell (1903), and Fall River (1904); the strike against John D. Rockefeller Jr.'s Colorado Iron and Fuel (1913); the silk mill strike in Paterson, New Jersey; and the Seattle General Strike (both in 1919) were among the largest and most dramatic strikes. The Homestead strike was especially notable because it gave the U.S. Supreme Court the opportunity to confirm that employers and their agents had exclusive control over divisions of labor and the geography of shop floor organization within factories. As described in the next chapter, this employer prerogative became especially important in the 1920s with the introduction of electric power in factories.

These spectacular and often violent strikes should not obscure the message in table 6.2: strikes, both large and small, were frequent. Unions called only a quarter of the strikes, and most were local affairs. But workers lost two-thirds of recorded strikes between 1881 and 1905 due to employers' capacity to draw on strikebreakers (hence workers' attempts to occupy workplaces via "sit-down strikes"), violence by hired thugs, vigilantes, police, militia, and occasionally federal troops, a coordinated antiunion drive by employers that reduced urban middle-class and church support of the labor movement, and finally, local injunctions and ordinances.

Changes in the Organization of Work

The gender, ethnic, and racial heterogeneity of the working class hindered effective cooperation; for example, the use of African American strikebreakers in the North exacerbated racial antagonism among workers. While biracial unionism was pretty much limited to longshoremen and miners, there were changes in the nature of work that increased the similarity of workers' workplace experiences and raised common issues around which people from disparate roots could rally.

At the end of the Civil War, factory workforces were divided into three fairly distinct groups: laborers, operatives, and craftspeople. In smaller and midsize factories, laborers were often hired by the day to move machinery and materials, clean, and perform other muscle-intensive chores. The casual nature of their employment encouraged frequent change of employer and locale. Stevedores were less peripatetic than most laborers and thus better able to organize unions. As the end of the century approached, laborers in the giant plants that developed in these decades experienced more stability in their work, making union organizing among laborers more feasible and desirable.

Operatives—machine tenders and assemblers—performed specialized and repetitive tasks. Textile mills were good examples of this mode of work in the middle of the nineteenth century, which already had workers performing specialized duties tending the machines that did the carding, spinning, and weaving. Weavers, one of the few crafts with substantial numbers of women, resisted being downgraded from craftspeople, whose experience and skill were necessary for smooth and efficient production. With the improvement of power looms, however, their work became increasingly like that of operatives, and employers were loath to pay them a premium over other machine tenders. Former craftspeople tended to join the ranks of operatives or to become supervisors.

As in the example of weavers, the declining need for workers' craft skills became evident throughout the economy. In steel production, Andrew Carnegie introduced the Bessemer process to the United States after the Civil War, thus increasing the scale of production and reducing the time and number of people required. Steel mills began to use open-hearth furnaces in 1910, and the use of recycled hot gasses made possible extremely high furnace temperatures that reduced the need for skilled workers to make judgments about impurities.

The use of mechanical shears and specialized functions in garment production contributed to the narrowing of garment workers' tasks. Instead of skilled tailors cutting and assembling a garment, somebody ran the cutting machine all day, another person made sleeves (or lapels, collars, and so on), and assembling the clothing also was done in specialized steps. Skilled tailors lost leverage on employers.

Continuous-flow production processes in chemical production and food processing made all workers machine tenders, and Henry Ford approximated the process in automobile production by introducing the moving assembly line in 1913. On such an assembly line, a worker might spend his or her work life mounting two wheels on the right-hand side of the car, and another worker, with a partner, would spend his or her time at work installing engines as each chassis moved by.

Deskilling workers' tasks had its limits. Mechanics who fixed and adjusted textile machinery, for instance, continually had to draw from experience and make sound judgments and thus retained much of their craft status. Railroad engineers, firemen, conductors, and trainmen established and maintained strong craft brotherhoods. In the building trades, carpenters, plumbers, and, later, steelworkers, cement workers, and electricians hung onto a traditional apprenticeship system for admission to the trade and preserved a good part of craft privileges.

Nevertheless, employers in factories devalued craft skills, and the distinction between unskilled laborers and semiskilled operatives became tenuous, as much a matter of negotiation as of real skill differences. But it is vital to understand that this was not the result of an immanent aspect of human progress. Employers working in highly competitive markets, even if there were only three or four competitors, deliberately put it in motion; cost cutting and efficiency were imperative. In the early twentieth century, larger employers began trying to make workers more productive by having people with stopwatches closely observe how workers performed each of their tasks. The purpose of these time-and-motion studies was to break each task down to its basic elements to enable decisions about whether a worker would be more efficient if he or she were to perform fewer, more specialized, repetitive tasks.

The move toward organizing factory work into increasingly specialized tasks was a logical development within the "American system of manufactures" that British observers had noted before the Civil War. The American system's distinctive traits were standardization of products, interchangeability of parts, and use of assembly lines, pioneered in the Springfield (Massachusetts) Armory in the early nineteenth century. This type of production was appropriate for the northern and western United States, which had a more evenly distributed prosperity than Europe and therefore bigger mass markets for inexpensive, standardized goods.

Corporate management aspired to organize work in a corresponding manner: if work consisted of routine and repetitive tasks requiring little judgment, workers became interchangeable. And breaking work down to basic components also facilitated the mechanization of more tasks and better surveillance by supervisors. As a graphic illustration of the importance that employers placed on surveillance of their workers, the number of production workers in manufacturing, mining, and transportation grew 27.7 percent between 1910 and 1920, and the same decade saw supervisory staff grow by 66 percent.

Time-and-motion studies were part of what was called "scientific management," a movement and profession closely associated with an engineer named Frederick Winslow Taylor. Workers hated Taylorism and resisted the loss of control over their work through routinization and supervision. Spotting someone on the factory floor with a stopwatch often triggered instant walkouts.

Male managers in the late nineteenth and early twentieth centuries increasingly considered women to be especially suited for clerical occupations, even though men had dominated the occupation of clerk up to the early nineteenth century. The increasing range of administrative functions in giant firms caused the number of clerical positions to expand more rapidly than the number of production workers. Almost 20 percent of women workers were in clerical occupations in offices and department stores by 1920, outstripping the 16 percent in domestic service—traditionally the largest category of women workers. The same kinds of scientific management could be applied to women workers—typists, stenographers, adding machine operators, and light manufacturing (e.g., lightbulbs) workers. Women employees were also vulnerable to the "marriage ban"—the firing of women workers when they married, which kept most women captive in low-paying jobs with little hope of promotion or higher pay.

Industrial and Financial Elites

The giant manufacturing firms, banks, and retailers of this era generated a new stratum of immensely wealthy people. The number of millionaires in the United States grew from about twenty in 1850 to more than three thousand in 1900, and Cornelius Vanderbilt (shipping and railroads), John D. Rockefeller (petroleum refining), Andrew Carnegie (steel), J. P. Morgan (finance), and Marshall Field (retail) were examples of the small group whose fortunes amounted to more than $100 million each. These men and their peers, considered entrepreneurial heroes by some and robber barons by others, possessed the resources to engage in large-scale consumption. Multiple extravagant houses, such as the "cottages" in

Newport, Rhode Island, magnificent yachts, racehorses, splendid art and book collections, large, manicured gardens, and elaborate balls defined a lifestyle aptly labelled by Thorstein Veblen in his book *The Theory of the Leisure Class* (1899) as conspicuous consumption. Also in response to the opulent lifestyles of the very rich, Mark Twain christened the three post–Civil War decades the Gilded Age, and the name stuck. But the rich and their families also engaged in large-scale philanthropy. Symphonies, museums, libraries, and universities as well as the Carnegie, Ford, and Rockefeller Foundations still stand as witnesses to the largesse of these men and their descendants.

The rich did not just indulge themselves and give away money; they and their firms' executives also were deeply involved in politics. To fight against unions and advance probusiness views and legislation, employers created a series of cross-industry associations, such as the National Association of Manufacturers (NAM, 1895), the Conference Board (1916), and the National Civic Federation (NCF, 1900). The Conference Board became a business-sponsored research organization best known now for its Consumer Confidence Index. The other two were politically more significant and exemplified the split within the business community concerning the appropriate stance toward labor unions.

The NCF favored recognizing and negotiating with unions, utilizing third-party mediation and arbitration when necessary. This approach conceded less to workers than it sounded; employers would negotiate only with "responsible" unions, such as the AFL and decidedly not the IWW, and try to educate workers and their organizations about the need to respect the rights and obligations of different parties within capitalism in order to reap mutual gains. Some employers saw material advantages to this strategy: reducing interfirm wage differentials would diminish the ability of low-cost producers to lower prices in an effort to increase market share, thus triggering price wars.

In sharp contrast to the NCF, the NAM vehemently opposed dealing with unions and advocated breaking them and maintaining so-called open shops that did not require any worker to join a union. The NAM was important in the aggressive open-shop drive that weakened unions in the early twentieth century, and despite some modest success in establishing mechanisms for arbitrating labor disputes, the NAM's hard line generally prevailed among business leaders.

The Urban Middle Class

The increasing predominance of wage labor in the nineteenth century produced a working class, whose combativeness changed industrial and political landscapes. In addition to the working class, typically earning an hourly wage, salaried white-collar employees paid by the week or month constituted another significant new segment of the working population. Emerging in cities and good-sized towns in the last decades of the nineteenth century, the salaried middle classes were, and continue to be, socially heterogeneous. The range of their occupations includes managers, journalists, teachers, administrators, bookkeepers, clerks in stores and offices, independent professionals, and the whole panoply of salaried employees in public and private bureaucracies, occupations that reflected the increasing scale and complexity of urban and economic life.

Like the working class, the modern middle class did not possess property in production and thus depended on the sale of the only commodity they possessed—their labor services—but only a few segments of white-collar workers formed unions to further their interests. Nevertheless, they denied that they were members of the working class and had an identity of interests with them. First of all, their work was different, usually requiring some formal education and often giving them opportunities for an upward mobility that sharply distinguished them from wage workers. Moreover, members of the middle class self-consciously spent time and energy in setting themselves apart, socially and culturally, from the working class, even when their earnings might be but little different from better-paid wage workers. Emulating consumption patterns of the elites helped to maintain the desired distance, and since consumption involved status and class identification, it assumed an importance for white-collar workers beyond creature comfort.

The distinctive type of work-related organizations for middle-class salaried and independent workers became the professional association. The late nineteenth and early twentieth centuries were the time these organizations grew rapidly, beginning with the traditional professions of medicine and law. These occupations, along with morticians, schoolteachers, social workers, architects, pharmacists, veterinarians, librarians, dentists, engineers, and so on sought to establish national and state bodies that regulated means of entry, standards of practice, and competition within and among occupations in the name of eliminating quackery and assuring sound, professional practice. Requiring the emerging universities to train and certify a standardized competence, monitored by each professional association, set these occupations apart from trades. The most successful professional projects convinced legislators to use the power of the law to close off whole sets of occupations to all but the properly certified.

Salaried workers' heterogeneity as well as their unclear relations to the means of production—or to production at all—make it difficult to regard them as a class, and technically they constitute a social stratum. Nevertheless, in order to avoid confusing terms, we will call them the modern middle class, but it is imperative to remember that they are not the middle class of the English Industrial Revolution. That middle class, between propertyless workers and landed gentry, was the industrial bourgeoisie that became the most powerful propertied class in the nation.

The modern middle class, interested in moving out of the crowded and polluted cities, propelled a new type of land speculation: the suburbs. The electric trolley contributed to the feasibility of living some distance from work, and developers of suburbs were often the owners of the trolley companies that built ahead of demand. The first electric trolley system began in Richmond, Virginia, in 1888, and there were fifteen thousand miles of trolley track, mostly in urban areas, by 1901. By 1916, investors added another fifteen thousand miles of interurban track. But most of the trolley companies quickly folded in the 1920s and 1930s with the availability of affordable automobiles; Henry Ford introduced the Model T in 1908.

THE REFORM IMPULSE

In 1880, there were more than three million workers in the U.S. manufacturing sector, around four million independently owned farms, and 750,000 small businesses. These people increasingly became aware that public policies supporting giant firms, western land speculators, railroad operators, and tight credit were not benefiting them. Farmers and wage workers, whether in unions or not, began to exert pressure on municipal, state, and federal governments to rein in what they regarded as the excesses resulting from the lack of restrictions on the rich and prosperous during the free-wheeling Gilded Age. This effort to exert more systematic political influence produced a set of reforms during what is known as the Progressive Era, roughly the 1880s through World War I.

In addition, the increasingly frequent and violent conflicts between workers and employers seemed to threaten another civil war, this time between classes rather than geographic sections. Fear about the potential for a general conflagration as well as genuine humanitarian sentiments energized the urban middle classes and some elements of the upper classes to become the principal faces and voices of Progressive Era reforms.

And these faces and voices more often than not were those of women, usually from the middle class. Women were the core of the middle-class involvement in the late nineteenth and early twentieth century reform movements, having been involved in abolition, prohibition of alcohol ("temperance"), and suffrage movements since the 1830s and active in a wide range of supporting capacities during the Civil War. As a result, many were experienced in organizing, lobbying, and (then still controversial) lecturing to mixed audiences. Often excluded from men's organizations, including political parties, women established (or resuscitated) and operated a number of influential nonpartisan volunteer organizations. These organizations served working women and promoted woman suffrage, temperance, improved working and housing conditions, public health, education, libraries, parks, and protections for working women and children.

One of the most famous of these activist women's organizations was the settlement house movement, which worked with new immigrants, most of whom, like many native-born urban workers, were making the transition from rural to urban life. In the 1880s, Jane Addams cofounded Hull House in Chicago, which became the model and inspiration for others. Young, educated women moved into impoverished working-class neighborhoods populated by recent immigrants. These settlement houses supplied a range of services primarily for women and children in the neighborhoods, including cooperative nurseries, instruction in hygiene and English language, shelters for women in need, working women's clubs, medications, and occasionally an inexpensive restaurant. Small beginnings turned into a movement; in 1911, 210 institutions in cities with large immigrant populations responded to a survey of settlement houses, a number generally agreed to be an undercount.

Woman suffrage was one issue involving activist women, and it was a central one. The suffrage movement's traditional argument was that women were citizens and shared a common humanity with men and therefore deserved voting rights through the broadly construed "natural human rights" stated in the Declaration of Independence and in the Seneca Falls Declaration of Sentiments of 1848. After the failure of women's efforts to include suffrage as a universal right for all citizens, black and white, male and female, in the Fourteenth and Fifteenth Amendments, women's rights leaders began to articulate a new theme.

Retreating from the argument that women's right to vote was due to their similarities to male citizens and thus deserving to vote, some leaders claimed that because women were different, possessing unique qualities and virtues (less venal and violent, more virtuous and patient, and so on) that their inclusion in politics was necessary to raise the level of U.S. politics. By the end of the 1870s, this position emerged as a leading argument for woman suffrage, even though the essentialist claims about difference were major aspects of the argument against woman suffrage before the Civil War.

Much of opponents' hostility to women's enfranchisement stemmed from a general resistance to broadening the electorate; native-born white men were increasingly desirous of narrowing it. Even Progressive Era reformers, men and women, tended to have deep reservations about the "limited civic capacity" of the vast majority of new immigrants, believing that the new arrivals were not prepared to vote responsibly because "those people" were genetically inferior and that no amount of socialization and education would enable them to make a positive contribution to political life. Thus the attraction of the eugenics movement, which advocated selective breeding in order to create an improved U.S. population with superior inherited qualities. Moreover, whether the northern Progressives believed that those unfit to vote could or could not be raised to a satisfactory level, they were mostly comfortable with white southerners' disenfranchisement of African American men.

In the North and the South, states used literacy requirements, poll taxes, residency requirements, and wide discretionary powers of local registrars to exclude those considered undesirable. California was more direct; in 1879, anyone born in China was excluded from the voting rolls. The ban was framed in terms of nationality in order to avoid conflicting with the Fifteenth Amendment, which prohibits exclusions based on race. Oregon and Washington followed the California example, and the voting ban was not repealed until 1926.

Suffrage spokespeople subscribed to these concerns about the fitness of the electorate and fitted them into their rhetoric in a couple of ominous ways. The first was that white women voters were needed to counter the influence of those incapable of exercising their voting rights responsibly. The second was to agree that the franchise should be limited to the qualified and that qualified women should constitute part of this new, superior category of voters in an "educated suffrage." Through this type of strategy, it was easy to bury the universal citizen suffrage approach that included black and Asian men and women. Most of the women's movement supported Prohibition, and that cause also had an anti-immigrant tone. But many suffragists participated in or supported the labor struggles of working-class immigrant women in the needle trades and textiles.

As important as middle-class leadership was in the Progressive reform movement at the end of the nineteenth century, it was organized farmers and U.S.-born workers who brought political muscle to reform efforts, and these two groups' goals occasionally went beyond what the middle-class reformers saw as right and proper. Other than the suffrage movement, middle-class reformers represented significant segments of both political parties, and they did not aspire to change the fundamental structures of social power. Their goal was to create governments in which experts would apply scientific principles to social problems in order to mitigate the conflicts and contradictions of social life and enhance social harmony. These bureaucratic experts were to be guided by a democratic electorate, comprising citizens with the civic capacity to work rationally toward goals of greater social harmony.

At the same time that many were trying to narrow the franchise, farmers, the native-born working class, and the middle class were turning to the ballot to offset the power of the wealthy and rectify what they saw as a destructive situation of class conflict and rising inequalities. Farmers were adamant that there be some relief from what they saw as their exploitation by railroads, banks, and large corporations and from declining agricultural prices. Native-born workers and their unions were frustrated by the failure of strikes to create permanent changes, and going beyond their usual political caution, the AFL's 1894 platform advocated public ownership of railroads, mines, telephones, and telegraph.

South American middle classes formed effective political parties (often named "Radical" this and that) that did well in the early decades of the twentieth century in the more developed and urbanized nations. The U.S. middle class never formed durable independent political parties, but its members understood that the ballot was the only way in which they could overcome their numerical and positional weakness and have any influence over political decisions. The urban middle classes were but small percentages of the national population in the post–Civil War decades and seldom occupied strategic positions from which to apply political pressure. On the other hand, their literacy, urban location, organization and communication skills, limited goals, and opportunistic alliances with fragments of employer, farmer, and working classes made them significant in a number of reformist programs, such as municipal civil service reform to rein in political machines dominated by non-Anglo ethnics.

Two kinds of new electoral practices were the result of reform efforts and at the same time made electoral politics a more feasible avenue of reform. The first set of policies increased voters' access to politicians and policies. Rather than party insiders nominating the political parties' candidates for office in conventions, the direct primary required a political party to hold a primary election to choose the party's candidates. This line of reform was expanded to amending the U.S. Constitution (the Seventeenth Amendment [1913]) so that U.S. senators were elected directly by the electorate rather than by state legislatures. In a similar change, many states and municipalities accepted petitions for initiatives, referenda, and recalls. A successful initiative uses an election by all eligible voters to require a particular proposal to be placed on a state legislature's agenda; a referendum is an election about a proposed law, which might be passed or defeated no matter what the legislature desires; and a recall is an election about whether a particular elected official should continue in office.

The second innovation was the secret ballot (the "Australian ballot"). The first U.S. experiment with the secret ballot was in Louisville in 1888, and the practice spread rapidly. The secret ballot required election officials to produce a standardized ballot with all candidates' names on it and to distribute them on Election Day. These standardized ballots supplanted old ballots that had been printed by political parties with only their candidates' names, and since they came in a variety of easily identified colors, sizes, and shapes, there was little doubt as to which candidates an individual voter was supporting. The secret ballot therefore severely reduced the usefulness of buying votes and intimidating voters, since one could not be sure the voter stayed bought or intimidated in the voting booth. This reduced the ability of political machines and employers to manipulate election results.

Another aspect of the secret ballot was that it required literacy on the part of the voter; the voter now had to be able to distinguish among the names of multiple candidates on a ballot slip. This conveniently helped to trim the voting numbers of illiterate new immigrants, African Americans, and other poor.

A series of powerful journalistic exposés during the late nineteenth and early twentieth centuries informed and further motivated middle-class and occasionally upper-class reformers at all three levels of government. These journalists, who became known as muckrakers (Theodore Roosevelt's term), documented the terrible conditions in tenements and poorhouses (Jacob Riis), Standard Oil Company practices (Ida Tarbell), the unsanitary and degrading conditions in slaughterhouses and meatpacking sheds (Upton Sinclair), and political corruption (Lincoln Steffans), among others. These books and articles stimulated the passing of new regulatory laws, including housing and factory inspection, the federal Meat Inspection Act, and the Pure Food and Drug Act (1906).

Tragedy also could trigger legislative responses. The Triangle Shirtwaist Company fire occurred in New York City's garment district late on the Saturday afternoon of March 25, 1911. Already known as particularly nasty employers, owners' managers had locked the escape doors to prevent pilfering, and 147 workers, mostly young immigrant women, died. A jury acquitted the employers of criminal charges, but in response to civil suits, the employers paid families seventy-five dollars per life lost. The result was increased momentum behind factory inspections and worker safety concerns.

Many of the successful reform efforts were at the municipal and state levels, and in addition to the new regulations already mentioned, there was significant movement behind public health measures, tenement standards, municipal ownership of utilities, public education, limitations on the hours women and children could work, and regulation of prostitution and utility, transportation, and insurance companies. Several of these reforms directly improved urban life for swaths of the population, but there were limits to the effectiveness of local and state regulations. Railroad operators, for example, had to deal with a wide variety of regulations, depending on which state they were in, and some favored federal legislation that would cut through the inconsistent patchwork of state regulations.

A second reason to push for reforms at the national level was that employers could not evade federal rules by simply moving their operations to another state with looser (and less expensive) regulations. This was the time that cotton textile mills (although not their ownership and financing) were beginning to move south to take advantage of cheaper labor and to avoid northeastern states' factory inspections for unsafe and unsanitary working conditions and women's and children's work hours.

PROGRESSIVES AND REFORM

In the reformist movement, farmers took the lead in pressuring their U.S. representatives and senators. Agrarians were exporters and received no benefit from tariffs, and they sold their products to giant meatpackers, grain elevators, and flour mills while buying products and services supplied by giant corporations in farm machinery and equipment, credit, fuel, freight haulage, and consumer goods. They became organized as a national political bloc after the Civil War, first in the Grange network and later in the more activist Populist (or People's) Party. Farmers continually complained that the railroads, along with banks and large corporations, were cheating them. There is no doubt that there was price gouging by railroads that enjoyed monopolies over service to particular communities, but freight rates generally declined in the last three decades of the nineteenth century. Farmers' political leverage at the state level led to establishing a number of state-level public-utility commissions to regulate railroad rates and service.

Farmers allied with middle-class reformers to oppose corruption and the spoils system at the federal level and to pass the 1883 Pendleton Civil Service Reform Act that created a Civil Service Commission to design and administer competitive examinations for about 10 percent of federal positions. The act also prohibited pressuring employees to donate to a political campaign and gave the president the power to expand the number of employees covered by the act. The last provision, along with subsequent legislation, was crucial in extending the reach of the initial act. Among the lowest-profile U.S. presidents, Vice President Chester A. Arthur assumed the presidency after the assassination of President James Garfield in 1881, and President Arthur surprised many by signing the act despite his tainted record of graft and political corruption as head of the New York City Customs House.

Farmers' support was the principal political force behind the 1887 creation of the U.S. Interstate Commerce Commission (ICC), signed into law by President Grover Cleveland, who was the first Democratic Party president after the Civil War. Although Congress did not grant the commission authority to enforce its rulings until 1906, the ICC cut through the confusing tangle of state public-utility commission regulations and helped reduce price wars.[2] In the process, the ICC was highly influenced by the railroads themselves. After all, if you wish to regulate a complex industry, the people who best understand that industry have to be drawn from the very industry being regulated, with all the accompanying attitudes and conflicts of interest.

Farmers also paid attention to more general, macroeconomic issues that they saw responsible for agricultural products' price declines. When the U.S. government returned its currency to convertibility in 1879, this new convertibility included only gold, not silver (apart from some silver coins). Farmers, with silver mine owners, pushed for returning the United States to a full bimetallic standard in the hopes that the increased money supply would reduce credit costs and restore the inflation that had benefited them during the Civil War. Populist movements going back to Andrew Jackson viewed banks, tight credit, and hard currency as enemies of the people.

One of the principal problems with this analysis was that sagging agricultural prices were in large part the result of the rapid expansion of wheat and corn harvests. The number of new farms continued to grow through the end of the nineteenth century, and the acreage devoted to growing wheat and corn more than doubled between 1870 and 1910. Yields (output per acre) on that land increased little, and labor productivity in agriculture grew significantly. This is consistent with the scarcity of labor that encouraged mechanization and with the abundance of land that encouraged little interest in caring for the land.

The bimetallic monetary standard was a major plank in the Populist Party's platform in the 1896 presidential election, and the effort to let silver circulate alongside gold as money stimulated one of the most famous speeches in U.S. history. William Jennings Bryan, the nominee for U.S. president by both the Populist and Democratic Parties, talking to those who supported a gold-only standard, declared in his usual inflammatory style, "You shall not press down upon the brow of labor this crown of thorns, you shall not crucify mankind upon a cross of gold." The Populists lost, but new gold discoveries in South Africa, Australia, Alaska, and elsewhere in addition to U.S. **balance-of-payments** surpluses led to more gold circulating and some inflation in the first decade of the twentieth century, and World War I brought more. While the Populist Party declined after its loss in the 1896 presidential election, farmers (and William Jennings Bryan) continued to be a potent force in national politics.

Antitrust

Farmers were again in the forefront of efforts to contain the power of giant corporations through federal legislation. They were not alone because all who bought mass-produced products disliked monopoly power. Automobile producers that bought steel and glass from concentrated producers and retailers selling consumer goods were both sources of antitrust support. The middle classes, on the other hand, stayed fairly much on the sidelines during the assault on big business because of corporate employment opportunities and growing stock ownership. The AFL also was not very active except to fight against the claim that labor unions restricted competition.

Popular reaction to the first wave of corporate consolidations in the 1880s enabled the passage of the Sherman Antitrust Act in 1890. The need to make concessions in the bill to overcome the resistance of representatives from industrial regions, however, weakened it severely. There were suspicions that key Republican lawmakers were trading a weak antitrust bill in exchange for supporting higher tariffs.

The most important section of the Sherman Act reads, "Every contract, combination in the form of trust or otherwise, or conspiracy, in restraint of trade or commerce among the several States, or with foreign nations, is declared to be illegal." The act did not outlaw giant corporations except when they deliberately used their market power to suppress competition and raise prices. In 1895, the Supreme Court narrowed the law's effectiveness, and the administrations of President Grover Cleveland's second term (1893–1897) and President William McKinley (1897–1901) seldom used it to prosecute corporations. But employers were successful in using it for injunctions against striking workers.

The Supreme Court's weakening of the Sherman Act, President McKinley's defeat of William Jennings Bryan, and the beginning of the recovery from the Panic of 1893 cleared the way for the second, larger wave of corporate consolidations from the end of the nineteenth century through the first decade of the twentieth. Popular outrage at the new concentrations of economic power and the high levels of fraud and corruption encouraged dramatic federal action. Congress passed the Clayton Antitrust Act (1914), which amended and strengthened the Sherman Act, created the Federal Trade Commission with the power to investigate illegal business practices, and explicitly excluded labor unions from the purview of antitrust laws. Congress provided a similar exclusion for professional baseball in 1922.

But the more dramatic action occurred earlier. When President McKinley was assassinated in the fourth month of his second term (September 1901) and Vice President Theodore Roosevelt became President Roosevelt (1901–1909), the stage was set for the flamboyant hero of the Spanish-American War to become the heroic trustbuster and extend the power of the executive branch. Republican Roosevelt created an antitrust division in the U.S. Justice Department, allocated $500 million for prosecutions under the Sherman Act, and proceeded with thirty-seven prosecutions during his seven and a half years in office. The administration of his Republican successor, President William Howard Taft (1909–1913), brought forty-three suits against corporations.

When the Republican Party convention met to nominate its candidate for the 1912 presidential election, it passed over Roosevelt in favor of the candidacy of the incumbent, William Howard Taft. Roosevelt broke with the party and joined a disparate group of reformers to establish the Progressive Party. To woo white southerners, Roosevelt insisted that the Progressive Party convention seat no African American delegates from the South, and middle-class delegates forcefully resisted a robust antitrust plank. The convention duly nominated Roosevelt, who was backed by the AFL and W. E. B. Du Bois of the newly founded National Association for the Advancement of Colored People (NAACP, founded in 1909). With two Republicans in the race, the middle-class vote was split, and with help from southern voters, the Democratic Party nominee, Woodrow Wilson, won the election: the first election in which all forty-eight contiguous states participated (Arizona and New Mexico achieved statehood early in the year).

Although Wilson did not receive a majority of the popular vote, his proportion of the popular vote was fifteen percentage points greater than that of the second-highest, Theodore Roosevelt, and he had a huge majority of the electoral votes. President Wilson was only the second Democrat to be elected president since the Civil War. The Wilson administration (1913–1921) took up many of Roosevelt's Progressive causes and initiated fifty-three Sherman and Clayton indictments during Wilson's first term.

In this heyday of antitrust activity, the Northern Securities Company (a huge railroad combination), the explosives division of DuPont, the American Tobacco Trust, International Harvester, Eastman Kodak, the Standard Oil Company, and other less well-known firms were found to be in violation of the antitrust acts and potentially broken into smaller companies. The United States Steel Company was never convicted.

But it is easy to exaggerate the effects of all this activity. There was no political will to halt or reverse corporate consolidations, and even President Theodore Roosevelt considered the consolidations to be inevitable and essentially beneficial by generating new efficiencies and reducing "ruinous competition." If the giant firms abused their power in some clear way, they could be indicted under the Sherman and Clayton Acts, but there was little stomach to change the entire structure of economic power.

Reforms at the Edge of World War I

In the late nineteenth century, the federal government expanded regulatory responsibilities, postal service, foreign involvements, and the U.S. military, raising the costs of doing the business of government. Another drain on the Treasury was Civil War Union veterans' pensions and disability payments, which for the United States was the first significant experiment with social insurance and the foundation of a large and loyal political constituency for the Republican Party. Federal law continued to govern grazing, lumbering, and mineral and water rights in the West. Between 1880 and 1919, the federal government had built enough holding dams to expand the number of irrigated acres from a bit over three million acres to nineteen million acres, winning the loyalty of important interests but also incurring continuing costs.

These growing responsibilities required a source of revenue larger and more reliable than tariffs and land sales. Congress had phased out the Civil War personal income tax by 1872, but a Democratic Congress brought it back in 1894, bitterly opposed by northeastern moneyed elites but enthusiastically endorsed by agrarians in the South, Midwest, and West. Organized labor saw the tax burden that fell more on those with "the ability to pay" as good social policy. The Supreme Court ruled the income tax law unconstitutional in 1895, and in response, Congress passed the Sixteenth Amendment, which permitted a personal income tax. Three-quarters of the states had ratified it by 1913, and Congress established the personal income tax in the same year. While this was going on, the Supreme Court in 1911 ruled that legislation providing for a corporate income tax (the Corporation Excise Tax Act [1909]) was constitutional.

While both the personal and corporate income taxes could be seen as levelers, the Federal Reserve Act (1913) brought banking back to Alexander Hamilton's vision of a federally regulated economy. The recurrence of financial panics—1873, 1893, and 1907—was understood to have been caused by the weakness of the banking system rather than the gold standard and reduced enthusiasm for a bimetallic currency. The Fed was to serve as a lender of last resort to national banks experiencing depositors' panicked withdrawals that threatened the banks' closing, monitor the adequacy of national banks' reserves, operate a check clearinghouse, and function as the banker to the U.S. Treasury. Unlike the first two Banks of the United States, the Fed did not compete with private banks, and after 1927, it had no expiration date. General wariness about political centralization caused Congress to insulate the Fed from immediate political influence by a presidential administration and to organize the Fed into twelve regional banks, although the headquarters and major policy-making boards that include representation by the regional banks are located in Washington, DC.

* * *

Along with the major changes in the domestic industrial sector, social structure, and politics, the United States became newly involved in international affairs. This involvement included both international trade and investment but also a form of reluctant colonialism in a surprising form.

7

—⁂—

The United States
in the World

The United States possessed what amounted to a continent-wide common market, but while foreign markets were not as important to the United States as they were to Europe, foreign trade and investment by the United States grew at the end of the nineteenth century. Tariffs continued to be a contentious political and fiscal issue, and by the end of the century, the United States had higher levels of tariff protection than any other industrialized nation.

Another aspect of international involvement at the end of the nineteenth century and early twentieth century was the vigorous advocacy by various constituencies for creating U.S. colonies in distant lands with nonwhite populations. Commercial and military interests felt threatened by competing nations dominating trade, trade routes, and coaling stations for merchant and military shipping. There was also the conviction that the United States had come of age and as a powerful and mature nation should demonstrate the ability to create an empire similar in reach to the European empires. There was strong pushback against pursuing such avenues.

INTERNATIONAL TRADE AND INVESTMENT

On average, annual exports accounted for a bit more than 6 percent of U.S. **gross national product (GNP)** throughout the nineteenth century, with comparable levels for imports. European nations, on the other hand, tended to export between 20 and 30 percent of their total output. The low

U.S. dependence on foreign markets masks the extent to which foreign markets were vital for some sectors. Exports constituted around 20 percent of U.S. agricultural production in these years, and U.S. exports on the eve of World War I made up more than one-twelfth of world exports, impressive for a nation with less than one-sixteenth of the world population. The real news about the U.S. engagement in international trade in these years is the change in the composition of that trade, which is shown in table 7.1. Raw materials and unprocessed food (**primary products**) declined as percentages of exports over the fifty-five-year period while manufactured goods and processed food (**secondary products**) rose to almost 60 percent of exports. (**Tertiary products** are services, and although they include transportation, their share was low at this time.) The changes in imports were the reverse: primary products as a percentage of all imports rose almost two and one-half times, while secondary products declined by more than twenty-six percentage points.

The tremendous growth of manufacturing during these years makes explicable the rise in manufactured exports and decline in imports of foreign manufactures. But what was going on with the rise of raw material and unprocessed food imports? Thinking just about Latin America, the

Table 7.1. Composition of U.S. Exports and Imports, 1850–1858 and 1904–1913

	Raw Materials and Unprocessed Food	Manufactured Goods and Processed Food	Total
Type of Exports as a Proportion of Total Exports*			
1850–1858	67.3	32.8	100.0
1904–1913	40.0	59.9	100.0
Type of Imports as a Proportion of Total Imports*			
1850–1858	19.9	80.1	100.0
1904–1913	46.5	53.6	100.0

	Total	Europe	Latin America and Caribbean	Canada
U.S. Exports by Destination (Percentages*)				
1849–1858	100	73	15	8
1904–1913	100	66	13	12

	Total	Europe	Latin America and Caribbean	Canada	Asia
1849–1858	100	66	22	4	7
1904–1913	100	50	26	6	15

* Proportions may not add to 100 because of omitted categories.

Source: Derived from Robert E. Lipsey, "U.S. Foreign Trade and the Balance of Payments," in *The Cambridge Economic History of the United States*, Vol. 2: *The Long Nineteenth Century*, ed. Stanley L. Engerman and Robert E. Gallman (New York: Cambridge University Press, 2000), 702, 714.

late nineteenth century was the beginning of large-scale coffee imports into the United States from Central America and Brazil, bananas from Jamaica and Honduras, nitrates and copper from Chile, chocolate and a range of minerals from Mexico, and petroleum from Mexico and Venezuela. The upper and urban middle classes wanted and could afford more exotic foodstuffs, and the industrialized United States needed a larger volume and wider range of raw materials as inputs for its industries.

A corresponding shift occurred in U.S. foreign investment. Foreign investment from the United States of both types—**foreign direct investment** and **foreign portfolio investment** (see the glossary for the difference)—was minuscule before 1897, but between 1897 and 1905, it rose quickly: foreign direct investment quadrupled between 1897 and 1905, and portfolio investment increased by a factor of seventeen. Remember that this is the period of the greatest consolidation of firms, with almost continuous acquisition of firms by other firms and the expansion of giant U.S. corporations.

Between 1897 and 1914, Mexico received the largest amount of U.S. foreign direct investment, mostly in railroads and mining. Investments in Canada, the second-largest recipient of U.S. investment, were more diversified, although paper and pulp was the largest single sector of U.S. direct investment. Despite this growing interest in foreign investment, compared with Great Britain, France, and Germany, the United States was a small player up to 1914. Table 7.2 is a good illustration of the relative scale of U.S. foreign investments compared with those of Europe.

On the receiving side of foreign investment, the United States was a net recipient of both kinds of foreign investment through the second half of the nineteenth century, and most of it came from Great Britain and went into U.S. railroads. But with U.S. investors' heightened interest in foreign investment at the end of the century, U.S. individuals and corporations began to invest more abroad than foreigners were investing in the United States. This did not mean that the United States suddenly became a net creditor nation. The annual amounts of new investments are flows—values measured over a period of time (year, month, and so on). The value of assets owned by foreigners (or anyone) is a stock—the value of all assets held, irrespective of when acquired, at a given point in time (for example, 12:00 midnight, December 31, 1896). The two are connected: when U.S. people and institutions began to buy more foreign assets than foreigners bought U.S. assets in a given year, it meant that the net balance of foreigners' holdings of U.S. assets and the stock of total U.S. holdings of foreign assets began to decline. That balance is what defines a creditor nation from a debtor nation, and the U.S. began to whittle down that difference. But the balance was big—$2.6 billion in 1914, and it was going to take some catastrophic event to shift that balance quickly. (Think World War I.)

Table 7.2. Distribution of Foreign Investment, 1914 ($ U.S. Millions)

Sources	Europe	United States and Canada	Destinations — Australia and N.Z.	Asia	Africa	Latin America	World (%)
Great Britain	1,050	7,050	2,200	3,550	2,450	3,700	19,500 (44%)
France	4,700	500	100	1,250	900	1,600	9,050 (20%)
Germany	2,550	1,150	—	700	500	900	5,800 (13%)
United States	700	900	—	250	—	1,650	3,500 (8%)
Other	3,000	1,500	—	1,350	200	1,050	7,700 (17%)
World (% distr.)	12,000 (26%)	11,100 (24%)	2,300 (5%)	7,100 (16%)	4,050 (9%)	8,900 (20%)	45,550 (100%)

Note: The "Other" row is principally from Belgium, Netherlands, Japan, Russia, and Portugal. Totals may not be the sum of parts due to rounding errors.

Source: Derived from William Woodruff, *Impact of Western Man: A Study of Europe's Role in the World Economy* (New York: St. Martin's, 1966), 154.

AMBIVALENT COLONIALISM

The Louisiana Purchase (1803) and the Treaty of Guadalupe Hidalgo that concluded the Mexican War (1846–1848) enabled the major expansions of U.S. territory. Both new areas were contiguous to the existing United States and regarded as empty. From the Mexican War, the cession was half the territory of Mexico but only 5 percent of its population. This was not an accident; when some U.S. politicians advocated taking more or even all the Mexican territory, opposition to incorporating into the United States a large population of mixed-race Mexicans torpedoed the more grandiose proposals.

The U.S. political leaders, reflecting their constituencies, were generally reluctant to take over nonwhite populations if the nonwhite populations had any chance of becoming voting citizens. The struggles over "the Negro Problem" in the South, the virulent anti-Chinese stance in California behind the Chinese Exclusion Acts (1882 and later), and the late nineteenth-century tidal waves of southern and eastern European immigrants, whom many believed were incapable of being assimilated into the U.S. (white) mainstream, hardened nativist and racist convictions among U.S. whites.

Although enjoying many of the same opinions about racial superiority and inferiority, Europeans did not have such strong reservations about taking over non-European peoples. While some European colonies in Africa and Asia went back centuries, Europeans' scramble for new territorial acquisitions in Africa and Southeast Asia accelerated sharply in the last half of the nineteenth century. Europeans' ravenous appetites for colonies meant that with a few minor exceptions, all of Africa, South Asia, Southeast Asia (including present-day Indonesia and the Philippines), Australia, New Zealand, and the South Pacific islands had been carved into European colonies by 1914. Great Britain and France reigned over the largest colonial empires, but Belgium, Germany, Italy, Portugal, and Holland all administered substantial overseas colonies full of non-European peoples.

The pattern in East Asia was dissimilar and diverse, and U.S. aggressiveness there demonstrated that while wary about establishing colonies of nonwhite peoples, the United States was most interested in access to trade and investment opportunities irrespective of locals' colors.[1] But getting that access in colonized areas was difficult or impossible and was not easy even in parts of East Asia that were not colonized. From the seventeenth century, the Chinese, Japanese, and Korean governments restricted all contacts with Western powers. When the Chinese government moved against British merchants smuggling opium into China, Britain's victory in the Opium War (1839–1840) led to a treaty in which China ceded the island of Hong Kong and generous commercial rights and privileges to the British. China soon extended these rights and privileges to the United States, France, and Russia, an arrangement that became formalized among the four Western powers (Open Door policy), giving equal access to the Chinese market. Despite the weakness of the Chinese central government, dissension among the Western powers and the Chinese people's strong hostility toward Western intrusions, expressed in two large, bloody, and popular anti-Western rebellions—the Taiping Rebellion (1850–1864) and the Boxer Rebellion (1900)—prevented westerners from dividing China into colonies.

The Japanese reaction to U.S. Admiral Matthew C. Perry bullying it into a commercial treaty with the United States between 1853 and 1858 was the polar opposite from that of the Chinese. The Japanese military and elements of the merchant and aristocratic landed classes were enraged at the unequal terms of the trade agreement. In 1868, they overthrew the Tokugawa dynasty that had ruled for more than 250 years, restoring the emperorship in the person of Emperor Meiji (the Meiji Restoration). Despite restoring the emperor, it was not a backward-looking rebellion, and the emperor spoke for the new leaders of their determination to learn from the West on their own terms, adapting institutions and techniques to defend themselves against westerners. The deliberate effort to fashion a modern industrial sector and a strong military resulted in an industrialization process in the late nineteenth and early twentieth century with the distinct hallmarks of Finance Capitalism. The irony is that the Perry incursion that "opened" Japan bred a reaction that enabled Japan to become a formidable imperialist competitor of the Western powers in East Asia. Japanese troops defeated China (1894–1895) and Russia (1904–1905), giving them a presence in Manchuria and control of Formosa (Taiwan) and Korea. The Japanese Empire was born.

The abortive 1871 attempt by the United States to force its way into Korea and open it for trade and investment was an unproductive military adventure. Modeled on Admiral Perry's approach to Japan in the 1850s, the invasion killed several hundred Korean soldiers, both sides claimed victory, and Korea remained secluded until taken over by Japan. And the only territory in the Pacific that the United States acquired before 1898 was the Midway Islands, a barren, uninhabited atoll of two and one-half square miles. Claimed by the United States in 1867, it is one-third of the way between Honolulu and Tokyo and was thought to have some military use.

Closer to home, William H. Seward, secretary of state for Presidents Abraham Lincoln and Andrew Johnson, bought Alaska in 1867 from the Russians for $7.2 million. By expanding into the area around the Black Sea, Russia encroached on some territory of the Ottoman Empire and touched off the Crimean War (1853–1856). The Ottomans with Great Britain and France defeated Russia, which sold Alaska to the United States in order to replenish its treasury. The purchase went through Congress easily because Alaska was thought to be empty and was considered a step toward taking over Canada. The U.S. government ignored Alaska for decades, but the Alaskan gold rush in 1897–1898 stimulated U.S. official interest and a border dispute with Canada.

In chapter 3, I described the U.S. filibustering attempts by private militias in the 1850s to invade Central America and Cuba. After the Civil War, the U.S. government continued to be intrigued by Caribbean possibilities. Secretary of State Seward, an ardent expansionist, negotiated treaties to buy pieces and then all of the Danish West Indies (now the Virgin Islands, east of Puerto Rico), a large harbor in northwest Santo Domingo (now the Dominican Republic), and U.S. control of the isthmus of Panama. The U.S. Senate refused to act on any of these treaties.

Another attempt to acquire Caribbean real estate occurred in the early 1870s, when two U.S. investors who had bought large tracts of land in Santo Domingo approached President Ulysses S. Grant on the behalf of Dominican officials and asked that the United States annex Santo Domingo. The investors and the local economic and political elites feared another invasion by the Haitians, whose nation constituted the western third of the island and was populated and governed by former slaves, and those same Dominican elites also worried about the potential for an uprising by local impoverished people. U.S. investors and Santo Domingo political elites were convinced that if the United States were to annex Santo Domingo, the result would be to secure the social and political structure on which they depended. U.S. media and citizens were indifferent to the proposal, and the Senate rejected it on the grounds of expense and unease about the prospects of Santo Domingo adding an infusion of nonwhite citizens. In addition, the old abolitionist and Radical Republican politicians feared this might be a new scheme for deporting newly free U.S. blacks.

Similar problems plagued efforts of expansionists to annex Hawaii, which was an independent monarchy until 1893. U.S. missionaries, mostly from New England, began arriving in 1820, and the Native Hawaiian population declined precipitously, as had been the case with American indigenous peoples defenseless against Eurasian diseases. The estimated 1832 Native Hawaiian population of over 130,000 had shrunk to little more than 34,000 by 1890.

U.S. missionaries and their descendants, however, thrived in Hawaii. After introducing the idea of private property in land, immigrants from the United States appropriated large tracts of land for plantations growing sugar, rice, and eventually pineapples and coffee for export. A reciprocity

treaty with the United States, ratified in 1875, opened the U.S. market to
Hawaiian agricultural products in exchange for a U.S. Navy base in Pearl
Harbor, few import restrictions on U.S. exports, and the promise that Ha-
waii would not enter into a similar treaty with any other nation.

The increased market for Hawaiian agriculture put intensive pressure on recruiting labor for the plantations. Chinese contract labor had
been the principal source to augment the dwindling numbers of Native Hawaiians, and in the late 1870s, planters began to recruit in the
Portuguese islands of Madeira, Azores, and Cape Verde in the Atlantic.
Between 1876 and 1913, over 17,000 Portuguese citizens immigrated to
Hawaii. In 1884, the Japanese government relaxed restrictions on its
subjects' ability to emigrate as contract laborers. Between 1885 and 1894,
over thirty thousand Japanese immigrants arrived in Hawaii, where, as
table 7.3 shows, they outnumbered any national-origin group other than
Native Hawaiians.

Queen Liliuokalani was interested in revising the 1887 Hawaiian Constitution, the infamous "Bayonet Constitution" forced on her brother, the
former King David Kamehameha, by wealthy whites and their militia.
Her proposed constitution would have broadened the electorate to the
pre-1887 levels, but it was not the assault on white freedoms and property that white leaders claimed. John L. Stevens, U.S. minister to Hawaii,
in concert with the wealthy whites, had the naval commander of a U.S.
warship in the Honolulu harbor dispatch two companies of armed sailors
and a company of marines, and the so-called Revolution of 1893 was swift
and bloodless.

Table 7.3. National Origins of Hawaii's
Population, 1896

National Origin	Number	Percentage
Native Hawaiian	31,000	28.5
Japan	24,400	22.5
China	21,600	19.9
Portugal	15,100	13.9
Mixed nationalities	8,400	7.7
United States	3,000	2.8
Great Britain	2,200	2.0
Germany	1,400	1.3
Norway and France	479	0.4
All others	1,055	1.0
Total	108,634	100.0

Source: Derived from Eric T. Love, *Race over Empire: Racism
and U.S. Imperialism, 1865–1900* (Chapel Hill: University of
North Carolina Press, 2004), 130.

The white revolutionaries, many of whom had held important posts in the royal government, organized a provisional government and applied for annexation to the United States in order to assure their control of Hawaii and to ensure their access to U.S. markets, which new U.S. legislation had made less certain. The lame-duck Republican government of President Benjamin Harrison tried to push annexation through Congress the month before the March 1893 inauguration of Democratic president-elect Grover Cleveland, but it failed. After the emissary that President Cleveland sent to Hawaii reported the illegal role of the U.S. military and the hostility of the majority of Native Hawaiians to the revolution, Cleveland replaced Minister Stevens, forced the retirement of the naval captain who cooperated with Stevens, and declared that the queen should be restored. But the leaders of the Hawaiian revolution did not restore the queen, waited until a Republican returned to the White House with a Republican congressional majority, and convened a constitutional convention of themselves. In 1894, Sanford Dole became the first and only president of the Republic of Hawaii, elected under a constitution that disenfranchised the vast majority of Native Hawaiians and Asians.

President William McKinley was elected with Republican majorities in both houses of Congress in 1896. But annexation was still not a sure thing. The Hawaiian whites' continuing need for Asian labor and the resulting influx of mostly Japanese workers heightened white mainlanders' unease about admitting such a heterogeneous population into the United States. The white Hawaiians and their allies tried to paper over this contradiction by discovering promising Anglo-Saxon traits in the Native Hawaiians and the Portuguese, both of whom Dole had earlier declared unfit to vote, the latter because Sanford Dole contended that the Portuguese from the Madeira and Azores islands were too tainted by African blood to have the franchise. A second major argument was that if the United States did not move quickly, another nation would take over Hawaii and represent a military threat to the West Coast of the United States. After all, the Japanese had always shown interest in Hawaii and in 1897 had gone so far as to encourage Japanese immigrants in Hawaii to demand the vote.

These arguments did not tip the balance in favor of annexation among U.S. labor unions in the West and farmers in the Midwest and South. The political landscape did shift remarkably, but not until after the United States entered the war of 1898 (known misleadingly as the Spanish-American War) on the side of Cuban independence. Patriotic fervor in the United States peaked when Commodore George Dewey sailed into Manila Bay on May 1, 1898, and destroyed a Spanish naval fleet without losing one U.S. life. But Dewey could not take the city of Manila until mid-August, when the necessary reinforcements of troops and supplies arrived. The United States captured Manila in time to block the entry of Filipino forces fighting for independence.

The need for a large military base and coaling station on the way to the Philippines was obvious, and Congress passed the treaty of Hawaiian annexation in July 1898. Even with the momentum from the war, supporters of annexation were so worried about the strength of the opposition that they used a possibly illegal legislative maneuver to avoid the usual two-thirds vote in the Senate needed to ratify a treaty.

The treaty stipulated that the Chinese in Hawaii were prohibited from immigrating to the continental United States, in line with the Chinese Exclusion Acts. Becoming a U.S. territory enfranchised Native Hawaiian men, but the Naturalization Act of 1790, reinforced by the 1882 and 1892 exclusion acts, prevented Chinese immigrants from becoming naturalized citizens in the United States. Asians born in Hawaii were automatically U.S. citizens after 1898, but it took decades for their numbers to increase. The McKinley administration appointed Sanford Dole as the first governor of Hawaii.

It was through the war of 1898 that the United States became a clearly defined colonial power. The Second Cuban War of Independence began in 1895, eighteen years after the first Cuban War of Independence (the Ten Years' War) ended in failure. A mixed bag of short-run occurrences and long-run interests and feelings lay behind the intervention. An intercepted letter written by the Spanish minister to the United States was insulting to President McKinley. Soon after, in February 1898, a mysterious explosion of a U.S. cruiser, the *Maine*, in Havana harbor killed 265 U.S. sailors and was widely and erroneously blamed on the Spaniards.

These incidents would not have triggered a war with Spain without a context of deeper and longer-standing pressures. There was a pervasive belief that the United States should join the Europeans in claiming distant regions in order to reap investment and commercial opportunities, to fulfill what was seen as a U.S. moral duty to bring civilization to benighted populations, and to establish strategically located bases for protecting U.S. citizens involved in economic and "civilizing" missions. Sensationalist and exaggerated reporting of Spanish atrocities by William Randolph Hearst's *New York Journal* and Joseph Pulitzer's *New York World*—the supermarket tabloids of the day—helped create widespread sympathy in the United States for the Cubans and antipathy for Spaniards.

The atrocities were not figments of newsmen's imaginations. The Spaniards, for example, rounded up a sizable proportion of the population in Cuba's countryside and placed them in concentration camps in order to block their support of the insurgents. This tactic has been used in other colonial wars, such as by the British in Malaya after World War II, the United States in Vietnam, and the Guatemalan military in the 1980s civil war. In Cuba, the *reconcentración* policy accounted for an estimated one hundred thousand to three hundred thousand deaths in the camps from starvation, disease, and abuse.

The United States' entry into the war on the side of the Cuban insurgents in April 1898 hastened the end of the Cuban war, and hostilities ceased in August 1898 with U.S. troops in control of Cuba, Puerto Rico, and Manila. Because yellow fever sickened and killed so many U.S. troops in Cuba, the U.S. government withdrew them quickly, leaving behind a regiment of African American soldiers whom white officials conveniently (and mistakenly) thought to be immune to the disease.

The U.S. Congress's joint resolution for war against Spain included the explicit proviso (Teller Amendment) that the United States had no intention of annexing Cuba and promised to contribute to a new and stable polity in independent Cuba. But it was not easy to establish a stable and legitimate Cuban national government. The Spanish colonial state was gone, and the earlier loss of privileged access to the U.S. sugar market and the wartime devastation of plantations handicapped the sugar elites' ability to assume that leadership in the new politics. The Catholic Church's unwavering support for the Spanish made it an unlikely source of acceptable leadership. The liberation army was the only credible and coherent Cuban national institution still standing, and U.S officials quickly disbanded it.

Other U.S. actions also impeded Cuban independence. In 1903, the Platt Amendment attached to an army financing bill stipulated narrow limits to Cuban governmental policy and finance and gave the United States the right to intervene any time that the U.S. government believed the Cuban government was not acting responsibly or was coming under the influence of another foreign power. The amendment also created the U.S. naval base in Guantánamo. Meanwhile, U.S. investors found that Cuban plantations were available from the ruined Spanish and Cuban owners, and sugar production on U.S.-owned Cuban plantations rose from 343,000 tons in 1900 to over four million tons after World War I.

The Puerto Rican populace welcomed U.S. troops as liberators, but on the other side of the world, the colonial project was not going as smoothly. Guam was the easy piece. It was a small Spanish colony with about ten thousand souls (see table 7.4 for 1910 population figures) located east of the Philippines. It was not difficult for a U.S. Navy ship to stop at Guam in June 1898 and without bloodshed capture the fifty or so Spanish colonial officers and soldiers, none of whom knew that the United States was at war with Spain. But the Philippines were another matter.

When Dewey sank the Spanish fleet in Manila Bay, it raised the issue of what to do with the Philippines. At that time, there were over seven million Filipinos of Negrito, Malay, and Indonesian descent in an archipelago of over seven thousand islands, with Muslims predominating in

Table 7.4. Population of the United States, Including Outlying Areas, 1910

Contiguous United States	91,972,266
Total outlying areas	10,342,144
Philippines	8,886,000
Puerto Rico	1,118,012
Hawaii	191,874
Alaska	64,356
Canal Zone	62,810
Virgin Islands	26,051
Guam	11,806
American Samoa	7,251
Midway Islands	31

Note: Populations of Canal Zone and American Samoa are for 1912.

Source: U.S. Census Bureau, *Historical Statistics of the United States: Colonial Times to 1970, Part I* (Washington, DC: Government Printing Office, 1975), 9.

the south and Roman Catholics in the north. And it was a long way from the United States, and, unlike Hawaii, it was not under sure white control and unlikely to attract many U.S. settlers. The racial mix was distasteful, but by the late nineteenth century, the United States had three models that had been sanctioned a number of times by the Supreme Court. The first was Native Americans, who were treated as foreign nations and denied citizenship until 1924. The second was white women, who were citizens but denied the vote. The third was African American men, who had formal rights of citizenship but were denied them by open racist practices.

President McKinley and his cabinet seemed to have trouble figuring out whether to take over the Philippines, keep just Manila, give it back to the weakened Spanish, or what. The fear was that any move other than annexation would leave the Philippines to be picked off by the British, German, French, or Japanese, not palatable to the U.S. public and government.

When President McKinley decided that the United States would keep the Philippines and pay Spain twenty million dollars for it, the final Treaty of Paris gave the United States control of the Philippines and Puerto Rico. The treaty angered many, including farmers and unionized workers, and it was ratified by the U.S. Senate on February 6, 1899, by a one-vote margin. The vote was preceded by a huge flow of legal tender, federal judgeships, and other favors for senators on the fence and their families.

In all of this, nobody asked the Filipinos. The Filipino liberation army regarded the U.S. military as allies in a war of independence against Spain, and the liberation army cleared most of the islands of what had always been a slight Spanish presence outside Manila. They had surrounded Manila readying for an assault when the U.S. troops arrived. The U.S. commander cut a deal with the Spanish commander, who was not looking forward to being killed or captured by an angry liberation army. He promised to make only a weak show of resistance. The U.S. commander tricked the liberation army to let U.S. troops through their lines and captured the city easily. The U.S. troops, on President McKinley's orders, forbade the liberation army from entering the city, just as it did with the Cuban liberation army in Santiago, Cuba.

It was clear to the liberation army that the United States was not interested in contributing to the formation of the independent Republic of the Philippines and putting into effect its new constitution. The contents of the Treaty of Paris were clear, and on December 4, open warfare between the liberation army and U.S. troops began in the outskirts of Manila. (The beginning of fighting and U.S. casualties added pressure on U.S. senators to vote for the ratification of the Treaty of Paris two days later.)

The liberation army, like the population, was a diverse mixture of people and motives, but like 1776–1783 in the United States and the 1820s in Spanish America, the independence movement was a political revolution, not a social revolution. For that reason, the landed, merchant, and professional elites had been sympathetic to the end of Spanish control. But these elites, trusting the U.S. forces' commitment to property rights, deserted the independence movement when it met U.S. opposition, reducing the movement's resources and freedom of movement. Nevertheless, it took seventy thousand U.S. troops until 1903 to conquer the Philippines in a nasty guerrilla war complete with burning villages, looting, and indiscriminate butchering by both sides. The final death tolls were over forty-two hundred U.S. soldiers, twenty thousand Filipino soldiers, and at least two hundred thousand Filipino civilians. Some serious scholars argue that all four of these numbers should be doubled.

There were striking differences between the Philippines and Puerto Rico, the two new colonies, and these differences were why Congress ignored the "free white" clause of the 1790 Naturalization Act and, as in the case of Hawaii, granted U.S. citizenship to Puerto Ricans and not to Filipinos. The size, geography, and multilingual and multicultural dimensions of the Philippines overwhelmed any commonalities from the new colonies' shared experience with Spanish colonial rule. Local markets were much more important for Philippine agricultural production, and Philippine exports were more diverse than Puerto Rico's heavy dependence on coffee and sugar. Puerto Rican elites were weakened by serious declines in export prices and market access, and on top of that, a hurricane in 1899 killed 2,500 Puerto Ricans and wreaked immense devastation on buildings and coffee bushes.

This combination of events practically wiped out the Puerto Rican landed and merchant elites. The destitution in the countryside and the lack of resources for the elites to sustain traditional patron-client relations led to serious unrest among rural workers, complete with burning plantations and violence against the privileged. This helped convince the Puerto Rican elites that their interests were in becoming a state in the United States rather than an independent nation. The Philippine elite, despite the failed war of independence, fared much better in being able to hang on to the resources necessary to reproduce customary social relationships and hierarchy, and they accepted the U.S. policy of no U.S. citizenship but eventual independence.

Despite the diverse political situations in Puerto Rico and the Philippines, the United States civilian government went ahead to transform both new colonies into modern societies along U.S. lines. In both places, the United States improved education facilities, medical care, sanitation, roads, and the availability of potable water in the cities. They launched tutelary efforts to teach democracy and democratic procedures. Often demonstrating an arrogant innocence, U.S. officials in both colonies were Progressive reformers who were going to show that their colonialism, unlike that of the Europeans and Japanese, would bring democracy and capitalism for the good of the colonial subjects. A minor but revealing example of ignorance coexisting with a sense of superiority was when the first U.S. military governor in Puerto Rico decided that Puerto Ricans did not spell the name of their island correctly and mandated that all official documents call it Porto Rico—a Portuguese-language corruption of Puerto Rico that lasted into the 1930s.

The U.S. colonial strategy to teach about democracy was to begin with the (male) elites in the belief that there would be a marked trickle-down effect. So those eligible to vote and run for office in the first municipal elections and subsequent provincial and national levels were the landed class, merchants, and professionals (lawyers, physicians, educators). This meant that "the eligible class" constituted around 2.5 percent of the Philippine population and around 5 percent in Puerto Rico. The U.S. officials believed that creating a democratic polity was a matter of injecting proper attitudes and institutions and then conducting elections. At the same time, defending and expanding property rights was seen as a necessary aspect of the civilizing mission, even though those property rights undergirded a distribution of economic power so unequal that it compromised the idea of representative government. This mindset is alive and well in the twenty-first century. Altogether the effort worked better in Puerto Rico than in the Philippines.

One unexpected consequence of the U.S. imperialist adventure in 1898 was that it expressed and promoted U.S. whites' sense of racial superior-

ity in a manner that intensified anti–African American feelings and behavior, despite the courage and reliability of African American volunteer
regiments in both Cuba and the Philippines.

In the year after the war of 1898, the United States acquired some additional Pacific islands: in 1899, Wake Island, an unpopulated atoll of
several small islands around a lagoon, as well as the brokered settlement
dividing the Samoan Islands between the United States and Germany.
The Samoa agreement resolved a conflict that had festered for a decade
and almost led to war. And in 1917, the United States bought the largest
of the Virgin Islands from the Danes.

The United States was now a growing colonial power, and at the turn
of the twentieth century, there were reasons to believe that its improved
military and administrative capabilities would propel additional expansion in the new century. McKinley's reelection in 1900 seemed to be an
affirmation of expansion, but soon after President McKinley's second
inauguration in 1901, he was assassinated. The vice president, Theodore
Roosevelt, succeeded McKinley. Roosevelt was a celebrated veteran of the
1898 war in Cuba, and he had been a consistent and bellicose expansionist
in the nineteenth century. Nevertheless, the United States annexed little
more real estate during his seven years in office or, for that matter, later.

As in President Roosevelt's antitrust efforts, he was aggressive in foreign
policy. While there are a number of examples of his Big Stick diplomacy,
none of them rivals the audacity of his obtaining the site of the Panama Canal. Ferdinand Marie de Lesseps was the world-famous engineer in charge
of the construction of the Suez Canal, which opened in 1869. For an encore,
he worked out an agreement with the Colombian government to build a
ship canal through the isthmus of Panama, then a province of Colombia.
Like the Suez Canal, it was to be a sea-level canal with no locks. They
worked between 1883 and 1893, when malaria, yellow fever, and flawed
designs drove them into bankruptcy. De Lesseps offered the partially dug
canal to the Roosevelt administration for $40 million. The annexation of
Hawaii and the Philippines and the lure of the Chinese market made it an
attractive proposition for the Roosevelt administration, and the U.S. Senate ratified a treaty with Colombia in January 1903. The Colombian Senate
would not ratify the treaty, protesting against the six-mile-wide stretch
across the isthmus that would be under U.S. control.

On December 2, 1903, Panama launched yet another attempt to separate from Colombia, and with President Roosevelt's coordinated support
for Panama and threats to Colombia, Panama became an independent
nation on December 3, 1903. The United States immediately offered diplomatic recognition to independent Panama, and within two weeks, the
two nations agreed on a canal treaty that would give the United States a
ten-mile-wide canal zone in perpetuity and rent and up-front payments

similar to those in the Colombian treaty. The de Lesseps company was also involved in the timing of the "spontaneous" Panamanian revolt against Colombia, and it was rewarded with its $40 million. The canal, with seven sets of locks, opened in August 1914, the same month as the military conflicts that escalated into World War I.

PART IV

INTO THE
TWENTIETH AND
TWENTY-FIRST CENTURIES

8

—∿∿—

War, Depression, War

The assassination of an Austrian archduke in Sarajevo, irreversible military mobilizations, and overlapping alliances propelled Europe into World War I. Armed conflict in the principal theaters of war began on August 4, 1914, when Germany invaded Belgium. After initial German victories, British and French troops—the Allies, which also included Russia, Italy, and nominally a number of Latin American and East Asian countries—stopped the German advance in France. This western front hardly moved for three and a half years, with each side literally entrenched and stalemated and suffering immense casualties.

The eastern front opened when Austria-Hungary, with support from the Ottoman Empire and Bulgaria (with Germany, the Central Powers), invaded Russia. After the 1917 Russian Revolution, the new Soviet government instituted war communism as an emergency program to ensure the provisioning of the villages and cities during the war with the Central Powers and the domestic civil war fought by those contesting the Soviet government. The infamous Treaty of Brest-Litovsk, negotiated between the revolutionary Soviet government and the Central Powers and signed on March 3, 1918, closed the eastern front at the price of the Soviet's losing much of its western and southern lands. The treaty was annulled when the Germans agreed to the armistice on November 11, 1918.

WORLD WAR I AND THE DOMESTIC REFORM AGENDA

U.S. politicians and civilians fiercely debated the dangers and responsibilities the European war presented to the United States, but in November 1915, President Woodrow Wilson ordered the beginning of U.S.
military preparedness. The sharp political divisions over entering the
war did not paralyze U.S. politics. Congress had passed the Sixteenth
Amendment (the income tax) and the Seventeenth Amendment (the
direct election of U.S. senators) and sent them to the states during the
previous administration of William Howard Taft (1909–1913), and the
required three-quarters of the states (thirty-six of forty-eight) ratified
both amendments in 1913.

Before 1913, state legislatures elected U.S. senators. The Seventeenth
Amendment gave states' voters the right to elect their U.S. senators
directly. Frequent political gridlocks, extended vacancies in Senate representation, bribery, and other bad behavior by state legislatures had
already inspired many states to adopt some form of direct election. But
the U.S. Senate continually blocked a proposed constitutional amendment
that would have made the process consistent and general. It was only
after two-thirds of the states threatened to call a constitutional convention that the Senate passed the amendment. Six southern states plus Utah
and Rhode Island never ratified the amendment, and some conservatives
continue to advocate its repeal.

In his first term (1913–1917), Woodrow Wilson also initiated and supported new legislation in the spirit of the Progressive Era, supported by
Democratic majorities in both houses. He convinced the U.S. Congress
to act on the new Sixteenth Amendment and create the legislation necessary for collecting taxes on income in 1913. The president also signed the
Federal Reserve Act (1913), the Clayton Antitrust Act (1914), the Federal
Trade Commission Act (1914), a series of legislative acts that lowered
tariffs to pre–Civil War levels, and a 1916 law restricting the employment
of children. The U.S. Supreme Court declared the last law unconstitutional in 1918. Foreshadowing what the federal role in labor-management
struggles was to become during the U.S. involvement in World War I,
Wilson initiated and signed a 1916 bill mandating an eight-hour day for
four railroad brotherhoods (around 20 percent of railroad workforces) to
forestall a paralyzing strike.

The United States entered the war on the side of the Allies in April 1917
because "the world must be made safe for democracy," in the words of
President Wilson, who had campaigned for reelection in 1916 and boasted
that he had kept the United States out of the war. The war was opposed
by large numbers of U.S. citizens, an opposition that increased when draft
calls arrived. Over the course of the war, the size of the U.S. Army grew

from around 128,000 to nearly five million, of which more than half were draftees. Two million U.S. soldiers, including 350,000 African Americans in segregated divisions, served in Europe, and more than fifty thousand of the two million were killed and more seriously wounded.

Table 8.1 shows how the U.S. government financed the war: The government relied more on taxes and new money than in the Civil War, and less on borrowing. The new income tax (supplemented for the war), a new estate tax, an excess profits tax on corporations, a special tax on munitions producers, and higher across-the-board rates of existing taxes account for the additional proportions of tax revenues. These tax revenues came disproportionately from the wealthy and amounted to a deliberate social policy to reduce income inequalities.

The production of new money did not come from printing greenbacks, as it did in the Civil War; most of the new money was from the Federal Reserve increasing bank assets available for lending. The new loans were made possible by suspending convertibility (paying out gold for U.S. dollars). The increased money supply promoted inflation, and price levels doubled between 1914 and 1920 (see table 8.1), constituting a kind of tax that fell on workers and the middle classes. Finally, borrowing abroad was more difficult than during the Civil War because the war restricted European purchases of U.S. bonds and forced many European investors to sell their U.S. financial assets to pay war expenses. To encourage domestic purchases of the bonds, the federal government engaged in large-scale, sophisticated bond drives that emphasized patriotism and sponsored the appearance of popular film stars and other celebrities at bond-selling rallies.

A series of new federal government agencies, such as the War Industries Board, the Shipping Board, and the National War Labor Board, allocated new capital to expand war-related production as well as controlled prices, production, and distribution of food, fuel, cattle feed, clothing, and other goods and services considered of strategic importance. The federal government took control of the railroad, telegraph, and telephone

Table 8.1. Sources of Financing for Three Wars (Percentages)

	Civil War	World War I	World War II
Taxes	20	25	43
Bond sales to public	70	61	34
Creating new money	10	14	24
Total	100	100	100

Note: Totals may not be the sum of parts due to rounding errors.
Source: Michael Edelstein, "War and the American Economy in the Twentieth Century," in *The Cambridge Economic History of the United States*, Vol. 3: *The Twentieth Century*, ed. Stanley L. Engerman and Robert E. Gallman (New York: Cambridge University Press, 2000), 351.

systems. The Wilson administration appointed these powerful boards' members, who were business leaders and cabinet secretaries but also included Samuel Gompers and a number of women reform leaders. Other appointees were employed to recruit women into the workforce, and four hundred thousand more women entered paid employment. Through the war, women constituted up to 8 percent of union membership, despite discrimination.

The entry into the war and subsequent mobilizations and deployments did not completely stifle reform momentum. In 1919, the required three-fourths of states (still thirty-six) ratified the Eighteenth Amendment, which prohibited "the manufacture, sale, or transportation of intoxicating liquors," including imports and exports. The temperance movement has a long history in the United States, and it had deep roots in and many overlaps with the Progressive movement. The subsequent enabling legislation (the Volstead Act of 1919) defined intoxicating liquors at 0.5 percent alcohol by volume and provided for enforcement and the punishment of violators.

Although Prohibition was presented as a patriotic act, the criminalization of alcohol eliminated the revenue stream from liquor excise taxes, created the financial incentives for powerful criminal gangs to battle in public over territories, corrupted law enforcement, intimidated citizens, and supplied toxic liquor. The repeal of Prohibition was a part of the platform of the Democratic Party in the election of 1932, and in 1933, the Twenty-First Amendment made the Eighteenth the only constitutional amendment to be repealed.

There were changing numbers of states, counties, and municipalities that had outlawed the manufacture and sale of liquor independent from the federal government. Woman suffrage was also granted by individual states on an uneven basis. In table 8.2, the geographical pattern of enfranchisement is striking: the states that passed woman suffrage before the Nineteenth Amendment were, with the exception of New York, in the Midwest, Rocky Mountains, and Far West. Apart from New York, none of the northeastern states and none of the former Confederate states are on the list. Northeastern states are better represented in the partial suffrage column, but even here, only two states in that column were former Confederate states.

The necessary three-quarters of states ratified the Nineteenth Amendment in 1920, and after seventy years of organization, agitation, and lobbying, "The right of citizens of the United States to vote shall not be denied or abridged by the United States or by any state on account of sex." While all forty-eight states eventually ratified the Nineteenth Amendment, most southern states did not ratify the amendment until the second half of the twentieth century.

Table 8.2.   States in Which Women Voted before the Nineteenth Amendment

Fully Enfranchised		Only Elections Concerning Schools		Only Municipal or Tax and Bond Elections	
State	Date	State	Date	State	Date
Territory of Wyoming	1869	Kentucky	1838	Kansas	1887
Territory of Utah	1870	Michigan	1855	Montana	1889
Territory of Washington	1883	Kansas	1861	Michigan	1893
Territory of Montana	1887	Colorado	1876	Iowa	1894
Wyoming	1889	Minnesota	1878	Louisiana	1898
Colorado	1893	Mississippi	1878	New York	1906
Idaho	1895	New Hampshire	1878	Illinois	1913
Utah	1896	Massachusetts	1879	Florida	1915
Arizona	1910	New York	1880	Indiana	1917
Washington	1910	Vermont	1880	No. Dakota	1917
California	1911	Oregon	1882	Nebraska	1917
Kansas	1912	Terr. of Dakota	1883	Vermont	1917
Oregon	1912	Nebraska	1883		
Territory of Alaska	1913	Wisconsin	1886		
Montana	1914	Terr. of Arizona	1887		
Nevada	1914	New Jersey	1887		
New York	1917	Idaho	1889		
Michigan	1918	Montana	1889		
Oklahoma	1918	No. Dakota	1889		
South Dakota	1918	Terr. of Oklahoma	1890		
		Washington	1890		
		Illinois	1891		
		Connecticut	1893		
		Kentucky	1893		
		Ohio	1894		
		Iowa	1895		
		Delaware	1898		
		New Mexico	1910		

Note: In the second and third of the three columns, women's eligibility was often circumscribed by such conditions as being a head of household (that is, single or widowed) and a taxpayer.

Source: Derived from Alexander Keyssar, *The Right to Vote: The Contested History of Democracy in the United States* (New York: Basic Books, 2000), tables A.17, A.18, and A.20 in the appendix.

Labor Unrest

More people were on strike in 1916 than ever before, and the number of strikes rose to a crescendo in 1917. In the first six months after the United States entered World War I, over six million workdays were lost due to strikes galvanized by inflation's outpacing of wages, displeasure about entering the war, and workers' improved bargaining position from the increased and urgent demand to produce war materials. The metal trades, shipbuilding, mining, textiles, and lumber, in descending order, led in numbers of strikes, and sixty-seven strikes involved more than ten thousand workers. Seventeen percent of the lost workdays were in IWW-led strikes, and 75 percent of the strikers in the first three leading sectors were in AFL affiliates.

The Wilson administration's response to workers' wartime demands for better wages, hours, and working conditions was rather conciliatory, and it allowed unionization of the federal civilian workforce, granted a wage increase, and made the eight-hour day a federal standard. President Wilson personally intervened in disputes to impose solutions often favoring workers.

On the other hand, federal officials responded harshly to antiwar sentiments in general and from the working class in particular. As part of war preparedness, new espionage and sedition laws were already on the books in 1917, and the federal government expanded the Secret Service in the Treasury Department and the new Bureau of Investigation (later the Federal Bureau of Investigation, or FBI) in the Justice Department to apply them. Officials organized 250,000 volunteers in state and local safety committees under the umbrella organization—the American Protective League—to uncover disloyalty in factories and neighborhoods. Presidential warrants detained six thousand aliens and more than two thousand others for disloyalty. The federal government muzzled any critical newspaper and magazine reporting by denying postal privileges and shut down foreign-language newspapers and magazines. The Socialist Party and the IWW were major targets.

POSTWAR TROUBLES AND ISSUES

The war ended with the armistice of November 11, 1918, but the relief was diminished, if not extinguished, by a series of postwar crises. The confluence of these problems from unresolved earlier conflicts and the economic and political contexts in which they erupted made them especially dangerous.

One of the most immediate and unsettling tribulations of the postwar era was the pandemic of the so-called Spanish flu (influenza) of 1918 and 1919. The flu is estimated to have killed between twenty-five million and one hundred million people throughout the world, including six hundred thousand in the United States, and disrupted every aspect of life.

After two years of wartime wage controls and inflation, four million workers struck in thousands of separate job actions in the months after the war. The most spectacular was the general strike in Seattle, Washington, where sixty-five thousand workers walked off their jobs in February 1919. Although the strike lasted less than a week and was nonviolent, many frightened government officials accused these strikers and all strikers of being part of a Moscow-directed communist conspiracy to take over the U.S. government. This political panic, known as the Red Scare, stemmed in good part from the 1917 Russian Revolution, and it was convenient for employers because it encouraged and helped justify the harshness with which hired thugs and local, state, and federal authorities crushed strikes.

The fears bred by the Red Scare went beyond the labor movement. African Americans striving for racial equality found themselves being painted as puppets of the Soviet conspiracy, and African American war veterans were considered especially threatening. Armed and uniformed black soldiers jarred the sensibilities of many whites. This fear of African American veterans went to the top of U.S. politics; President Wilson, the first southerner elected president since the Civil War, stated in 1919 that "the American Negro returning from abroad would be our greatest medium in conveying bolshevism to America" (quoted in McWhirter 2011: 56).

Claims linking black aspirations for equality with a communist revolution were mere pretenses taken from the playbook of the Mississippi Plan. Racial tensions had risen in northern and midwestern cities due to the increased presence of black workers migrating from the South during the war. The government's demobilization of more than two and a half million active-duty military personnel, white and black, between 1918 and 1920, with no plans for incorporating them back into civilian life, exacerbated tensions around jobs and housing. The resurgence of the Ku Klux Klan was one of the clearest expressions of white ethnic sentiment toward African Americans, Jews, Catholics, and recent immigrants. The Klan was mobilized in the South, Midwest, and somewhat in the Far West and at its peak in the mid-1920s claimed something like two million members.

April to November, 1919, often called the Red Summer, saw the largest number of "race riots" and lynchings in U.S. history. In at least thirty-eight settings, white mobs invaded black neighborhoods and commercial districts and looted, burned, and murdered. Sometimes an incident, real or imagined, triggered the mob violence, but often whites claimed that their attacks were necessary defenses against blacks plotting to kill whites— that time-worn fabrication. The worst of the race riots in the summer of 1919 were in Washington, DC; Omaha, Nebraska; Charleston, South Carolina; Longview, Texas; Knoxville, Tennessee; and especially Chicago. Elaine, Arkansas, also belongs on the list, although it was unusual in that it was a rural area in which lynchings and individual shooting deaths of African Americans were more common. But in 1919, Arkansas whites killed between one hundred and two hundred black sharecroppers who were meeting to form a union. These postwar disturbances were different from earlier riots in that blacks were willing and able to fight back, resulting in some white casualties.

Probably the worst race riot in the nation occurred on May 31 and June 1, 1921, in Tulsa, Oklahoma, the locale of one of the most prosperous African American communities in the United States. Blacks challenged a white mob's lynching of a black man and set off a white invasion of black neighborhoods and the black business district. Twelve hundred buildings were torched, and as many as three hundred African Americans were killed. The riot drove many, if not most, African Americans from Tulsa.

The decade of the 1920s saw petroleum production in Oklahoma, Texas, and Louisiana grow enormously. Since state and local governments did not obtain a large piece of the new riches in order to improve education, libraries, parks, physical infrastructure, public health, and judicial systems, the natural-resource bonanza was not the foundation on which a high-wage economy with general and enduring prosperity could be built. As so often in such oil booms, whether in U.S. states or abroad, the oil resulted in a handful of very rich individuals and a majority of low-wage workers and poor rural dwellers. The three states continue to have per-capita incomes and per-pupil education expenditures well below national averages.

The portrayal of the 1920s as the "Roaring Twenties"—a carefree time of jazz, flappers, Prohibition-era speakeasies, bootleg whisky, fast cars, and colorful gangsters—masks the difficulties of the decade. While the Nineteenth Amendment was one of the crowning achievements of the Progressive Era, it was not a harbinger of new and more inclusive federal reforms in the following decade. The Red Scare and anti-Bolshevik domestic crackdowns enabled the U.S. government to use the Espionage and Sedition Acts of World War I to deport immigrants active in the U.S. labor movement, crush strikes, deter political dissidence in general, and ignore the murder of African Americans and the destruction of their communities. New heights of income inequality obliterated and reversed the wartime reductions in income inequality. The repressive political and economic environment was not conducive to widening and deepening the democratic reach of public policy.

One positive accomplishment of the decade was the expansion of public high schools. In the 1920s, public high school enrollment doubled, and high school graduates as a proportion of seventeen-year-olds rose from 16 to 24 percent.

An Isolationist Program

The 1920s retreat from domestic reform politics was complemented by a strong desire to avoid foreign entanglements. There was a sharp division, even contradiction, between the outsized U.S. participation in postwar international trade and finance and a political reaction in the United States against participation in international affairs outside the Americas. This isolationism was clear when the U.S. Congress refused to implement President Woodrow Wilson's vision of a League of Nations. Subsequent Republican Congresses and administrations of Presidents Warren Harding (1921–1923), Calvin Coolidge (1923–1929), and Herbert Hoover (1929–1933), appalled by continuing and potentially violent quarrels among European nations, raised tariffs in 1920, 1921, and 1930, discouraged official U.S. participation in international conferences, and stepped away from the potential risks, obligations, and rewards of the U.S. dollar becoming a key international currency. One of the principal moves in an isolationist direction was to place more restrictions on immigration and naturalization.

Chinese and Japanese immigration was a thing of the past. Nativist reactions to the Italians, Jews, Poles, Slavs, Greeks, and other immigrants of late the nineteenth and early twentieth centuries demanded similar measures. Eastern and southern Europeans were declared incapable of assimilation and were thought to harbor dangerous political views. In the Emergency Quota Act (1921), the U.S. Congress created a new tool to restrict the immigration of undesirables—quotas based on national origins. These quotas were based on census counts of U.S. foreign-born residents.

The Second Quota Act of 1924 reduced national quotas from 3 percent of the share of each nation's foreign born in the United States to 2 percent, and the count was based on the census of 1890, thereby further decreasing the quotas for southern and eastern Europeans. It allocated 86 percent of available visas to western and northern Europe and 12 percent to eastern and southern Europe. And it gave explicit legal standing to the principle that "no alien ineligible to citizenship" be allowed to immigrate. There were a few exemptions: occupations and professions deemed valuable; family reunification; and continuing open immigration from the Americas.

Tensions around Foreign Financial Pressures

A major exception to the U.S. isolationist policy concerned the war loans to the Allies that U.S. lenders wanted repaid. In order to finance World War I, Great Britain and France borrowed heavily from U.S. public and private sources as well as drawing down their investments in the United States. Between 1914 and 1919, U.S. investment abroad rose by more than two and a half times, and foreign investment in the United States declined almost 25 percent, creating an $8.5 billion U.S. net international credit balance. The United States had gone from the world's largest international net debtor to the largest international net creditor in five years.

The Treaty of Versailles at the end of World War I redrew the map of Europe by dissolving the empires of the Central Powers—the German Empire, the Austro-Hungarian Empire, and the Ottoman Empire. It did this by establishing new nations, granting German colonies to the French and British, and distributing sizable pieces of the former empires and Bulgaria to neighboring nations.

In other negotiations around the Versailles Treaty, France, Belgium, and Great Britain, under pressure to repay their $10 billion wartime debt to U.S. creditors, led a successful effort to impose draconian war reparations on the Germans of £6.6 billion as well as lesser amounts on other Central Powers belligerents. These payments caused economic havoc in Germany and throughout central and eastern Europe, weakening fledgling democracies forced to pay for the misdeeds of former militaristic imperial governments.

Postwar European Politics

Financial stresses added to general instability, complete with region-wide insurrectionary and interethnic turmoil, exacerbated by the Great Depression after 1930. The consequence was a fertile field for the growth of fascism, and by 1939, every nation in southern, central, and eastern Europe, with the exception of Czechoslovakia, followed the lead of Italy and established nationalist right-wing authoritarian governments that were fascist, protofascist, or semifascist. They smashed labor movements and any hint of socialism or communism. The 1933 election led to Adolf Hitler's becoming Germany's chancellor, illustrating the desperation of the period.

These nationalist governments pursued an economic policy of autarky—self-sufficiency. They went off the gold standard, repudiated foreign debts and reparation payments, and centralized and militarized political power, often at the expense of the large industrialists and landowners who initially supported them. Japan underwent a similar process when the Japanese military, allied with important big business interests, assumed political control in the 1930s and destroyed the last vestiges of political moderation.

By the early 1920s, the Soviet army had contained the Russian counterrevolutionaries and defeated the 120,000 troops deployed by Japan, Greece, France, Great Britain, the United States, and other governments that had tried to destroy the Bolshevik state. This victory allowed the Soviets to inaugurate the New Economic Policy (1921–1928), which combined private and government ownership. With Lenin's death in 1924 and the ascendance of Joseph Stalin, the first five-year plan (1928–1933) established almost complete state control and central planning in the economy.

The principal goal of the five-year plans was to create a modern industrial sector that could supply the materiel to defend the Soviet Union against an expected invasion by capitalist nations.

The Soviet industrial sector grew rapidly in a decade, financed in large part by the agricultural sector, where a brutal collectivization program led to the deaths of four to ten million people from food shortages, state violence, and disease. Tens of thousands were imprisoned or deported to Siberia. Consumer products were scarce, although standards of living did rise somewhat in urban areas. While it came at great cost, industrial development occurred during the Great Depression, when the capitalist world continued to be mired in stagnation.

NEW TENDENCIES IN THE U.S. ECONOMY

U.S. economic growth during World War I came to a screeching halt after the war with a short, sharp recession in 1921 and 1922. The rest of the decade experienced steady economic expansion, although agricultural prices continued to drag farm incomes down below their 1920 level. The major economic developments in the 1920s were not the quantitative; they were discernible structural trends that continued to mature throughout the twentieth century.

Mass Production–Mass Consumption

The early decades of the twentieth century marked the appearance of a new form of capitalist industrial development organized around mass production and mass consumption. That is, the production and sale of consumer goods were becoming the principal source of economic dynamism, and the United States was the leader in this new source of economic dynamism. Machine-tool and chemical firms were innovative leaders that transformed the technical conditions of production in some already-existing consumer goods, and significant innovations were apparent in the production of new kinds of consumer products.

Large, machine-using firms became predominant in such traditional products as processed foods, cigarettes, soap powders, shoes, spirits, pharmaceuticals, and cosmetics as well as in new consumer goods such as rayon, nylon, paper, plastics, electrical appliances, and the automobile—that ultimate symbol of U.S. consumer civilization. Since both sets of consumer goods were produced for national markets by firms with similar capital intensities, large-scale plants, organizations of work, and market structures, I include both in a single category—modern consumer goods.

The use of electric power facilitated innovations in production. Electric power had been used in factories at least for lighting during the late nineteenth and early twentieth centuries, but with the greater availability of reliable and lower-cost electrical power, whether through in-house generators or purchases from utility companies developed to supply power to residences and trolleys, the use of electricity to run plants' machinery accelerated during World War I. By 1919, 50 percent of power supplied to manufacturing establishments was from electricity rather than from central power sources, such as water-powered turbines or steam engines. A central power source required belts and shafts to transmit power to factories' machines, and friction and slippage rendered this transmission inefficient. Belts and shafts constrained the positioning of power-using equipment, the flow of the product, and thereby the organization of work. Electric power, by contrast, gave managers new flexibility in determining the placement of equipment and flow of materials and enabled the adoption of new production organizations and technologies.

Large manufacturing corporations became larger through mergers, acquisitions, and bankruptcies, and most product lines were tending toward domination by a few large firms, say, two to five—a **market structure** that economists call oligopolistic. Several manufacturing firms went into direct retailing, but the principal consolidation in retailing during the 1920s occurred through such chain stores as the Great Atlantic & Pacific Tea Co. (A&P), Kohler, Grand Union, F. W. Woolworth, and Sprouse-Reitz.

A market controlled by a few firms did not mean that they were uncompetitive. Cutthroat price competition had been a problem for large corporations producing consumer goods in the late nineteenth and early twentieth centuries, but with the expanded capacity of manufacturing plants during the war, it became more intense and destabilizing in the 1920s. The goal was to reduce the dangers of price wars without creating monopolies or interfirm collaborations that flagrantly violated the Sherman Antitrust Act, the Clayton Antitrust Act, and the Federal Trade Commission Act. Aggressive large-scale mergers and acquisitions would have forced even the pro-big-business Republican administrations of Presidents Harding, Coolidge, and Hoover (1921–1933) to intervene.

As in the case of railroads in the middle to later nineteenth century and then the intermediate and capital goods firms in the late nineteenth and early twentieth centuries, mass-consumer goods firms in the third decade of the twentieth century turned to business trade associations that tried to promote orderly markets through coordinating prices, production, and marketing, tiptoeing around antitrust legislation. But again, the inability to enforce agreements crippled such efforts, and state governments' attempts to regulate markets were ineffective. The federal government in the 1920s did little beyond raising tariffs at the beginning and end of the decade and establishing a small agricultural price support program in the late 1920s. The solution to cutthroat competition was not obvious or easy, and it was several decades until the United States was able to institutionalize a structure more appropriate for this new phase of capitalist development.

One promising path for business emerged from employers' and government officials' having defeated the strikes after World War I. Undergirded by the anticommunist Red Scare, the persecution of the labor movement created a climate of fear and intimidation in which unions were on the defensive and divided. A few business leaders began to think beyond their implacable hostility toward labor unions, recognizing that some form of unionization was inevitable and that the pummeling of workers and unions had weakened and fragmented the labor movement to the point that workers would be receptive to a business-oriented unionism. They concluded that it was an opportune time to recognize a few well-behaved unions that would not impinge on managerial prerogatives.

The incentives for employers to move in such a direction were to avoid the costliness of breaking strikes and the likelihood that a set of politically safe, industry-wide unions could perform a useful regulatory function. If unions could establish uniform wages, hours, and work conditions in the principal firms within each product line, they would remove one of the foremost sources of differential production costs that encouraged price competition. Moreover, as long as higher wages did not disadvantage important fractions of capital, greater working-class purchasing power could expand mass markets for modern consumer goods.

Corporate Governance

As employers mulled over such a change in strategy, they were a part of a major transformation in corporate governance: the people making such suggestions and even decisions were increasingly not the corporations' owners. The entrepreneurial heroes or robber barons of mid- to late nineteenth-century capitalism were involved in running their firms, but by the 1920s, a fundamental shift was evident.

As the nineteenth century turned into the twentieth, the role of professional managers in day-to-day operations increased, and the role of owners—stockholders, represented by boards of directors—in operational decisions receded. Boards of directors were supposed to supervise management, but even large stockholders were coming to regard their holdings as one component of their financial portfolios, and their interest in running the business was slight as long as stock price and **dividends** were satisfactory. As the role of professional managers increased in day-to-day operations, the operational role of owners receded.

On the other side, the complexity of these giant organizations did require a range of expertise, and educational institutions were beginning to include new business and personnel management programs in their curricula. Professional corporate executives and managers were not enthusiastic about meddling or even scrutiny by amateurs, rich or not. The effect was the beginning of the separation of corporate control from corporate ownership, a tendency that continued to grow through the twentieth century. The clearest sign of this tendency is the frequency with which a corporation's chief executive officer (CEO), technically a hired hand responsible to the board of directors, is often now also the chairperson of the board of directors.

THE GREAT DEPRESSION

A spectacular stock market bubble in the late 1920s doubled the Dow Jones industrial stock index in eighteen months. When the bubble burst in 1929, stock market values fell almost 80 percent. The fragility of the domestic banking system and the inability to match levels of mass consumption with capacities for mass production in a chaotically changing economic landscape converged to create the most serious capitalist crisis ever. Between 1929 and 1933, U.S. real GNP declined by a third, official nonfarm unemployment rates rose to over 25 percent, thousands of banks closed, deflation pressed consumer prices down by a quarter and wholesale prices down a third, and consumption expenditures declined 43 percent. U.S. exports declined by 44 percent, suffering not only from reduced foreign income and demand but also from desperate national governments' uses of tariffs, quotas, exchange controls, and competitive **devaluations** to stimulate their domestic economies at the expense of trading partners. The steep economic decline over four years was unprecedented and traumatized most nations of the world.

Although urgent action was needed, U.S. political decentralization, capitalists' disarray, and the belief in the healing power of deflation obstructed an effective political response. The United States, like most western European governments, adhered to the conventional thinking that governments should balance their budgets to create a stable monetary environment and engage in little else in the way of **macroeconomic policy** (see the glossary). By relying on market mechanisms, the standard analysis went, the Depression would drive wages and prices down to the point that employers would resume hiring and consumers would once again purchase goods and services.

One problem with this analysis was that the deflation was uneven. Between 1929 and 1934, agricultural prices in the United States declined

50 percent from already depressed post–World War I prices. On the other hand, oligopolistic manufacturing firms had considerable market power and preferred cutting back production rather than engaging in dangerous price cutting. As a result, the prices of manufactured products declined only 20 percent.

A second flaw in waiting for a self-correcting deflation was that producers would not resume hiring until there was adequate demand for their products. On the other side of the market, consumers would not resume buying consumer goods and services until they had adequate income from employment and production. Moreover, even if markets could overcome the chicken-and-egg dilemma and pull the economy out of the depression in the long run, the observation by the respected British economist John Maynard Keynes ([1923] 1971: 65) is apt: "In the long run we are all dead." But conflicting policy ideas are not dead; similar convictions about appropriate policy are still alive and well in the eurozone, the International Monetary Fund (IMF), and conservative U.S. legislators.

When it became clear in the first three or four years of the Depression that the traditional prescription was not working, the United States and western Europe, as opposed to the rest of Europe, moved toward social democracy by incorporating labor movements into politics and creating social insurance, relief programs, pensions, and other supports for their hard-pressed citizens.

The administration of President Franklin Delano Roosevelt, which lasted into four terms (1933 to his death in 1945), and the solid Democratic Party majorities that the 1932 election swept into both houses of Congress moved quickly to stem the banking crisis. Three weeks before President Roosevelt's inauguration, the lack of confidence in banks caused depositors to withdraw their money from the banks at a time in which the banks' own loans were not being paid back. In these self-fulfilling prophecies, thousands of banks failed. President Roosevelt was inaugurated on March 4, 1933, and two days later, he followed the lead of thirty-eight states and declared a national "bank holiday" that closed all banks in the United States in order to stop these damaging runs.

Four days later, with the assurance of temporary deposit insurance, banks reopened without public panic, and much of the withdrawn cash was redeposited. By then, Roosevelt had issued an executive order in April 1933 that took the United States off the gold standard. By breaking the link between the volume of U.S. currency and the Treasury's holding of gold, the value of the U.S. dollar vis-à-vis the British pound (already off the gold standard) declined 30 to 40 percent.

The Roosevelt administration and Congress also initiated a number of experimental policies known as the New Deal. The short-lived National Recovery Administration (NRA), created in 1933, was an attempt at national industrial planning and coordination of manufacturing production, pricing, and employment. The agency backed up with federal law what industrial business and trade associations had tried in the 1920s. In effect, the NRA was to create cartels among the largest firms in every line of industry, and as in late nineteenth-century Germany, the price and production agreements among firms were to be legally binding. Even though business leaders dominated the councils empowered to make decisions about prices, wages, and output levels, the NRA's failure to bring order into markets turned the business community's support into opposition. The U.S. Supreme Court ruled the act unconstitutional in 1935.

Other policies enjoyed greater success. The Banking Act of 1933 (also known as the Glass-Steagall Act) established the Federal Deposit Insurance Corporation to sustain depositors' confidence in banks and gave new regulatory powers to the Federal Reserve System. The most controversial part of the act defined specific financial activities, and only those activities, as appropriate for brokerage houses, commercial banks receiving deposits, and investment banks, which did not have depositors but engaged in corporate finance, mergers and acquisitions, initial public offerings, and trading on their own accounts in a wide range of securities. Limiting commercial banks' risky behavior was a major goal of separating these activities into different, unaffiliated institutions. Twenty years later, insurance companies were walled off from other financial institutions in a similar manner.

The National Labor Relations Act (1935) legalized and regulated union organization, clearing the way for the Congress of Industrial Organizations (CIO) to begin organizing workers in mass-production plants. In doing so, they brought in all the plants' workers, skilled and unskilled, rather than having separate unions for such crafts as electricians, machine tenders, carpenters, and so on.

The Social Security Act (1935) mandated a national pension system, some limited social insurance, and the beginnings of a federal-state partnership for offering unemployment insurance. The act excluded agricultural and domestic-service workers from coverage, thus neglecting large numbers of minorities, women, and the poor. The New Deal also included a myriad of more focused programs, ranging from agricultural price and income support to a moratorium on farm foreclosures, the Civilian Conservation Corps, the Work Projects Administration, the Tennessee Valley Administration (conservation, reclamation, and hydroelectric power), the Securities and Exchange Commission, the Fair Labor Standards Act, the Rural Electrification Administration, and other regulatory, public works, and relief projects. One special program was directed to farmers and ranchers whose dire Depression-induced plights were exacerbated by terrible drought, soil erosion, and high winds (the "Dust Bowl") in

Colorado, Kansas, New Mexico, Oklahoma, and Texas. There was a mass exodus from these states, mostly to California.

During the Depression, John Maynard Keynes published *A General Theory of Employment, Interest, and Money* (1936). He advocated the use of governmental budgetary deficits and surpluses—**fiscal policy**—to affect aggregate demand in positive ways to reduce unemployment or negative ways to fight inflation. The argument was controversial in its rejection of conventional economic thinking, and President Roosevelt, elected on a balanced-budget platform, did not deliberately use fiscal policy to stimulate the economy.

Although the federal budget was in **fiscal deficit** through the six years of the Roosevelt administration before World War II, the deficits were small, and the national debt as a percentage of GNP rose only four percentage points in these years. In fact, the effort to balance the federal budget in 1937 and 1938, along with some mistaken Federal Reserve decisions, reversed the economic growth and recovery that had occurred since 1933.

Some business leaders supported some New Deal acts, but most opposed them as steps toward socialism. Their opinions, however, had less political influence than in the 1920s. The Depression had undermined the hold of business ideology and increased the power of the federal government, which in turn strengthened labor unions and popular electoral power. The entire New Deal endeavor has to be understood as an effort to put the business system back on its feet, even while it had to overcome opposition by the business community to do so. Nevertheless, when World War II began in 1939, the U.S. unemployment rate of the nonfarm workforce was still 17 percent.

WORLD WAR II AND WAR CAPITALISM

World War II rescued U.S. capitalism from the Great Depression. The war began when Hitler invaded Poland in September 1939; Italy and then Japan, which had invaded China in 1937 and perpetrated the Nanking Massacre,[1] joined Germany and Italy as the Axis Powers that also included Bulgaria, Hungary, Romania, Croatia, and Slovakia. The fascist governments of Spain and Portugal rooted for Nazi Germany but remained officially neutral. The United States entered the war after Japan's attack on the U.S. naval base at Pearl Harbor, Hawaii, in December 1941 and joined the Allies (United Kingdom, Soviet Union, and members of the British Commonwealth—Australia, Canada, India, and South Africa).

The belligerents fought on three massive fronts—western Europe, eastern Europe, and East and Southeast Asia, with spillovers to other locales.

Axis troops had captured almost all of these three regions in the early days of the war, and wherever the Nazi Germans took over, they, as they did in Germany, killed Jewish and Rom (Gypsy) peoples, political dissidents, and other groups deemed undesirable. These mass murders are estimated to have been around eleven million people, including six million Jews. The Allies drove Axis troops back on all three fronts. Germany surrendered in May 1945, and after the United States dropped atomic bombs on the cities of Hiroshima and Nagasaki, Japan surrendered in September 1945.

In order to achieve this victory, the United States had to engage in a huge mobilization of people and resources. The U.S. financial cost of World War II was more than six times that of World War I, accounting for over 40 percent of total U.S. production. The U.S. military grew from 334,473 in 1939 to 12,123,455 in 1945, of which 83 percent were inducted by the draft. World War II lasted a bit more than twice as long as World War I, but the number of U.S. military deaths (405,399) was three and a half times greater than in World War I.

Looking back at table 8.1, you can see that financing of the war continued earlier trends of relying more on taxes, less on borrowing from the public, and more on the creation of new money. Borrowing was proportionally a smaller source of financing; there was an almost sixfold increase in federal debt, from 46 percent of GNP in 1939 to 116 percent in 1946. The fact that these massive deficits did not destroy the financial system contributed to the acceptance of Keynes's arguments, which became part of mainstream professional economics after the war.

Although there was idle productive capacity at the beginning of the war, it soon was brought into full production, and inflationary pressures became evident. In order to suppress inflation, the federal government imposed wage and price controls and rationed food, fuel, and a range of other consumer products. The government also prohibited the production and sale of automobiles, refrigerators, and other appliances in order to devote more manufacturing capacity to the war effort, and by constructing and equipping new manufacturing plants, the federal government owned around half of all U.S. industry by the end of the war. The government also raised taxes and innovated by establishing mechanisms for withholding a portion of wages and salaries against future tax liabilities. This enabled the federal government to avoid waiting until the tax deadline into the next year for a good part of individuals' tax payments.

The downside of concentrated political power in the federal government, and in the executive branch in particular, was evident two months after the Japanese attack on Pearl Harbor. On February 19, 1942, President Roosevelt issued Executive Order 9066 that forced 120,000 Japanese Americans on the West Coast and in southern Arizona into concentration camps that were still being constructed in isolated and barren settings, camps surrounded by barbed wire and armed guards. Two-thirds of the "internees" in these harsh camps were native-born U.S. citizens—Japanese immigrants were prohibited from becoming naturalized citizens until 1952. U.S. officials gave people little time to get their affairs in order and restricted the few possessions that could be taken to the camps. As a result, and a not-unanticipated one, Japanese Americans lost large proportions of the value of their homes, businesses, and agricultural property.

The federal government also interned more than eleven thousand German nationals and three hundred Italian nationals, the principal targets being noncitizen residents. As in the case with Japanese camps, some of the internees were sent to camps in the United States. Cooperating Latin American governments also shipped some of their residents with ties to Japan, Germany, and Italy. Executive Order 9006 did not include Hawaii, where around 150,000 Japanese Americans and Japanese nationals constituted more than one-third of the territory's population. Fewer than two thousand Japanese Americans in Hawaii were sent to camps.

At the end of the war, most of the internees were released, but the Japanese were not warmly received by the general population despite their being treated so shabbily and in spite of the World War II Japanese-American 442nd Regimental Combat Team, the most decorated unit in U.S. history for its size and duration of service. It was not until 1988 that Congress apologized for the detentions and provided some financial redress. President Ronald Reagan signed the law. The German and Italian internees have been ignored by Congress, except for some failed attempts in the late 2000s to pass a bill entitled the "European Americans and Refugees Wartime Treatment and Study Act." These camps were not on the scale of the horror of Auschwitz, but like Jim Crow laws, they are testimonies to how fear, prejudice, and ignorance can trump what we call national values.

Business opposition to wartime federal regulation and control all but evaporated as soon as large federal expenditures for war materiel raised profit prospects and unions agreed to a no-strike pledge. During the war, the federal government operated a successful regime of war capitalism that went far beyond measures taken during World War I or the New Deal in its comprehensiveness, tight controls, top-down commands, and rationing. These wartime controls and management raised U.S. production by 2.3 times in four years, reduced U.S. unemployment to 1.2 percent in 1944, created new occupational opportunities for women, achieved modest reductions in income inequalities, and held out new possibilities of civil rights for African Americans.

Despite the Cold War, struggles around decolonization, renewed business assault on New Deal reforms, inflation and recession, and the Korean War, a number of these gains lasted for decades after the war.

9

—m—

Post–World War II Recovery and Modern Times, 1945–1980s

Significant postwar renovations in international and domestic political economies encouraged the emergence of a new economic structure in the United States. The structure had its roots in the previous century and came to full fruition in the postwar world. Although it appeared robust and durable, there were some strict conditions necessary to sustain it.

POSTWAR RECONSTRUCTION OF THE INTERNATIONAL POLITICAL ECONOMY

At the end of World War I, the United States had pressured the Allies to pay their debts, and the Allies imposed heavy reparation payments on Germany and others. Both moves proved to be mistakes, and the United States took the opposite tack in the decade after World War II. The United States canceled much of the Allies' public debts and sponsored the Marshall Plan for Europe and smaller programs for Japan, which was occupied and administered by U.S. military authorities until 1952. Between 1948 and 1951, the Marshall Plan pumped around $14 billion (5 percent of U.S. **gross domestic product**, or **GDP**, in 1948) into Europe. This first large-scale experiment in foreign aid was successful in rebuilding war-ravaged economies and in inoculating these regions against anticapitalist movements in general and communist influence in particular.

These programs' achievements in Germany and Japan were due in good part to both already being modern industrialized societies and needing principally to repair and rework physical plants, equipment, and

infrastructure. The reorientation of the two economies toward mass production and mass consumption with an emphasis on exports meant that
both soon became formidable competitors in the international economy.

The Bretton Woods Conference and the Dollar-Exchange Standard

Again in contrast to the aftermath of World War I, the U.S. government
asserted a new determination to shape international affairs in the post–
World War II world, buttressed by its dominant economic and military
power. One major concern was to fashion an international financial
framework robust enough to support a vigorous postwar expansion of
international trade and investment. When an Allied victory became imminent, U.S. Treasury Department officials convened a 1944 international
conference in **Bretton Woods**, New Hampshire, with representatives of
forty-three Allied nations, one neutral (Argentina), and a handful from
European colonies in Africa, South Asia, and Southeast Asia. U.S. Treasury officials and a British representative, John Maynard Keynes, were
the principal architects of the new international framework, which was
approved by the conference.

Except for the Soviet representatives, who attended Bretton Woods but
did not join the new pact, there were some general areas of agreement
among the principal representatives. One was that international trade
and investment were mutually beneficial for all participants and that a
new framework was needed to replace the previous framework that was
shattered in the 1930s. (See "comparative advantage" in the glossary.)
The second area of general agreement among political and economic
elites of the leading capitalist nations was severe doubt about the ability
of unregulated markets to generate stability and prosperity. This was
expressed as a new willingness to rely on discretionary interventions by
public authorities.

Skepticism about the efficacy of unregulated markets included doubt-
ing the effectiveness of either the **gold standard** or flexible exchange rates,
both free-market adjustment mechanisms to rectify imbalances in a nation's exports and imports—the **balance of trade**. (See "balance of trade"
in the glossary.) The actual operation of the nineteenth-century gold standard was uneven, but even when it did work with textbook tidiness, it
produced inflation in the economies with export surpluses and deflation
in economies importing more than they exported. Neither inflation nor
deflation made a government popular with citizens.

Flexible exchange-rate systems operate through international currency markets, raising the prices of a balance-of-trade surplus nation's
currency with respect to other currencies—its **exchange rate**—and reducing a balance-of-trade deficit nation's exchange rate. As a consequence,

prices of the surplus nation's exports rise in foreign markets and import prices decline in its home market, both reducing exports and increasing imports and thereby contributing to a reduced surplus. With the other side of adjustment, the reduction of the price of a deficit nation's currency leads to lower prices of the deficit nation's exports in foreign markets and prices of imports in the home market rise, thus increasing exports, reducing imports, and moving toward a balance. The expectation, then, is that both deficit and surplus nations will be propelled closer to balance. One problem with flexible exchange rates for the conference participants in the early 1940s was that it sounded too much like the competitive devaluations and exchange-rate volatility that had contributed to international economic instability during the 1930s.

The adjustment mechanism established by the Bretton Woods Conference was known as the **dollar-exchange standard**, and it was closer to the gold standard than a flexible exchange-rate system even though the volume of gold held by a national treasury no longer affected the quantity of money circulating in its national economy. The U.S. dollar became the new key currency—an international legal tender—to which all other currencies were pegged and defended by their governments. For foreign central banks and only foreign central banks, dollars were convertible to gold at thirty-five dollars per ounce.

The principal Bretton Woods innovations were to sever the link between holdings of gold and the volume of national money and to create two new international financial institutions: the **International Monetary Fund** (IMF) and the International Bank for Reconstruction and Development (later known as the **World Bank**). These two new institutions were charged with monitoring and stabilizing the international trade and payments system, focusing on nations running persistent balance-of-trade deficits.

A third institution, the International Trade Organization, was proposed right after the war to complement the IMF and World Bank by reducing tariffs. The U.S. Congress refused to ratify the agreement, maintaining that it involved too great an infringement on U.S. sovereignty. This left the General Agreement on Tariffs and Trade (GATT), a forum for discussing and negotiating tariff reductions.

The IMF's principal responsibility was to deal with imbalances considered to be of a short-term, cyclical nature by lending hard currency (for example, U.S. dollars) to a nation running a deficit in its international payments. Borrowing beyond a certain point, however, often required the borrowing government to agree to certain conditions—the IMF's "conditionality."

Similar to the medicine of the gold standard, the IMF's standard prescriptions to reduce a balance-of-trade deficit were to enact deflationary domestic policies, emphasizing reductions in government expenditures such as social services and subsidized urban food and transportation. In addition, the IMF pressured nations to abolish government regulations such as workers' protections and controls over domestic and international merchandise and financial transactions, and to privatize government-owned firms such as steel mills, petroleum refineries, and airlines. These were steps seen as necessary for efficient markets.

The World Bank, in contrast to the IMF, made long-term loans to countries where chronic balance-of-payments deficits were seen to be due to the structure of the deficit nation's economy. The purpose of these loans was to help nations change the domestic composition of their production, create new patterns of comparative international trade advantage, become more competitive internationally, and thus bring their international payments into balance.

Measures that directly attacked an individual nation's payments deficits, such as exchange-rate devaluations or tariffs, were to be used as a last resort and then through orderly, managed, and approved procedures that did not destabilize the dollar-exchange standard. But the principal point was the substantial change in the definition of the problem. The gold standard and flexible exchange-rate systems force adjustments on both deficit and surplus nations as constituent parts of destabilizing imbalances. Although it is obvious that there cannot be balance-of-payments deficits without equal balance-of-payments surpluses in the world, the Bretton Woods agreement placed the burden of adjustment entirely on deficit nations. A second major drawback to the entire enterprise was paying insufficient attention to international investment and its destabilizing potential. This became clear decades later.

The United Nations

The United Nations, also founded in 1944, was another important postwar international organization, but its influence on the world economy has been less than that of the IMF and the World Bank. Since the Soviet Union chose to join neither the IMF nor the World Bank, the United States and its allies and clients have had little trouble dominating both institutions, where voting power is proportional to the quota each nation pays into the institutions. The decisive influence by the United States in the IMF and the World Bank, then, was different from its position in the United Nations, where the Soviet Union had veto power in the Security Council. As a consequence, the U.S. government has preferred to work through the IMF and World Bank, ensuring the Bretton Woods institutions' place as the premier international economic institutions.

The European Economic Community

The North Atlantic Treaty Organization (NATO), established in 1949, was a military alliance between the United States and western European nations, but beyond comforting U.S. allies and deterring Soviet aggressiveness, it had little widespread impact. The more important international institution in the early post–World War II years was the European Economic Community. The first step occurred in 1952, when France, Germany, Italy, Belgium, the Netherlands, and Luxembourg, with U.S. support, established the European Steel and Coal Community. This was a common market in coal, iron ore, steel, and scrap that could be traded among the six signatories without customs or taxes while erecting common tariffs against outside products.

The community worked so well that in 1957, the same six nations formed the European Economic Community, a more ambitious effort to create a comprehensive common market that was the second-largest integrated market in the world. The goal was to reduce or eliminate tariffs on all traded goods within the community while maintaining a common external tariff, which, as in the case of Japan, was tolerated by the United States as a part of the reconstruction agenda. In 1971 Ireland, Denmark, and, after considerable British dithering and French resistance, Great Britain joined the European Economic Community. The nine-member community was as large an economy as the United States, with 125 percent of the U.S. population.

The Development Project

The geographic expansion of the Cold War compelled U.S. officials to pay more attention to Africa, Asia, and Latin America—the so-called **less developed countries (LDCs)**—in order to counter Soviet inroads. President Harry Truman, in his 1949 Point Four doctrine, announced the intention of the U.S. government to promote poor nations' economic growth and to alleviate worldwide poverty and misery—conditions that were considered "breeding grounds for communism."

The resulting development program underwrote an elaborate and interlocked development establishment of U.S. government agencies, universities, and foundations, as well as some international and foreign agencies, all of which dispensed foreign aid, loans, expert advice, and sponsored research. The principal intellectual paradigms that informed U.S. thought about economic development framed the issues in terms of "poor nations" and "rich nations" rather than of poor peoples and rich peoples, thus avoiding uncomfortable questions about class disparities at home and abroad.

U.S. support for industrial development was in line with nationalist ambitions of LDC leaders, including newly decolonized states. The strategy chosen by most of them was called **import-substituting industrialization** (ISI), which was a formalization of the ad hoc defensive package of tariffs, currency controls, and subsidies used by governments of the more urbanized and industrialized LDCs to survive the crisis of the Great Depression. Unlike Central American nations that were small, rural, and contracted during the Depression, the larger and more urbanized national economies of Latin America, Turkey, Egypt, Thailand, and even British India could not shrink without severe social and political disruptions. The local business class of producers and retailers, the urban working class, and a middle class of public and private white-collar employees were not likely to slink quietly away into subsistence agriculture. A sudden and severe decline of these urban groups' standards of living would have torn apart these more complex societies.

During the Great Depression, the political weakening of LDC elites who were based on primary-product exports and the concomitant strengthening of urban-industrial interests, including the political incorporation of labor unions, made import-substituting industrialization politically attractive and feasible. ISI shared the nineteenth-century U.S. and German officials' conviction that primary-product exports had not been and would continue not to be capable of propelling nations into modern and prosperous societies. In this scheme of things, the proper role of primary-product exports was to finance the imports necessary for urban and industrial development, and the government had to manage foreign trade and investment for this to occur. The IMF disapproved.

The U.S. government's Cold War development project involved active promotion of economic reform and LDC market expansion, but the reformist and developmental impulse of U.S. government officials and transnational corporations was not all that strong. The development project, if it worked, too often produced a politics unacceptable to transnational corporations and the U.S. government.

Because of increasing internal political conflicts and unwillingness of LDCs to adhere to the U.S. line, the United States government soon subordinated its reform and development efforts to those in counterinsurgency, suppression of popular movements, and formation of national security states.

THE TUMULTUOUS POST–WORLD WAR II
YEARS IN THE UNITED STATES

Between 1945 and 1948, the federal government cut military expenditures from $83 billion (37.5 percent of GDP) to $9.1 billion (3.5 percent) and demobilized 10.7 million active-duty military personnel. The result was a sharp contraction of output as firms converted to peacetime production of goods and services.

Laying off so many workers for conversion enabled employers to change the composition of their workforces where women had been hired into production jobs (for example, "Rosie the Riveter"). But after the conversions were completed, women tended not to be called back despite the high praise women had earned in these positions during the war. African American men were hired back at higher rates than women. Employers were acceding to political pressure from returning veterans, mostly men, and to the statement "for the duration" when women were being hired for formerly male-segregated positions.

At the same time, the federal government dismantled its mechanisms of direct economic controls of wages and prices, causing sharp rises in prices. Most observers expected these effects, and many believed that returning to the prewar Great Depression was likely. The surprise was the rapid rebound of economic growth after the transition period. Through the Great Depression and World War II, families had been unable to purchase consumer goods, including housing, and the war had enabled many of them to acquire the financial resources, but the desired products had not been available.

The pent-up demand for housing was important for general economic expansion; think of the materials used to construct a house, its financing, and new appliances and furnishings. The demand for housing was not just pent-up demand; it was supported by generous federal mortgage programs and the availability of inexpensive tract housing and propelled by the large increase in family formation and birth rates—the so-called baby boom that lasted from 1946 to 1964, after which birth rates fell.

So the postwar explosion of suburban housing, exemplified by Levittowns with their identical floor plans and inexpensive construction, stimulated production from a wide swath of suppliers, and the demand for new automobiles, washing machines, and other consumer **durable goods** also stimulated a wide range of industries. Complementing pent-up demand for familiar products, there were new products, such as television sets, nylon clothing, stereo phonographs, and medicines as well as products using new materials such as petroleum-based plastics.

The postwar transition was made smoother by generous veterans' benefits, which subsidized education, home purchases, and other help for veterans easing back into civilian life. Veterans' return from World War II was difficult, but it was a more humane process than experienced by World War I veterans, who often encountered outright hostility.

The idea of pent-up demand applied also to labor relations. After the war, released from their no-strike pledges and facing rising prices, workers participated in an unprecedented wave of strikes, and while better wages, salaries, and work conditions were part of strikers' goals, a number of unions, led by the United Auto Workers, demanded changes more threatening to business leaders: profit sharing and union participation in management.

Business leaders had begun to push back against the New Deal and union strength in the late 1930s, and while the antiunion and anti-New Deal crusade paused during World War II, the backlash by capital became broader and more resolute in the late 1940s and 1950s. Business leaders desired to disrupt the 1930s alliance among the labor unions, the Democratic Party, and the federal government in order to undermine and weaken the union movement and roll back New Deal reforms.

Corporations sponsored free classes for their workers during working hours, with introductions to economics that stressed mutual responsibilities and benefits of labor-management cooperation. Corporate managers made similar efforts at the community level, influencing schools, churches, and local charities. At the national level, such organizations as the National Association of Manufacturers (NAM), the Advertising Council, the Committee for Economic Development (CED), the United States Chamber of Commerce, and the Iron and Steel Institute lobbied politicians, targeted campaign contributions, litigated, and mounted extensive and expensive public relations programs stressing free enterprise, individualism, and property rights ("Americanism") to displace unions' emphases on equal rights, worker solidarity, and fairness (another kind of Americanism).

The left wing of the unions, mostly in the Congress of Industrial Organizations (CIO), went further and proposed federal economic planning, the resumption of direct economic controls, and the redistribution of income. None of this came about, but the Employment Act of 1946 was a victory for the unions and their allies. The act obligated the federal government to ensure full employment by managing effective demand through fiscal and monetary policies. But the Employment Act was followed by the 1946 midterm elections that brought Republican majorities to both houses of Congress for the first time since 1928 with the election of President Herbert Hoover. The Republican majority soon proposed and passed the Taft-Hartley Act of 1947, a victory for capital. The act constrained freedoms to organize and strike that the Wagner Act had accorded organized labor, strengthened conservative union leaders' control over members, and mandated purging unions of left-wing troublemakers. The Taft-Hartley Act was a direct response to the postwar strikes set off by the rank-and-file membership despite opposition by union leaders and to employers' fears that the Employment Act would strengthen labor's bargaining position. The bipartisan nature of the assault on labor unions became clear when the majority of Democratic members of the

House, mostly from the South, voted with Republicans to override President Truman's veto of the Taft-Hartley Act. Senate Democrats were also split in their voting, allowing the override to succeed.

The business agenda against the unions was buttressed by domestic anticommunism and worries about internal security. The Cold War began in 1947 with President Truman's declaration that the principal goal of U.S. foreign policy would be to "contain" the influence of the Soviet Union and its allies. The internal repercussion of this foreign policy was to encourage the official pursuit of subversive people and organizations, which intensified with heightened international turbulence and power shifts in the rest of the world. The convulsions of independence and violent, bloody partition of India and Pakistan (1947); the Berlin blockade (1948); the creation of Israel in Palestine (1948); the communist coup in Czechoslovakia (1948); the triumph of the communist revolution in China (1949); the Soviet Union's detonation of an atom bomb (1949); and bitter anticolonial struggles in Greece, Malaya (now Malaysia), Indonesia, Vietnam, and Algeria added up to the appearance of a world out of control. With the Chinese revolution, the scope of the Cold War became global.

The election of 1948 was a setback for the business campaign. To the surprise of most observers, President Truman was elected and the Democratic Party regained majorities in both houses of Congress. Nevertheless, the business agenda had a strong wind at its back. Allegations of and convictions for spying in the United States built support for the Internal Security Act of 1950 (a.k.a. the McCarran Act). The act established a national registry for all Communist organizations, a Subversive Activities Control Board with broad powers to investigate individuals and groups, and an emergency detention provision. It was passed by both Democrat-controlled houses of Congress, which again overrode President Truman's veto. The persecutions of individuals and organizations by the House Un-American Activities Committee, Senator Joseph McCarthy, immigration and naturalization officials, the FBI, and other federal and state agencies reflected the poisonous political climate prevailing and demonstrated one more time how vulnerable U.S. freedoms are to generalized fear.

Anti-communism was not limited to the government and business interest groups. Fear of anticapitalist ideas were alive in the CIO, which after a bitter internal struggle expelled eleven of its unions in 1949 on the grounds of undue Communist influence. This divisive action, together with continuing competition with the AFL, weakened the ability of the labor movement to engage in concerted actions to defend itself and its vision from the business onslaught and to mount a major organizing drive in the South. In 1955, the CIO and the AFL merged, forming the AFL-CIO umbrella organization of labor unions.

The resurgence of business influence in national politics was expressed in the Eisenhower years when such interests prevailed—declining anti-trust prosecutions, coastal oil drilling, National Labor Relations Board's restrictions on union organizing, and other administrative and legislative changes favoring capital. Although there were few new business regulations and welfare-state initiatives, existing ones were not repealed.

So despite bluster, rhetoric, and some significant steps away from New Deal policies, federal economic involvement and regulation (often called "the mixed economy") continued to characterize the first three postwar decades. An important step in that direction was the 1951 "accord" between the Treasury Department and the Federal Reserve. The accord freed the Federal Reserve from the wartime mandate to keep interest rates low to ease financing the federal debt, and the Fed once again became an active policy-making body governing interest rates and credit availability.

THE STRUCTURE OF MODERN TIMES

Within the political back-and-forth gyrations of postwar politics, there emerged an economic structure and institutions, some deliberately created and others emerging in a more serendipitous fashion, that supported a new form of capitalist dynamics. I have called this new economic formation "Modern Times," the title of Charlie Chaplin's brilliant 1936 movie about working on an assembly line, and the name evokes the entire era of modernity.[1]

The construction and operation of the postwar Modern-Times model was made possible by a unique and stringent condition: the United States was the preeminent industrial producer of the world. In the early 1950s, manufacturing accounted for almost 30 percent of total U.S. output, and although it grew fairly steadily into the twenty-first century, it did not grow as fast as other sectors, reducing its share of total output. U.S. industrial dominance complemented its military power, including an initial monopoly of atomic weapons, and the United States had the will to exercise its preeminence in the international realm. In addition, the lack of significant foreign competition in domestic U.S. markets enabled the United States to avoid a conflict between promoting unrestricted international trade and investment and preserving and expanding a modest system of national welfare capitalism.

In presenting the central elements and interrelationships of Modern Times, I employ a stylized version of it by grouping the economy into three sectors, drawing on Averitt (1968), O'Connor (1973), Gordon, Edwards, and Reich (1982), and others. I name the three sectors the Core, Competitive, and Public Sectors. While it is occasionally difficult to draw precise lines dividing sectors, the general contours are clear.

The Core Sector

The Core Sector is the distinctive, even defining, element of Modern Times. The tendencies apparent in the 1920s developed further during World War II, and by the 1950s, there was a stable set of highly profitable U.S. manufacturing corporations producing mass-consumption goods with sophisticated, capital-intensive production technologies. These corporations, the principal source of economic growth, had systems of work divided and supervised along the principles of scientific management, unionized labor forces, and rising labor productivity. Corporations producing modern consumer goods—standardized consumer durables (automobiles, electrical appliances, and so on) and mass-produced nondurable consumer goods (pharmaceuticals, cosmetics, detergents, cigarettes, processed foods, for example)—made up the Core Sector's dynamic center.

Firms that produced intermediate and capital goods, such as steel and other metals, fuel, power, plastics, glass, chemicals, and machinery, had similar organizations of work and market power and sold most of their output to modern consumer-goods producers, thus deserving to be included in the Core Sector. Added to the mass consumer-goods firms and their input producers were the large industrial corporations devoted to manufacturing armaments for the federal government's pursuit of the Cold War and occasional hot wars—the "military-industrial complex" noted by President Eisenhower in his 1961 farewell speech. Finally, many firms supplying a range of services for Core-Sector firms, such as finance, communications, transportation, and marketing, can usefully be considered part of the sector.

Core firms' oligopolistic market organization governed their capital-capital relationships, obliging the few large corporations that dominated each market to engage in corespective non–price competition through advertising, product differentiation, and distribution and product services in an effort to avoid price competition's leading to price wars. The lack of aggressive price competition among large corporations became so evident in the 1950s and 1960s that the professional economics literature contained frequent contentions that corporate managers had opted to achieve an easy life rather than aggressively pursue maximum profits.

The absence of foreign competition along with wages constituting smaller proportions of total costs in large corporations than in smaller enterprises produced historically new relations. Once unions' agendas and leadership had been cleansed of leftist influences through the Taft-Hartley Act (1947) and political purges, it was in the interest of corporate managers to strike an implicit bargain with unions, a capital-labor relationship that included high wages and benefits in exchange for control over the organization of work. Capital's pro-business campaign and rising prosperity were having their effect on organized labor, and standardizing workers' wages, benefits, and work conditions across the major firms in an industry removed a source of differential production costs that tempted price competition.

A wage increase, felt throughout an industry through industry-wide unions, would signal all three or four or five major producers to exert their market power and recover the higher labor costs by raising product prices. Moreover, above-market remuneration in the Core Sector meant that more people were willing to work at the Core Sector's desirable administrative and production jobs than positions were available. Once obtained, the jobs could become work-life careers in the firm. With the exception of clerical work, the occasional director of personnel, and a handful of firms, production and administrative positions were mostly men, and white men.

The New Transnational Corporation

In the post–World War II period, U.S. foreign direct investment surpassed U.S. foreign portfolio investment, becoming larger by a factor of four. In 1938, U.S. foreign direct investment in LDCs, typically in Latin American mines, oil wells, plantations, ranches, forestry, and the occasional urban utility, was three times the level of U.S. foreign direct investment in Europe. By the early 1970s, however, U.S. foreign direct investment in Japan and Europe was three times the U.S. foreign direct investment in Latin America. (See "foreign direct investment" and "foreign portfolio investment" in the glossary.)

These geographical shifts are explained by sectoral shifts: the predominant form of postwar U.S. foreign direct investment was to create the capacity to manufacture modern consumer goods abroad to sell in those foreign markets. That is, a U.S. manufacturer invested (built a plant) in Brazil and made automobiles (or electrical appliances, pharmaceuticals, cosmetics, breakfast cereal, and so on) to sell to Brazilians. That is, no longer was U.S. foreign direct investment in LDCs dominated by investments abroad in the production and transportation of resource-based primary products for the markets of the United States and other industrialized nations. This is what was new about the new **transnational corporation**.

U.S.-based transnational corporations expanded during the 1950s and 1960s, and in the mid-1970s, half of world transnational corporation investment was still from the United States, although that proportion was declining. By 1971, foreign production of U.S. transnational corporations was almost four times the value of U.S. exports, and of the nine largest manufacturing firms in the United States for which data are available, profits derived from foreign operations averaged well over 50 percent of total profits between 1957 and 1974. Transnational corporations were almost exclusively Core-Sector firms.

This change in the character of U.S. foreign direct investment from primary to secondary sectors derived from the competitive structure of the U.S. Modern-Times economy. The avoidance of price competition inhibited increasing domestic market share for individual firms, and another strategy was needed to expand sales. Export markets were a possible avenue for sales expansion, but there were trade barriers, and exports still raised the specter of potential price wars with other large U.S. exporters. Becoming a diversified conglomerate was one avenue around the obstacles to increasing market size. Ling-Temco-Vaught was the outstanding example of a conglomerate: by the late 1960s, Ling-Temco-Vaught had acquired firms involved in electronics, aerospace, cable service, plumbing appliances, sporting goods, meat packing, pharmaceuticals, airlines, car rentals, resorts, and steel.

Another option for increasing market size was to become a transnational corporation. By establishing production operations in a foreign site, U.S. producers could expand sales without disrupting market arrangements within the United States, neutralize other competition, and exercise significant market power in foreign venues. Modern-Times transnational corporations were not seeking cheap labor, nor were they looking for resource-based export possibilities; they sought actual and potential markets for modern consumer goods by establishing production facilities in those markets.

Transnational corporations were quite selective about the choice of location. What the transnational corporations wanted, first of all, was a stable and promising domestic market. This criterion meant that transnational corporations were attracted to places such as Canada, Australia, and Europe, which were prosperous, or to countries like Brazil, India, and South Africa, which were less prosperous but had affluent minorities that could be substantial markets for modern consumer goods. On the negative side, post–World War II uncertainties and instabilities in the recently independent nations of Africa and Southeast Asia discouraged transnational corporations, and, of course, they were not welcome in communist countries at this time. Finally, India and the fast-growing East Asian economies could have been desirable locations, but their closely regulated domestic markets restricted transnational corporations' freedom of action.

The bulk of foreign direct investment by U.S. transnational corporations was in Europe, but the change in the sectoral composition of foreign direct investment was striking in Latin America, where foreign investors had traditionally favored mineral and agricultural products by wide margins. The shift in U.S. direct investment toward manufacturing altered foreign firms' interests in local politics. The United Fruit Company, Anaconda Copper, and Standard Oil are examples of the older pattern. These firms produced resource-based exports in Latin America for industrialized nations' markets, and their interests in the host nations were narrow. Vigorous domestic economic growth would have caused unwanted complications and raised the cost of doing business.

On the other hand, foreign investors like General Electric, Chevrolet, General Foods, Bayer, and Procter & Gamble, which were selling in the markets of their foreign hosts, had a direct stake in expanding local markets for their products. Modern-Times transnational corporations became supporters of national economic development as long as they were in a position to profit from domestic economic growth.

This was not always the case. The International Telephone and Telegraph Company (now ITT Corporation) was and is a diversified manufacturing and communications U.S. transnational corporation. In 1973 it worked with the Chilean military to overthrow and assassinate the democratically elected president, Salvador Allende, leader of the Socialist Party. The succeeding brutal military dictatorship lasted almost twenty years, demonstrating that new forms of transnational corporations could behave in a traditional manner when they believed their interests were threatened.

The Competitive Sector

The Core Sector was the leading force in the economy, but it was not the only way in which commodity production was organized. Most U.S. employees worked in small, low-profit, and low-wage enterprises with high rates of failure. These enterprises, many using both wage and family labor, included small factories, laundries, artisanal enterprises, retail stores, restaurants, small farms, and a wide range of services in both formal and informal work situations. They operated in competitive markets with little or no market power, and this capital-capital relationship governed their capital-labor relations.

Competitive-Sector firms tended to be more labor intensive, employed the majority of minority and women workers, and experienced high turnover of employees. The scale, structure, instability, and fluidity of competitive markets at work in the Competitive Sector were as severe an obstacle as employer resistance to organizing effective labor unions.

Not everyone in the Competitive Sector was struggling. Many independent professionals, such as physicians, lawyers, morticians, accountants, and financial advisers, made comfortable livings and bought modern consumer goods. Some employers who operated in competitive markets and a range of tradespeople, such as electricians, plumbers, machinists, and surveyors, also did well in the Competitive Sector. In both the professions and the trades, those most likely to flourish were in occupations in which government-enforced certification and licensing requirements limited new entrants and constrained competitive market forces.

The Public Sector

While most of the Public Sector's activities were not productive in the conventional market sense, all three levels of government were major employers. Supported by rising unionization and the explicit use of parity principles linking wages, salaries, and work conditions with those in the Core Sector, Public-Sector employment was like Core-Sector employment in that there were always more people desiring those jobs than there were vacancies.

One of the Public Sector's principal functions was to sustain Core-Sector firms' profitability through subsidies, protections, and lucrative contracts, especially for defense justified by the Cold War and occasional hot wars. These expenditures to keep the United States and its allies and clients safe from anticapitalist movements, all labeled communist no matter their nature, also contributed to stabilizing effective demand for corporate products through Keynesian-style demand management. The massive federal armament expenditures were politically palatable because they did not compete with significant private interests at either the local or national level.

The second function was to dampen political unrest and disaffection. Programs to achieve these goals were initiated and administrated at the federal level, but local and state governments were often enlisted to administer and support these programs.

MODERN TIMES IN MOTION

The Modern-Times economy was generally buoyant, supported in part by rapid expansion of international trade and investment. It was not a smooth ride, but the economic growth contributed to some new social policies as well as to some major changes in the parameters of U.S. politics.

Despite occasional reverses and a weakening of economic growth in the late 1960s, Modern Times' real economic growth (corrected for inflation) averaged just under 4 percent per year between 1948 and 1970; real GDP in 1970 was 2.3 times GDP in 1948, and 1970 per-capita GDP was 1.72 times the 1948 level. Fueled by the Cold War, the Korean War, the Vietnam War (1965–1973), and expanded social programs, the federal debt grew between

1948 and 1970, but GDP grew more quickly. As a result, the size of the federal debt declined from roughly equal to GDP to less than 30 percent of GDP in these years.[2] In addition, inflation reduced the real burden of the national debt since bonds are denominated in fixed-dollar terms.

Economic expansion accompanied by widespread increases in employment in the three post–World War II decades enabled record numbers of women to enter the peacetime wage-labor force in the Competitive Sector or in gender-segregated occupations in the Core and Public Sectors. Women's greatest opportunities for professional employment were in the Public Sector, where more effective fair employment and promotion practices were in place. The prosperity and optimism of the period, in conjunction with a Public Sector politically empowered to regulate social processes to maintain social peace, also encouraged those excluded for reasons of race and gender from many occupations, schools, and public services and accommodations to struggle against discrimination. These pressures to counter discrimination by race and gender, as uneven as their successes were, bred deep resentments among large numbers of white men.

Economic growth's positive trend was periodically interrupted by mild recessions in 1949 and after the end of the Korean War (1950–1953) and by a more serious setback in 1957–1958. The 1957–1958 recession included an unemployment rate of almost 7 percent—the highest since before the United States entered World War II and not equaled until the mid-1970s. The 1957 inflation rate of 3.3 percent was the highest since the Korean War and was not topped for a decade. Simultaneous rises in unemployment and inflation rates, called **stagflation**, were common in the larger, semi-industrialized Latin American nations since the 1930s, but stagflation was a puzzle to standard Keynesian analysis, which sees **inflation** as too much demand and unemployment as too little demand. The stagflation helped John F. Kennedy's narrow defeat of Richard M. Nixon in the 1960 presidential election.

Core-Sector Dynamics

Aggregate numbers obscure the significance of how the sectors functioned. Core firms' market power enabled them to capture and retain within the enterprises the fruits of cost reductions, whether the reductions stemmed from higher labor productivity, technical or organizational innovation, or materials prices. These increased earnings were then distributed, albeit not evenly, among corporate managers, owners, and workers, and here the capital-labor struggle occasionally turned nasty. Nevertheless, the struggles were set within narrow parameters: wages, benefits, hours, working conditions, and seniority rights, not what was going to be made and how it was made.

One of the most notable social features of the Modern-Times social formation was to propel large swaths of the unionized Core-Sector working class into the middle ranks of income receivers. This was a family wage—a wage high enough to have only one member of a family employed—that complemented the postwar revitalization of the ideology of domesticity, with the father as the breadwinner and the mother as the homemaker. The extent to which reality reflected this ideology is doubtful: the 1950s were the beginning of women's large-scale return to paid work outside of the house. Nevertheless, historical misconstructions about the 1950s family continue to enjoy considerable political salience, even though they contain a profound irony for those who laud the *Leave It to Beaver/Father Knows Best/Brady Bunch* model of white middle-class families. If such family life did exist in statistically significant numbers, this family model had produced by the late 1960s and early 1970s the white middle-class political radicals, counterculture young adults, Vietnam War protestors, and many of the shock troops in the civil rights and feminist movements.

Another aspect of Core-Sector firms' ability to secure higher profits and distribute them within the corporation was that it prevented the benefits of productivity increases in the Core Sector from being diffused throughout the economy and society through lower product prices. Making products more accessible for more people through lower prices and creating new jobs making those added products are two dimensions of the diffusion of benefits. In markets dominated by oligopolies, which are loath to drop prices and are protected from new entrants by barriers to entry (daunting start-up costs for a new firm of an efficient scale, well-developed distribution and service channels, and brand recognition and loyalties), the trickle-down effects were sharply curtailed.

Agricultural Transformations

The Core Sector was not the only economic sphere generating significant changes; developments in agricultural production in the twenty-five years after World War II transformed U.S. agriculture. Federal price-support programs begun in the 1930s generated surplus crops after World War II despite acreage limitations. These surpluses, either stored, **dumped** on international markets at below-market prices, or granted to domestic and foreign consumers (Food for Peace), were the result of rapid increases in yields (per acre) and productivity (per worker) in crops like wheat, corn, and cotton, yields that rose faster than acreage limits were reduced. These yield increases were due to having a predictable and guaranteed price for a crop that made borrowing (and lending) for machinery and chemicals (fertilizers, insecticides, and herbicides) more attractive.

One result of these striking gains in yields was the growth of large farms at the expense of farms too small to use modern machinery to good effect and with less access to credit at favorable terms. Between 1945 and 1974, the number of farms in the United States shrank more than 60 percent, and during the same years, the number of farms over one thousand acres grew to 37 percent. These larger farms constituted 59 percent of total agricultural acreage in 1974, up from 40.1 percent in 1945. These developments led to a demographic upheaval that shrank agricultural employment from 24.4 million people in 1945 (17.5 percent of the civilian workforce) to 9.7 million in 1970 (4.8 percent of the civilian workforce), and farm output continued to grow.

The political influence of the agricultural sector had been declining for a century as the numbers of rural residents continued to be fewer in absolute and relative terms, but the decline was accelerated by three separate decisions by the U.S. Supreme Court in the 1960s.[3] These decisions mandated that voting districts for U.S. House representatives be of equal numbers of constituents, voting districts for both houses of state legislatures contain equal numbers of constituents, and federal courts could interfere with state-drawn district maps if they were found to be imbalanced. These rulings soon ended the overrepresentation of rural voters and the underrepresentation of urban voters in those legislative bodies.[4]

Immigration Reform

Despite continuing fears about allowing anarchists and communists into the country and not deporting them fast enough, there was an uneven move toward relaxing some of the most restrictive and discriminatory provisions in immigration and naturalization laws of the late nineteenth century and early twentieth century. The Magnuson Act (1943) repealed the Chinese Exclusion Act, fixed a token quota on Chinese immigrants (105 per year), and enabled Chinese residents of the United States to become naturalized citizens. After all, China was an ally in the war against Japan. In 1946, immigrants from India and the Philippines were accorded privileges similar to those accorded the Chinese.

The Cold War, however, led to some countermovements. In line with the Smith Act of 1940 and the Internal Security Act of 1950, the Immigration and Nationality Act (1952, also known as the McCarran-Walter Act) created harsh criteria and procedures for exclusion and deportation in order to make immigration politically pure. The act continued national origins quotas and retained the almost thirty-year-old quota imbalance between eastern Europe and western and northern Europe. But it also prohibited racial or gender discrimination in immigration or naturalization decisions, gave the first preference to those with professional and technical competences and the second to reuniting families, nullified all Asian exclusions (including a small quota for Japanese immigrants and a path to citizenship for foreign-born Japanese immigrants), and kept immigrants from the Americas outside quota limits. Congress again overrode President Truman's veto.

In addition to Cold War concerns, Congress considered illegal immigration from Mexico and Central America to be a threat to U.S. economic interests and national values in the decades after World War II. Nevertheless, there were no serious efforts to estimate the number of illegal residents, although many dubious numbers were thrown around.[5] This did not deter the U.S. Justice Department from engaging in wholesale deportations that harked back to the 1920s. The U.S. attorney general formed a multiagency program called Operation Wetback (that is really what they called it) in 1954. The operation coordinated an assault on Mexican neighborhoods and workplaces in the United States, and by 1959, the operation had rounded up and returned to Mexico more than one million Mexicans. One needs to be somewhat skeptical about this number, because those doing the detaining and deporting did not screen individuals carefully, treat them respectfully, or record them reliably.

The Hart-Cellar Act of 1965, reflecting the antidiscriminatory spirit of the civil rights era, abolished discriminatory national origins quotas, including those for European colonies. It gave preference to reuniting families and thus allowed large-scale legal immigrations from Mexico and Asia. But at the same time, it also erected new barriers for Mexican immigrants without close relatives in the United States by imposing immigration quotas for the Americas for the first time. These new quotas came a year after the cancellation of the Bracero program, which had granted 4.4 million temporary work permits for Mexican agricultural workers between 1942 and 1964.

César Chavez and Dolores Huerta formed what became the United Farm Workers (UFW) in 1962, and they were critical of the Bracero program, referring to it as "indentured servitude." The absence of temporary migrant labor and the new quotas were factors in the success of UFW walkouts, boycotts, and sponsored legislation to organize agricultural workers and gain better working and living conditions (wages, hours, sanitation, safety, education of children, and so on). The new quotas and termination of the Bracero program also made circumventing immigration rules more attractive.

Riots and Federal Activism

When agricultural employment lost fifteen million workers in twenty-five years, where did all these former agricultural workers go? By and large, they went to medium-sized and large cities, although it often took more than one generation. In those cities, they replaced more prosperous city dwellers who were creating the new suburbs at this time. But employment opportunities were often too few for the new entrants to the urban workforces, many of whom were further handicapped by racial discrimination. The outcome was a growing underclass that appeared in the inner cities, an underclass whose poverty was due not to an exploitation that enabled greater accumulation and growth but rather to their being outside of and irrelevant to the circuits of profit-driven production.

These conditions produced the 1960s race riots, which were different from the historical pattern of whites invading black neighborhoods, burning, looting, and assaulting. The 1960s riots were by African Americans living in de facto segregated communities of mostly northern cities, culminating in the "long hot summer of 1967." The assassination of Dr. Martin Luther King Jr. in 1968, accusations of police brutality, and displacement by urban renewal triggered many of the riots, but the underlying causes were persistent poverty and indifferent and often hostile state and local public policies.

Fears of social instability raised by the inner-city convulsions, antiwar protests, and the civil rights movement stimulated federal policies to ease some of the worst pressures on poor residents who benefited little from weak Modern-Times trickle-down effects. Government sponsorship of core firms' profitability and core firms' ability to pass on increased tax costs to consumers kept significant fragments of Core-Sector capital—the "liberal corporation"—in favor of an active Public Sector. In addition, Modern-Times structures and the federal government created a more even political balance between labor and capital, and the expansion of agreed-upon government functions enabled the federal government apparatus itself to exercise more influence.

During President Lyndon B. Johnson's administration (1963–1969), the federal government allocated increased resources for safety-net programs by expanding some existing programs, such as Aid to Families with Dependent Children (1961, 1964, 1968) and the Food Stamp Act (1964), and establishing new ones—Job Corps (1964), Head Start (1965), Medicaid (1965), and Medicare (1965). In addition, the government expanded unemployment benefits.

Cold War ideological pressure helped to assure that welfare capitalism remained modest. Any domestic political initiative that threatened to redistribute power or more than a small amount of income could be labeled socialist or communist and defined as like the enemy—illegitimate, un-American, and traitorous.

But the Cold War did not stifle new federal regulations. In the six years of Lyndon Johnson's presidency and the first four years of President

Richard Nixon's administration, the following were made law: the Water Quality Act (1965), the Fair Packaging and Labeling Act (1966), the Child Protection Act (1966), the Traffic Safety Act (1966), the Agricultural Fair Practices Act (1967), the Flammable Products Act (1967), the Truth-in-Lending Act (1968), the National Environmental Policy Act (1969), the Securities Investors Protection Act (1970), the National Air Quality Act (1970), the Occupational Safety and Health Act (1970), the Noise Pollution and Control Act (1972), the Consumer Products Safety Commission (1972), and the Pure Air Tax Act (1972).

In addition, the Twenty-Fourth Amendment to the U.S. Constitution (1964) outlawed requiring the payment of poll taxes in order to vote, and the Twenty-Sixth Amendment (1971) reduced the minimum voting age from twenty-one years to eighteen years.

Civil Rights and Political Geography

The civil rights acts of the 1960s were built on a century of African American struggles against Jim Crow laws in the South and extralegal racial discrimination in the North. The slightly later surge by the women's rights movement also built on a century of agitation and politicking by women for more opportunities in education, careers, and health care.

The 1954 Supreme Court opinion in *Brown v. Board of Education* (Topeka, Kansas), which declared racial segregation in public schools to be a violation of the U.S. Constitution, was a major national-level victory for the civil rights movement.[6] There were several federal legislative steps from there, and the principal watersheds were the Civil Rights Act of 1964, hesitantly contemplated by President John F. Kennedy and pushed through by President Lyndon B. Johnson after Kennedy's assassination, and the Voting Rights Act of 1965.[7] The Civil Rights Act went beyond race, the principal focus, and contained a prohibition of discrimination on the basis of "sex" (gender) by employers. This item was inserted into the act by an ardent segregationist senator from Virginia who voted against the act.

Federal agencies and courts rather vigorously enforced both the Civil Rights Act and the Voting Rights Act for fifteen years, up to the inauguration of President Ronald Reagan. The young, white, middle-class political activists who grew up in the 1950s were important supporters of the civil rights and women's movements, although political energy was drawn off by anti–Vietnam War and antidraft struggles.

The acts remade race relations in the South, although southern whites, including politicians, employers, and most church leaders and educators, resisted strenuously. In this pushback, white southerners evoked "states' rights," the early nineteenth-century defense of slavery, to mask the substance of what they wanted state governments to be able to do. There has been a fair amount of historical rewriting about the extent and depth of white resistance, and one recurring trope was that race relations in the South were already changing, and the coercive acts were unnecessary and made desegregation more difficult. More specifically, a number of economists deduced from the logic and assumptions of micro-economic theory that competitive markets would force employers to hire the best workers despite skin color in order to maintain profitability.[8] For good reason, none of the antidesegregation forces at the time appeared to believe this.

White southern politicians' dislike and fear of federal attempts to provide civil rights protections and, to a lesser degree, women's rights made them ripe for seceding from the Democratic Party. An early move in that direction was the short-lived States' Rights Democratic Party ("Dixiecrats"), created to support the 1948 presidential candidacy of former South Carolina governor and future U.S. senator Strom Thurmond in the wake of President Harry S. Truman's executive order prohibiting racial segregation and discrimination in the U.S. military. The Dixiecrats carried four of the eleven former Confederate states and soon disappeared.

Richard Nixon, President Eisenhower's vice president, narrowly lost the presidential election of 1960 to John F. Kennedy. In 1968, Nixon campaigned the second time for president, and he and his circle of advisers decided that white segregationist Democrats in the South would be vulnerable to a Republican appeal based on race, coded to varying degrees, along with adamant anticommunism. This "southern strategy" was tricky; many Republicans at that time still proudly proclaimed themselves to be of the "party of Lincoln," and President Eisenhower, a Republican, sent U.S. Army troops into Arkansas to integrate Little Rock Central High School in 1957. The southern strategy was further complicated by Alabama governor George C. Wallace's segregationist third-party candidacy.

Wallace won five southern states, but by 1972 the Republicans' southern strategy was beginning to work. Although the Watergate scandal forced President Nixon to resign in 1974, white elected officials in the South were switching from the Democratic Party to the Republican Party, and new candidates for elected office opted for the Republican label. Southern states again became one-party states, although of a different party.

Jimmy Carter carried all eleven former Confederate states in 1976 in his narrow defeat of President Gerald Ford. Well, yes, he is a Georgian, but he was still a Georgian in 1980 when he carried Georgia but not one of the other ten former Confederate states and lost to Ronald Reagan. That election reflected a general conservative electoral tide that swept over industrialized nations in the 1980s, but it also demonstrated that the southern strategy was taking hold in the United States. Whites in formerly

Confederate states—just over one-fifth of the U.S. population—have been much more successful in putting their sectional stamp on federal policies through the Republican Party than they had through the Democratic Party or third parties. What had been a sectional strategy soon became more generalized and more overt, as with President Reagan's "welfare queens" with Cadillacs, and "strapping young bucks" buying steaks with their food stamps. These images were unsubtle and were aimed at a national audience of whites.

Harbingers of the Future in the Modern-Times Era

Modern-Times agriculture and some service enterprises exemplified a tendency that became stronger at the end of the twentieth century and beginning of the twenty-first century. While some food processing and the production of agricultural inputs (machinery, fuels, fertilizers, herbicides, and insecticides) were securely Core-Sector activities, Core-type production processes ("factories in the field") became important in chicken and lettuce production. The competitiveness of agricultural product markets, however, prevented agricultural capital from controlling its markets and from constructing Core-type accords with labor. But in the name of the increasingly scarce family farm and despite declining rural populations, big agricultural capital still wielded enough political clout to ensure government price supports, acreage limits, tariffs, and subsidized research, credit, and crop insurance as well as the seasonal immigration of Mexican *braceros* in the program terminated in 1965. These policies helped significant fractions of agricultural capital to reap incomes more like those of Core capital while agricultural labor and food-processing workers in meat and chicken packing worked and lived under conditions more like those in the Competitive Sector.

The service sector, including restaurants, hotels/motels, and retail stores, traditionally was populated by small local firms solidly in the Competitive Sector, but as noted earlier, several giant retail firms emerged in the late nineteenth century and early twentieth century. Sears Roebuck, J. C. Penney, and Montgomery Ward, with their branch stores and catalog business dependent on telephone and mail orders, began to apply Core organizational forms.

Even more dynamic retail growth and consolidations occurred in the 1950s and 1960s when McDonald's fast-food chain and Holiday Inn's hotel chain began expanding by using combinations of corporate-owned stores along with franchisee-owned stores. In corporate size, profits, and work organization, McDonald's fast-food chain and Holiday Inn's hotel chain were clearly Core, but in other key features—labor intensity, general work conditions (such as pay and job stability), and therefore the composition of its labor force—they more closely resembled the Competitive Sector. In the early 1960s, Kmart, Target, and Walmart launched the era of big-box discount retailers with comparable hybrid characteristics. These mixed features were a portent of a new set of economic arrangements that was to develop more fully in following decades.

* * *

The transformation of international trade and investment and of the structure of U.S. Modern Times in the next three decades exposed the underlying economic and political frailties of what had seemed to be a vigorous, durable, and progressive social formation.

10

—⚟—

The Dissolution of U.S. Modern Times, 1980s into the Twenty-First Century

In the 1950s and 1960s, the dynamic international economy contributed to the U.S. economy's vitality and the Modern-Times system, but by the end of the 1960s, the positive influence of a growing and developing international economy was turning into its opposite. In the 1970s, the strength of the international economy eroded the foundations of both the Bretton Woods agreement and the Modern-Times social formation. The dollar-exchange standard of the Bretton Woods agreement disappeared suddenly, and the Modern-Times structure began to come apart at the seams.

THE SUCCESS AND FAILURE OF THE BRETTON WOODS SYSTEM

In its own terms, the Bretton Woods system succeeded. Average tariffs on manufactured goods declined sharply, foreign trade and investment grew rapidly, and exchange rates and the international economy as a whole achieved a decent level of stability. The proportion of total exports to world GDP rose from 7 percent in 1950 to over 11 percent by 1973. Exports as a proportion of each nation's GDP rose for most countries, some doubling or tripling, while the U.S. proportion rose more modestly from 3 percent to 5 percent of GDP. In sharp contrast to this general trend, the export-GDP ratios declined in Latin America and India—the effect of import-substituting industrialization policies. Foreign investment also rose, and, as noted earlier, U.S. foreign direct investment in new transnational corporations

(TNCs) surged until it was four times the value of U.S.-owned foreign portfolio investment.

German and Japanese manufacturing firms, jump-started by U.S. aid in the immediate post–World War II years, rebuilt using newer and more efficient production processes often developed in the United States but ahead of what many U.S. firms were willing to finance and install. The more centralized political and economic institutions of Germany and Japan were capable of coordinating capital-capital and capital-labor relationships to maintain economic growth and social peace without the nuisance of antitrust laws. These economies became tough competitors in international markets for modern consumer products and intermediate and capital goods. In addition, they were able to accommodate electoral politics.

While German exporters began selling goods with a range of qualities, the Japanese began with inexpensive, simple manufactured items often of poor quality. Guided, subsidized, and encouraged by government policy, Japanese industries moved up the ladders of product quality and complexity, and by the 1970s, Honda, Toyota, Sony, and other Japanese brands were becoming respected and desired throughout the world.

After employing import-substituting industrialization policies, the authoritarian governments of South Korea and Taiwan (a.k.a. "Nationalist China") also began encouraging industrial exports as a platform for general economic development, and they adapted to electoral politics. The city-states of Singapore and Hong Kong, without primary products to export but with productive workforces, joined in this strategy. As in the case of Germany and Japan, they were aided in this project by receiving millions upon millions in U.S. aid and privileged access to U.S. markets because of their status as frontline nations in the Cold War. They successfully created dynamic export-manufacturing sectors, working up from textiles and stuffed animals to steel, electronics, and in the case of South Korea, shipbuilding.

These four nations as well as Japan, Germany, and later China are another expression of the mass production–mass consumption era of manufacturing. The principal difference from the Modern-Times formation in the United States is that they are producing primarily for consumers in other countries.

To protect U.S. markets from aggressive foreign exporters, U.S. firms might have used their financial clout to lobby for rising trade barriers against foreign products, but the U.S. business community with rapidly increasing stakes in foreign firms was divided on this issue. In addition, foreign companies followed the U.S. example by engaging in foreign direct investment in the United States to produce manufactured goods for U.S. markets. These so-called transplants further complicated the design of protectionist legislation.

The success of the Bretton Woods system in supporting a vigorous general international economic expansion and the emergence of new national economic powerhouses undermined the necessary condition of that success: confidence in the strength of the U.S. dollar. International competition eroded U.S. balance-of-trade surpluses that were further weakened by the war in Vietnam and heightened social expenditures, both of which fueled U.S. inflation.

As the head Cold War warrior, the U.S. government spent millions of dollars abroad on U.S. troops, on military assistance, and on open warfare in Korea and Vietnam. Maintaining these large unilateral outflows required a substantial balance of exports over imports, but the surplus in the U.S. balance of trade disappeared in the late 1960s and became negative in the early 1970s. The U.S. dollar could not devalue, and none of the surplus nations was willing to appreciate its currency to rectify the dollar glut. The Bretton Woods agreements, made at a time when the United States was the principal surplus nation, had avoided formal provisions to pressure them to do so.

By 1971 the value of U.S. gold reserves was down to one-third the value of U.S. dollar reserves held in foreign central banks. Unpopular anti-inflation policies one year before U.S. presidential and congressional elections were politically unpalatable, so President Richard Nixon's administration unilaterally abrogated the Bretton Woods convention by suspending the convertibility of the dollar into gold in August 1971.

The exchange rate for the U.S. dollar in leading foreign currencies fell almost 20 percent over the next few months, and the price of gold rose. While these price changes gave U.S. producers some protection from imports and encouraged U.S. exports, the same changes effectively punished those governments (e.g., Italy) that had cooperated with the United States by holding unwanted dollars and rewarded the uncooperative governments (e.g., France) that had cashed in dollars for gold. After a failed effort to reinstate something formal in the place of the dollar-exchange standard, leading governments agreed to work with the default position—a flexible exchange-rate system for the currencies of the international economy's largest trading and investing nations, and the other currencies remained pegged (that is, fixed) to one of the major currencies—the U.S. dollar, deutsche mark, yen, and so on.

Unforeseen Consequences

Since the international price of oil was denominated in U.S. dollars, the devaluation of the dollar reduced oil-exporting nations' purchasing power. This contributed to galvanizing oil-exporting nations, especially Middle Eastern members of the Organization of Petroleum Exporting

Countries (OPEC) that were already unhappy with U.S. support for Israel in the recent Yom Kippur War. OPEC declared a temporary oil-export boycott in 1973 and then quadrupled the price of oil. It was a successful exercise of market power, and OPEC's success led to imitations by exporters of copper, bananas, coffee, and other commodities, but none achieved the necessary cohesion and market power of OPEC.

Thinly populated Middle Eastern nations received large portions of the new bonanza and, being unable to spend all of it, deposited millions and millions of dollars of enhanced oil receipts (petrodollars) in large, carefully screened international banks. Since banks' profits depend on their being able to lend funds at higher interest rates than they pay depositors, these huge new deposits posed a problem. The rise in oil prices that created the deposits also contributed to recessions in the industrialized nations, thus limiting the number of attractive lending opportunities. There were, however, many willing borrowers in Africa, Asia, and especially Latin America, where military governments had little popular support. Peddlers of bank credit pressed everyone in sight, independent of risk or record, to borrow as much as they could be talked into borrowing. And since the borrowers did not have to pretend to pay attention to IMF injunctions and bureaucracy, the commercial banks' lending practices eclipsed IMF authority.

The Reagan administration's early 1980s fight against inflation, coordinated with the Fed, drove interest rates to almost 20 percent and threw the U.S. economy into recession with high unemployment rates. These policies made high-yield U.S. government bonds so attractive that foreign portfolio investment poured into the United States, which became a net debtor for the first time since World War I. Since interest rates on the bank loans to the LDC governments were variable (that is, they rose and fell with current interest rates), the rising interest costs squeezed debtor governments, and Mexico in 1982 was the first to declare that it could no longer pay even the interest charges on its foreign debt. All continental Latin American nations except Colombia and several of the other indebted LDC governments soon followed. The debt crisis had arrived.

The possibility of billions of dollars lent to LDC governments turning into bad debts was said to threaten the survival of the large international banks and therefore the stability of the entire international financial system. This "too-big-to-fail" story justified interventions by the metropolitan nations' governments, led by the United States, to save the banks from the consequences of their bad decisions. The governments from nations in which the large international banks were based designated the IMF as the chief collection agent for the big banks.

These governments and the IMF had clear and complementary views about the reforms that they wished to promote in LDCs by using the leverage of the debt. The so-called Washington Consensus offered longer debt repayment schedules, some new loans, minor discounting of debt, and fixed (nonvariable) interest rates in exchange for the governments' commitment to a series of reforms.[1]

There were to be strict limits on nonmilitary government spending with no taxes more than "moderate." Governments were required to relax controls on interest rates, exchange rates, and foreign trade and investment and to abolish price controls, workers' protections, and subsidized food and public services (for example, urban transportation, health, and utilities). Governments were to sell government-owned enterprises such as airlines, steel mills, and oil refineries to private buyers and generally to strengthen property rights.

The reform package was justified by the contention that free-market mechanisms are the most effective way to promote exports, that a strong export orientation is the most effective source of general economic expansion, and that import-substituting industrialization had failed. Although the causal chain from unregulated markets to export promotion of primary products to broadly based economic growth is murky at best, it is crystal clear that the policy prescriptions coincided precisely with what was necessary for LDC debt repayment to the large international banks. LDC governments could pay off the loans to the banks in hard currencies if and only if they were able to run significant surpluses of exports over imports for extended periods. The 1980s were dubbed "the lost decade" in Latin America, with stagnant GDPs and declining per capita incomes through most of the decade.

By the beginning of the 1990s, the debts had not gone away, but the debt crisis had become muted to the point that it was regarded as debt problems for individual LDCs. Three continuing legacies of the debt crisis and resulting reforms were clear: the LDCs had been more tightly integrated into the global economy; employers were in a much stronger position than workers; and LDC governments' ability to shape their nations' economic futures had been diminished. These outcomes were clear within the nations, and in the twenty-first century, nations such as Venezuela, Ecuador, Bolivia, Brazil, and Nicaragua rejected a good number of the prescribed policies.

PRESIDENT RONALD REAGAN'S TWO TERMS

President Reagan continues to be revered in certain political circles. He and his administration created a record of reducing taxes for the wealthiest, running record peacetime fiscal deficits, slashing federal assistance to local governments, reducing budgets for public housing and rent subsidies, eliminating the antipoverty block grant program, and articulating a strong antigovernment and pro–free market ideology that produced the savings and loan crises.

One bright spot in President Reagan's second term was the Immigration Reform and Control Act (IRCA) of 1986. It was a three-pronged approach to monitor and control illegal immigration; the IRCA levied sanctions against employers who hired workers who did not have proper permits, bolstered border security, and permitted two categories of illegal immigrants—those who had been in the country since January 1982 and those who had worked in agriculture—to be eligible for legalization and eventually citizenship. Three million people applied for legalization, almost 2.7 million of them were approved, and by the early 2000s, a third of the approved had become naturalized citizens.

The Republican-controlled Senate passed IRCA, the Democrat-controlled House passed IRCA, and President Reagan signed it. By the late 1990s and early 2000s, "amnesty" had become a dirty word for Republicans, who blocked President George W. Bush's effort to create a path to legal residence for those in the country without proper papers.

On the international front, the Reagan administration carried out a disastrous military adventure in Lebanon, the bombing of Libya, the invasion of Grenada, and a ratcheting up of the Cold War by supporting anti-Communists anywhere despite their records and aspirations. For example, the Reagan administration led in contributing weapons, CIA trainers, and billions of dollars to the multinational forces fighting against the Russian invasion of Afghanistan. After nine years, the Russians withdrew from Afghanistan, and the Taliban, generously armed by the U.S. government, emerged out of the subsequent civil war and chaos as the most capable of governing. The United States had worn Cold War blinders to believe that all enemies of our enemies should be supported.

The most bizarre and dramatic scandal surfaced in President Reagan's second term. In 1986, a Lebanese newspaper broke the news that high-level officials in President Reagan's administration had secretly pulled off three stunning breaches of law and trust. The first was to sell missiles to Iran while engaged in the Iran-Iraq War, in which the United States was helping Iraq. The U.S. officials used Israel as an intermediary and blatantly contravened the U.S. arms embargo against the Iranian revolutionary government.

The second was that the sale was in exchange for the revolutionary government's release of U.S. hostages. This was an unequivocal violation of repeated assurances by the president and some of those involved in the conspiracy that the United States would never pay ransom to the Iranians for the hostages.

The third was to use the money from the missile sales to support the anti-Sandinista troops ("Contras") fighting to reverse the 1979 Sandinista Revolution in Nicaragua. The Contras were led by officers of Nicaragua's notorious National Guard, which had brutally protected the dictatorships of Anastasio Somoza Debayle and his brother and father before him. The Boland amendments of 1982 and 1984 forbade any further U.S. government support for the Contras, and President Reagan, angered by the ban, told his national security adviser to get support to the Contras in any way possible.

By the time that these machinations became public, 1,500 missiles had been shipped to Iran, but $18 million of the $30 million paid to U.S. officials could not be found. Various judiciaries indicted fourteen people involved in the enterprise, but when President George W. H. Bush pardoned those who had been convicted, it was clear that it was futile to take the others to trial. President Reagan plausibly claimed that he did not remember hearing about the scheme.

THE END OF U.S. MODERN TIMES

There is no question that internal, dialectical pressures within U.S. Modern-Times structures constituted a serious problem. The political system struggled to promote economic growth in the Core Sector while sustaining political legitimacy or at least quiescence among those outside the Core Sector. Nevertheless, the principal forces for economic change within the United States came from abrupt changes in the economic relations among capitalist economies, affecting the U.S. economy in ways as radical and far-reaching as the watershed changes of the 1930s. The shattering effects of foreign competition at the level of individual product lines went far beyond problems with overall balances of trade and exchange rates that brought down the Bretton Woods dollar-exchange standard.

The New International Economy and Changing Capital-Capital Relationships

The insulation of U.S. Core-Sector capital from international competition in the immediate post–World War II years enabled Core-Sector oligopolies to agree tacitly to avoid price competition. The oligopolistic organization of domestic product markets in the Core Sector paved the way for the next step: establishing relatively peaceful and mutually advantageous relationships with industry-wide unions—once those unions' agendas and leadership had been cleared of leftist influences.

U.S. firms had been losing to international competition in such products as textiles, apparel, shoes, and toys for some time. But the more widespread foreign penetration of U.S. manufacturing markets began in the 1960s and produced qualitative changes. Foreign firms were increasingly competing, and competing successfully, with U.S. producers in such Core manufacturing lines as automobiles, steel, and electrical appliances. It was becoming clear that U.S. international preeminence in these and other Core-Sector product lines—necessary for U.S. Modern Times as we knew it—was over and that new sets of relationships and rhythms were emerging.

Table 10.1 shows how hard and fast new foreign competition struck U.S. core manufacturing. In addition to the products listed there, imports by the mid-1970s had risen to about half of U.S. consumption of sewing machines, motorcycles, and bicycles, and the proportions of imports were high and growing in important branches of chemicals, pharmaceuticals, and electronics. Imported steel had supplied less than 5 percent of the U.S. market in the late 1950s, but that proportion rose to 40 percent in 1982, and U.S. steel production declined precipitously.

In addition, television receivers and automobiles with high proportions of foreign-made parts were being assembled in foreign-owned plants located in the United States. Some of this movement of foreign transplant firms into the United States was in cooperation with U.S. firms (for example, the GM-Toyota and Ford-Mazda joint ventures), but in any case, the competitive threat from without had, to an extent, moved within, and as table 10.2 shows, foreign firms domiciled in the United States accounted for almost 15 percent of U.S. manufactured output by 1990, and this was in addition to imports of competitive finished products.[2]

The effects of increased price competitiveness of U.S. Core-Sector markets went far beyond reduced sales, profits, and employment. By transforming the Core Sector's capital-capital relationship that underlay the

Table 10.1. **Imports as a Percentage of U.S. Sales by Product**

	1959	1976
Radios and televisions	1	43
Automobiles	6	20
Tires and tubes	1	12
Textile machinery	5	30

Sources: U.S. Department of Commerce, *U.S. Commodity Exports and Imports as Related to Output, 1960 & 1959* (Washington, DC: U.S. Government Printing Office, 1962), 19–33; U.S. Department of Commerce, *U.S. Commodity Exports and Imports as Related to Output, 1976 & 1975* (Washington, DC: U.S. Government Printing Office, 1979), 18–20.

Table 10.2. Percentage of U.S. Manufacturing Production by Foreign-Owned Transplants, 1990

Chemicals	32
Rubber and plastics	19
Stone, clay, and glass	25
Primary metals	19
Electronics and electrical equipment	16
Passenger cars	13
Industrial machinery and equipment	12
Total U.S. manufacturing production	15

Source: Ned G. Howenstine and William J. Zeile, "Characteristics of Foreign-Owned U.S. Manufacturing Establishments," *Survey of Current Business* 74, no. 1 (Jan. 1994): 53–59.

Modern-Times moment, the new price competition irrevocably altered the structure of the U.S. economy and led to the end of Modern Times.

The 1970s and 1980s was a time of successive waves of speculative activity, including real estate ventures, LDC debt, and mergers and acquisitions financed by junk bonds ("non–investment grade bonds"). But a number of U.S. firms did respond to the new competitive milieu by adopting some shop floor reorganizations, robotic production technologies, and such practices as just-in-time inventory control. In addition, there were some significant downsizing and outsourcing of in-house functions. U.S. firms had an advantage over their European and Japanese counterparts in these rearrangements because the U.S. labor market was more flexible—a euphemism for the ease with which U.S. employers could reassign or fire employees.

At the same time, corporations seized the opportunity to weaken unions and reduce labor costs by forcing givebacks and other concessions from employees and seeking new sources of labor with lower wages and benefits and without expensive health, safety, and other labor protections. As part of cost-reducing strategies, companies began to increase contracted outwork and to move operations within the United States from unionized areas of the Rust Belt (the Great Lakes to New England) to the Sunbelt (the U.S. South and Southwest) with little union strength. Soon the major push was to relocate production abroad, where in addition to lower direct and indirect labor costs there were numerous other cost-saving advantages, such as the ability to operate without regard to environmental damage.

The first important wave of the late 1960s created the publicized *maquiladoras* that were just over the U.S. border in Mexico. In a few years, however, U.S. firms initiated large-scale movements of assembly production to the Caribbean, northern Latin America, and Southeast Asia in search of low wages and what were perceived to be docile workers, facilitated by declines in transportation and communication costs.

The initial pattern was for a firm to export U.S.-made components to a foreign subsidiary for assembly and packaging—the most labor-intensive stages of the production process—and then import the assembled and packaged product back into the United States. Under special provisions of the customs code, U.S.-made components are not subject to duty, and what is subject to duty—the value added to them by foreign assembling and packaging—are intrafirm transfers easily undervalued for tariff purposes. Although Japanese firms using East and Southeast Asian labor for the assembly of exports were pioneers in this pattern, when U.S. firms began to adopt foreign assembly, what had been sporadic forays became a new international system of production.

A consistent aspect of this geographic decentralization of manufacturing production has been the use of women workers. And in considering this, one must understand that low-wage labor is not the same as unskilled labor. In explaining employers' preference for women workers, it is important to avoid a "psychology of women" even when it does not deteriorate into essentialism. The key phenomenon is that women have less social and political leverage and thus are vulnerable to exploitation no matter what skills they have.

Although apparel and electronics products dominated foreign assembly production in the 1970s, cost-reducing innovations in communications (telecommunications, computers, and satellites), transportation (containerization, supertankers, and air cargo networks), integrated international financial markets, and production technology increased the range of industrial products and parts that were feasible to produce abroad. The technology of Core corporations during Modern Times promoted long runs of products that enabled lower average production costs through economies of large-scale production and made it likely that there were cost advantages from internal (to the firm) production of components as well. By the 1970s and 1980s, however, it was becoming evident that less rigid production processes were reducing **economies of scale** in production and allowing economies of scope—flexible production processes that can rapidly and inexpensively be reconfigured to produce differently designed goods. These innovations make shorter production runs economically feasible.

Flexible production technologies were in part a response to new market opportunities in which increasing concentrations of income throughout the world were heightening demand for less standardized, more specialized products. As the system became better tuned, flexible production processes and growing markets for niche products with short product life cycles encouraged greater use of foreign-origin components and routinized more parts of production processes.

New Players in the International Economy

In order to institutionalize the new international economy, the Uruguay Round of GATT negotiations in 1995 established the World Trade Organization (WTO), a new international organization to promote the expansion of free trade by discouraging government policies judged to be illegitimate trade restrictions. This function is quite similar to that of the International Trade Organization proposed by the Bretton Woods conference more than fifty years earlier but rejected by the U.S. Congress as conceding too much national sovereignty to a supranational organization. In the 1990s and the first decades of the twenty-first century, however, the U.S. government has been a major supporter of the existence and authority of the WTO.

The WTO gained notoriety over the years for ruling against efforts by some national governments to restrict imports of goods made under conditions that violate protective standards for workers, the environment, and human rights. The sole WTO provision of this kind makes it possible to exclude imports made by prisoners. The United States has proposed allowing nations to prohibit imports that involve severe human and ecological degradation, but LDC members are adamantly opposed to such rules. As a result, the WTO has preferred ruling against restrictions rather than attempting to draw meaningful lines.

In early 2013, the WTO membership had grown to 159 nations, reflecting the dynamism of the new international economy. Some important players joined rather recently, illustrating their increased engagement in international trade and investment and at least nominally open trade and investment policies. The outstanding example, of course, is China.

From the mid-1950s to the early 1960s, China went through the Great Leap Forward, in which thirty to fifty million people died of starvation. In the mid-1960s, Mao Zedong and his allies regained control of events and declared the Cultural Revolution (1966–1976) to purify the revolution from creeping capitalism, bureaucratic corruption, and increasing regional and individual inequalities. The result was a decade of drastic leveling, forced relocations, and chaotic vigilantism and violence that paralyzed the nation. Mao's political influence, like his health, declined, and he died in 1976.

The new leadership included some of the principal targets of the Cultural Revolution, most notably Deng Xiaoping, and that leadership pursued policies that did indeed have a capitalist resonance and enabled economic recovery. A principal element of the strategy was to move aggressively into manufactured exports for prosperous nations' markets by strengthening private property rights and material incentives. China's exports grew from one billion dollars in 1978 to fifty billion dollars in 1988 and rose to one and a half trillion dollars in 2008, surpassing U.S. exports.[3]

Liberalizing the economy did not mean political liberalization. The Communist Party's fear of losing its monopoly on political power accounts for the fierceness of the crackdown on pro-democracy movements, such as in Tiananmen Square in 1989, and dissident religious groups, such as the Falun Gong, beginning in 1999.

I have already described the emergence the Four Asian Tigers—South Korea, Taiwan, Hong Kong, and Singapore—as important new players in the international economy. Their impressive success with sophisticated export manufactures depended on more experienced, better-educated, and higher-paid workforces, thus opening space for low-wage competition in apparel, textiles, furniture, and other products by new entries into the market. By the mid-1990s, Malaysia, Thailand, and Indonesia had become integrated into international product and financial markets, frequently with foreign direct investments from Japan and the Four Asian Tigers. Vietnam shows some signs of also becoming a more significant trading partner, employing the familiar Asian route with some differences in details. The Philippines offer a more uncertain picture because continuing internal political divisions produced economic stagnation. The per capita incomes of Thailand and the Philippines were comparable in 1980, but by 2008 Thailand's per capita income was twice that of the Philippines.

China's per capita income in 1970 was roughly equal to that of India, by 2000 it was twice India's, and by 2008 it was three times India's per capita income. The Indian government, threatened and encouraged by China's example, began a cautious reform program in the mid-1980s, loosening strict licensing requirements on domestic firms and beginning to open the Indian economy to international trade and foreign direct investment. As in China, India's billion-plus population indicates a potentially huge domestic market, but 76 percent of the population lives on less than two dollars a day. Changing such deep poverty will entail political and social perils far greater than fashioning export-oriented platforms or relaxing controls on foreign direct investment.

Beginning with reforms on foreign trade and finance in the 1980s, Russia has established a substantial presence in the international economy. Manufactured goods made up 17 percent of merchandise exports, and Russia depends to a large degree on the export of nonrenewable resources. Although Russia has used its vast pools of oil and natural gas to good political effect in Europe, it is difficult to use exporting a natural resource as a platform for general prosperity.

Much of what Russians have to overcome is the advice pushed on them by the IMF and the U.S. government of President Clinton, when the Russians were prostrate from the collapse of communism in the early 1990s, a collapse unforeseen by practically all, including the Central Intelligence Agency. The IMF and U.S. officials apparently believed that all that was needed to create a viable market system was to remove government controls and transfer the means of production to private ownership. In doing this, they ignored the need to create regulatory institutions like a central bank, a strong judicial system, and a fiscal structure capable of collecting taxes, providing public services, and supporting other national priorities.

Distributing state-owned assets to private owners at fire-sale prices was fully agreeable with those in a position to benefit—often senior Communist Party apparatchiks—and it was done in a rush-through executive fiat that bypassed and weakened fledgling democratic institutions. As a result, the reforms created a small cadre of the superrich (oligarchs), and the distribution of Russian personal income went from looking like Sweden's to being one of the most skewed in the world. The resulting unstable conditions in finance, production, and marketing encouraged corruption, speculation, and criminal activities more than they did productive investment. So much of what had been achieved at terrible human cost in Soviet industrialization was squandered, and the massive inequalities, insecurity, loss of public services, authoritarian governance, and decline of life expectancy in Russia continue to have frightening implications for the world as a whole.[4]

Mexico is an economic powerhouse, and a good part of its manufacturing exports is enabled by its membership in the North American Free Trade Agreement (NAFTA) and fueled by U.S. direct foreign investment. Brazil resembles Russia in its relatively low proportion of manufactured exports, but Brazil's nonmanufactured exports are renewable agricultural products: soybeans, sugar, coffee, orange juice, and cellulose. Furthermore, the manufacturing sector is growing and serves domestic and foreign markets in transport equipment (including automobiles and aircraft) and armaments.

The entry of new trading partners added complexity and range to the new international economy, but at the same time, the new additions also made the entire project amorphous and vulnerable to individual national problems affecting multiple economies. Moreover, geographical dispersion, competitive markets, and interdependence cannot be mistaken for dispersion of control; large corporations are still the major players. Innovations in information and control technologies that lessened the cost advantages of large-scale operations in production were the same ones that have heightened the cost advantages of large-scale operations in financing, communications, and marketing, which includes product design and brand-name identification.

The shift in the ways in which firms could reap economies of scale, then, means that while U.S. firms sometimes own foreign production sites, there is a considerable variation in ownership of foreign plants producing items with U.S. brands. There often is no more than a contractual (albeit often captive) relationship with a local national or with an entrepreneur from elsewhere (such as Taiwanese firms in Nicaragua and South Africa). For instance, Benetton, Schwinn, and Nike are U.S. firms with prominent brand names that do not own any production facilities but design and market goods produced by foreign contractors, and giant discount retailers like Walmart and Target are contracting with foreign producers in a similar manner.

By investing in or contracting with foreign operations to produce for global markets, the newest transnational corporations differ in a number of ways from Modern-Times TNCs that invested in foreign sites to produce for those foreign markets. The newest TNCs come out of a different set of dynamics within the advanced industrial nations and amid greater competition among firms, and one would expect the rhythms of their expansion and contraction to be distinct from their Modern-Times counterparts.

U.S. firms are less dominant, and the newest TNCs' foreign direct investment is more oriented toward poor LDCs than were Modern-Times TNCs. Perhaps the most important difference from Modern-Times TNCs, however, is that the new manufacturing TNCs have little immediate concern for the economic growth of the region in which the goods are being produced. These firms' chief interest in their foreign locations is as repositories of inexpensive but better educated and productive labor along with reasonable transportation facilities; both the education levels and developed infrastructures are legacies of successful import-substituting policies. In their lack of interest in the nations where their goods are produced, the newest TNCs are like earlier U.S. foreign direct investment in resource-based exports by Anaconda, Standard Oil, and United Fruit. Substantial local economic growth is likely to be a disadvantage for these export-oriented corporations because development and change could raise the price of local labor and create political movements and a stronger government apparatus that would not be to the TNCs' advantage.

There are still U.S. TNCs that produce abroad and sell to local markets in such products as soft drinks, cigarettes, plumbing fixtures, and pharmaceuticals or that supply such services as fast food, car rentals, finance, entertainment, communication, and transportation. Whether their production is sited in the United States or elsewhere, some firms are still interested in LDC markets' growth, but this is a much diluted set of interests.

The combination of the changed interests by TNCs and the implosion of the Soviet Union, and thus the end of the Cold War, have led to major contractions in what I called the development project. While the United States and other metropolitan nations can respond generously to natural disasters such as tsunamis, volcanoes, earthquakes, and floods, their long-run concerns about the people of the poorer countries seem limited to warding off threats of disease and massive emigrations from less prosperous regions.

Changing Capital-Labor Relationships

U.S. economic growth during the 1950s and 1960s, along with unemployment insurance, reduced the threat of unemployment, encouraged a series of strikes in the Core Sector, and fostered a decline in labor productivity that corporate managers believed required new ways to encourage more intensified efforts by employees. There was quite a bit of excitement in the 1970s and early 1980s about new kinds of work organization, such as worker self-management, corporate stock options for workers, new kinds of teamwork, and quality of work life (QWL) efforts, which would encourage workers to work harder. By the 1990s, however, after workers throughout the world became available to U.S. employers, the balance of bargaining power between capital and labor tipped so much toward capital that the attraction of these experiments waned among employers.

What had been a convergence of interests between U.S. Core capital and labor—the basis of the implicit capital-labor accord—began to unravel in the late 1960s and early 1970s as international and domestic capital-capital competition sharpened. Significant international competition reduced the market power of domestic firms and prevented U.S. corporations from passing on increased labor costs through higher product prices.

Union membership in the United States as a proportion of the nonagricultural labor force plummeted from its 1954 peak of 34.7 percent to 11.3 percent at the end of 2012. These aggregate figures include Public-Sector unionization and thus mask the severity of the decline in private employees' rate of unionization, which dropped to 6.6 percent of private-firm employees in 2012. It is no surprise, then, to learn that the number of strikes by units of one thousand or more workers declined from an average of more than 270 a year in the 1960s to five in 2009, eleven in 2010, and nineteen in 2011.

Not all the labor movement was in decline. Some services, such as tourism, insurance, and other financial products, are involved in international trade and investment and are subject to international competition. Others, however, are insulated from international competition by the fact that their services have to be performed on the spot, as it were—they produce "nontradable" goods and services. Catalog and e-commerce companies can sell clothes made in Honduras, use telephone operators in Jamaica, and farm out data entry and web design to workers in India. Nevertheless, packages have to be delivered in the here and now, and that service cannot be imported. In a similar manner, hospitals can bring in Filipina nurses, and janitorial and security-service companies can hire immigrants, but the actual services—patient care and cleaning buildings—like service-producing public employees (e.g., police, firefighters, classroom teachers, bus drivers, and those who plow and repair roads) are not amenable to foreign production, although their pensions, benefits, and rights to collective bargaining are under serious attack. Strikes by nurses, janitors, teachers, police, airline employees, telephone workers, and United Parcel Service workers, all providing nontradable services, have been the most effective. This is a reversal of historical patterns in which industrial workers were at the forefront of fighting back against employers.

Despite the vitality of union organizing in a few specific areas, average hourly earnings (corrected for inflation) for U.S. production and non-supervisory employees on private nonfarm payrolls have not fared well. Real earnings did grow between 1947 and 1973, when they peaked at a 75 percent increase over 1947. Then they fell and rose, with a net loss of 11 percent at a low point in 1986. From then, real earnings grew slowly until 1998, and a small uptick peaked in 2007. The Great Recession of 2008–2009 forced real earnings down, and they continued to decline through 2012. Median household income (the halfway point between the 50 percent of the higher income receivers and the 50 percent receiving lower incomes) in 2012 was 8.9 percent less than in 1995. It is not surprising, then, to find that almost half of the reduction in the gender gap in wages was due to declines in men's wages.

Downward pressures on earnings were felt beyond blue-collar work; the restructuring and downsizing of corporations in the 1980s and 1990s increased outsourcing for clerical services. This general process has reduced and degraded white-collar work, including middle management, and created somewhat less rigidity in gendered and racial definitions of job categories. Some of these changes have been due to fewer opportunities for white men, who have had to seek work in previously female-stereotyped occupations and to patch together multiple part-time jobs without benefits. "Men's work" has become more like "women's work."

International economic integration and the weakening of labor unions held down U.S. workers' wages, and on the flip side, corporate profits as proportions of national income, along with stock market price indices, hit all-time highs. Another record was also broken: wage and salary incomes sagged to below 50 percent of national income.

In addition, deregulation, hostility toward labor unions, and growing service occupations have contributed to the distribution of wage and salary income becoming more uneven. Wages and salaries in unionized firms were more evenly distributed than in nonunion firms, so the decline of unions registers in the distribution of wages as well as levels. Moreover, the distribution of wages and salaries among service workers has chronically been more uneven than among workers producing goods (e.g., manufacturing and mining), so it is no surprise to find that the rapidly rising numbers and proportions of service occupations have led to more variability in wages and salaries than when the numbers of jobs were more evenly divided between goods and services.

Corporate salaries and bonuses, driven by record-breaking profits, are the most visible example of high incomes. And among firms, the financial industry is the poster child of salary excess. Up to 1980, compensation in the sector was roughly comparable to that in other sectors, but it has grown so quickly that it is now 70 percent higher.

Despite the diversion of discussing financial-sector salaries, the principal point of this section is that Core-Sector capital-labor relationships have become more like those in the Competitive Sector. As the Core Sector moves closer to the McDonald's and Walmart models, the assumption that long-term capitalist development in the United States will improve the income, opportunities, and security of succeeding generations of U.S. workers is in serious doubt.

Changing Public Sector–Citizen Relationships

As international competition sharpened and disciplining labor could be left to what was a buyers' market for labor, the liberal corporation as a political force quietly disappeared and became politically indistinguishable from members of conservative business groups such as the National Association of Manufacturers and the U.S. Chamber of Commerce. The way in which the Modern-Times period produced a consumer and taxpayer identity among much of the white male working class meant that their populist anger and anxiety could be deflected toward foreign competitors, African Americans, immigrants, uppity women, and the poor.

In all this anger and fear, a special animus is reserved for the federal government, seen as parasitic and intrusive, and worse, as the protector of undeserving women and minorities who are given unfair advantages in the job market. The conviction that on balance, government policy is oppressive and unfairly privileges some groups is deeply embedded in the U.S. individualism derived from classical liberal thought, and such antigovernment sentiments inform the work of writers from all points of the political spectrum. A wide range of Marxists, feminists, neoliberals, postmodernists, hippies, Tea Partiers, militias, and survivalists argue trenchantly against the regulatory authority of the U.S. government, even though they have very different views about whom the Public Sector privileges.[5]

In the new era, governments have diluted the force of labor legislation and even mounted explicit attacks on the institution of collective bargaining. And it was a Democratic president, over the fervent opposition of organized labor, who championed the North American Free Trade Agreement (Canada, United States, and Mexico [1994]) with its weak provisions to protect U.S. workers, much less the natural environment.

The push for **deregulation** reflects the conviction that competitive market forces promote society's welfare, security, and freedom and that government intervention hinders the benign magic of the markets. This was an ideological sea change, and it means that those with economic and social advantages could take full benefit of those advantages with little restraint or consideration for others.

Deregulation was and continues to be a bipartisan movement. The current foray into deregulation began during the administration of President Jimmy Carter and involved airlines and some financial institutions. And with the encouragement of his treasury secretary Robert E. Rubin, a former head of Goldman Sachs, President Bill Clinton signed the legislation that repealed the Glass-Steagall Act of 1933. This act created a strong boundary between commercial banks that received deposits insured by the federal government and lent them to borrowers and investment banks that brought initial public offerings (IPOs) onto a stock exchange, brokered mergers and acquisitions, traded in financial markets with their own resources, and were not insured by the federal government. The Glass-Steagall Act had hobbled large financial institutions' efforts to engage in wider and more diverse types of financial gaming.

Before the U.S. Supreme Court selected George W. Bush to be president in 2000, Governor Bush indicated in his campaign that he intended to engage in several dimensions of deregulation. His aspirations were derailed by the terrorist attacks of September 11, 2001, and by a host of massive frauds and accounting scandals. The revelations about Enron, Tyco International, Adelphia, and WorldCom were shocking, and the list continued to grow. There were new instances of serious misconduct in such major corporations as the Federal Home Loan Mortgage Association (Freddie Mac), HealthSouth, Westar, the Federal National Mortgage Association (Fannie Mae), Nortel Networks, and Refco. In addition, it turned out that major accounting firms' activities contained severe conflicts of interest, stock analysts for brokerage and investment banking firms lied to their clients, mutual funds firms were caught in unethical trading, and one of the largest insurance companies was rigging bids.

This is a wide variety of misdeeds, but they all had one thing in common: they were not the actions of the economically marginal who were bending rules in order to get by. These were and are transgressions conducted by prominent and wealthy businesspeople. The ability of the competitive market to discipline such unbecoming behavior is limited, and it did not take a subtle mind to realize that the first years of the twenty-first century were not a propitious time to weaken business regulation. In fact, President Bush took a hard line on white-collar crime, establishing the Corporate Fraud Task Force that led to 1,200 convictions, including more than two hundred corporate presidents, chief executive officers, and chief financial officers. In addition, Congress passed and the president signed the 2002 Sarbanes-Oxley Act that turned a series of unethical practices and conflicts of interest by auditors and corporate managers into federal crimes.

There is, however, another, more insidious type of deregulation that does not involve new rules legislation or public announcements. The second type of deregulation is to appoint to regulatory agencies incompetent party hacks or people who are opposed to any sort of government regulations restricting the free play of the market. The administration of President Ronald Reagan did this well, but the administration of President George W Bush (2001–2009) developed it into a true art form. Appointments to the Federal Emergency Management Agency, Justice Department, Securities and Exchange Commission, Minerals Management Service, and Food and Drug Administration were the most blatant examples of this type of deregulation.

The track record of deregulation is not without some severe glitches. More than one thousand recently deregulated savings and loan associations, plagued by record-high interest rates and mismanagement, collapsed in the late 1980s. The bailouts cost U.S. taxpayers $124 billion in the 1980s and early 1990s. In the name of creating more competitive marketplaces, deregulation of the airlines has yielded a situation in which United, Delta, American, and Southwest provide 71 percent of domestic air traffic. It used to be 55 percent. Cell telephone service is dominated by AT&T and Verizon. In the provision of TV cable service, Comcast recently acquired NBC Universal studios and attempted to acquire Time Warner Cable, although it was not approved by federal regulators. AT&T has completed a merger with Direct TV.

One aspect of all this coziness is that broadband Internet in the United States is the sixth-slowest and the seventh-most-expensive among the twenty-one most prosperous countries. Amazon, Google, Microsoft, and Facebook dominate their markets. Monsanto has legal monopolies (patents) on key genetic traits of most corn and soybeans grown in the United States. And after years of hand-wringing about banks that were "too big to fail," the five largest banks possess half of the total banking assets, up from 30 percent in 2000.

The point is not that regulation is good and deregulation is bad. The point is that in some circumstances unregulated markets work quite well, and in other circumstances they work poorly and can threaten the performance of the entire economy. There is no universal truth in these matters, regardless of what economic theory and self-interested advocates purport to demonstrate.

Another illustration of the termination of Public Sector–citizen relationships is that in the middle of 2013, four years after the Great Recession, there were still almost twelve million workers out of work and two million fewer U.S. jobs than there were in 2007. Half of those unemployed had been unemployed for more than six months, and one-half of that half had been unemployed for more than a year. These numbers do not include those who have given up looking for work, those unwillingly in part-time jobs, those who have had to accept jobs that pay substantially less than their previous work, and those forced to take "independent contractor" status, thus denied mandatory employee benefits such as workers' compensation, overtime pay, minimum wage, unemployment insurance, and Social Security contributions.

Another aspect of the employment picture is the declining proportions of people between the ages of twenty years and fifty-nine years who are active members of the workforce, employed or unemployed. Certain U.S. political factions project their own inclinations and claim that because U.S. taxes are so high and social services so generous, they encourage significant numbers of people to stay out of the workforce. Neil Irwin (in the *New York Times*, Dec. 17, 2014: B2) reports on recent cross-national research on cohorts between twenty and fifty-nine years of age, the group most likely to be in the workforce. Compared with the United States, the higher-tax nations of Denmark, Norway, Netherlands, Sweden, and Germany, with broadly available social services—generous subsidized care for children and the elderly, maternity and paternity leaves, unemployment insurance, safety-net programs, accessible public transportation, together with high minimum wages—have higher labor force participation rates than the United States. In other words, when high taxes go for programs that make participation in the workforce more attractive and feasible, people choose to work.

The small and ineffective policies implemented in the name of saving householders from foreclosure was another example of governments' indifference. There is a general reluctance to help the poor and unlucky, who are often thought to be alien to U.S. values and skin color. The Republican Party has led the charge against the poor, restricting Medicare and fighting extensions of unemployment insurance and subsidized health insurance. In the election of 2012, the Mitt Romney campaign, according to Jill Lepore's story in the *New Yorker* (Dec. 2, 2013: 75–79), "ran to the right of the breakdown lane," and Republicans lost the total popular vote for U.S. representatives, U.S. senators, and the presidency.[6] They retained a majority in the House of Representatives through gerrymandered districts, and overall, a bipartisan indifference to the plight of millions of U.S. citizens reigns.

As the political parties compete with each other in attacking citizens' protections and benefits, the Public Sector–citizen relationships of Modern Times, like the related Core-Sector accord between capital and labor, are in tatters.

NEW PATTERNS IN THE U.S. ECONOMY

Accelerated international economic integration over the past two decades along with weakened market regulations have generated economic patterns different from those of earlier post–World War II decades. In the first few decades after World War II, inflation appeared to be the consequence of too much aggregate demand, and recession and unemployment were the mirror image—caused by too little aggregate demand. The notion of demand-based causation for inflation and recession, consistent with John Maynard Keynes's *A General Theory of Employment, Interest, and Money* (1936) and refined through observations of the 1950s and 1960s, suggested that public policy of demand management must guide aggregate economic activity along a narrow path between the dangers of inflation on one side and recession and unemployment on the other and that there are definite trade-offs between the two.

The problem with this straightforward formulation is that the U.S. economy has generated two kinds of anomalies that undermine the idea of an orderly universe in which relationships between inflation and unemployment are regular, stable, and inverse. The first aberration was that the U.S. economy went through a couple of periods of stagflation—simultaneous inflation and recession—in 1958 and the 1970s. The first bout with stagflation was short, and one contribution to it was Core-firm unions pushing up wages and Core firms passing the increased cost to product purchasers by raising prices, which priced many consumers out of their markets, leading to economic decline, unemployment, and price rises.

The stagflation of the 1970s was longer and caused by the supply-side shock of OPEC's oil embargo and subsequent quadrupling of the price of petroleum. The price hike led to cost increases for the chief source of energy as well as for fertilizer, paints, and the many chemicals and plastics for which petroleum is an important ingredient. Producers of these products and power-using firms in general struggled to recover their higher costs, disrupting markets and leading to bankruptcies, unemployment, recession, and higher prices.

A new anomaly appeared in the 1990s. Instead of the abnormal appearance of inflation and unemployment together in stagflation, we saw the abnormal *absence* of both inflation and unemployment. During most of the 1990s and the early 2000s, the U.S. economy grew well with low rates of unemployment and inflation.

By the 1990s, employers' threats to send production offshore were real and plausible, and U.S. wages stagnated, relieving employers of the cost-push wage demands of the 1950s. Chairman Alan Greenspan of the Federal Reserve System repeatedly evoked the frightening specter of rising wages and salaries that would create inflation if economic growth did not slow down. Nevertheless, the new international dynamic avoided the disaster of increasing wages for working families. In addition to the lack of pressure from wage increases, heightened price competition from foreign producers in Core-Sector markets formerly dominated by U.S. oligopolies kept down the domestic prices of goods, while prices of several nontradable services (notably medical) rose.

Price competition in product and labor markets underlay the economic expansion in the 1990s that dampened the inflation-unemployment trade-off, and the increased concentration of income among the top income receivers in the top brackets generated rising income-tax revenues that created federal budget surpluses. Even with the technology bubble that popped in 2000–2001 and the terrorist attacks of September 11, 2001, the George W. Bush administration and Republican congressional majorities created large federal deficits, including two wars essentially financed by credit cards. The deficits did provide a fiscal stimulus that helped sustain general economic expansion.

Another major change in the U.S. economy is the manner in which international integration of product and financial markets reduced the effectiveness of domestic demand-management tools. On the fiscal policy side, as imports became larger proportions of U.S. purchases, more and more of any increase in domestic demand created by government policies goes to the purchase of imports, leaking off to foreign producers instead of stimulating local production and employment.

In the realm of monetary policy, the Fed's policy of low interest rates created easy credit, and credit markets were awash with financial capital seeking short-term profits throughout the world. Since most industrialized nations' governments had lowered barriers against the instantaneous movement of financial capital, the Fed had less control over U.S. credit markets. Global financial markets thus gained influence over the volume and the terms (interest rates) of loanable funds available to U.S. borrowers.

In the competitive international economy, cost cutting is the rule, and nations with the fewest protections for their citizens and workers set global standards. This race to the bottom is illustrated domestically by Alabama's strenuous efforts to land a new Mercedes-Benz factory (opened 1993), South Carolina's successful courting of BMW (opened 1994), Mississippi's determination to be the site of a new Toyota plant (opened 2011), and Tennessee's landing a new Volkswagen assembly plant (opened in 2011). State officials promised a combination of docile, inexpensive, and nonunionized workers, lax enforcement of worker safety and environmental regulations, low or zero taxes, few social services, and free land and infrastructure.

11

—ʍ—

The Great Recession, Austerity, and Three Worrisome Tendencies

U nregulated market capitalism is capable of generating bursts of vigorous economic expansion and dire contractions. In the most dramatic fashion, financial markets in particular have demonstrated their inability to correct themselves and function in a manner that supports economic prosperity beyond the salaries, bonuses, and capital gains of a select few. I conclude the chapter and the book with three trends that are troublesome.

THE GENESIS OF THE GREAT RECESSION

One response by financial investors to historic low interest rates was to engage in making bets on riskier ventures, such as the prices of foreign currencies. Currency speculation has a long history of folks making money by buying and selling currencies that had little to do with the exchange of real goods. It requires ready access to cross-border portfolios of currencies, fixed exchange rates, and ease of converting from one currency to another. These conditions appeared in the European Union in the early 1990s, when speculators attacked the currencies of EU members who had pegged their currencies to the German deutsche mark, forcing devaluations. In 1994, the year that NAFTA began, speculators turned to the Mexican peso, which fell 50 percent in a month.

In the mid-1990s, Thailand, Malaysia, Indonesia, Taiwan, and South Korea were fiscally conservative and stingy with workers' rights and social policies. The five economies were booming, led by export platforms that generated domestic investment bubbles in stock markets and real estate. Wall Street pressured the U.S. Treasury to pressure the IMF to pressure the countries to relax their controls on foreign investment. In 1997 speculators took advantage of the newly opened financial systems and attacked Thailand's currency (the baht), and the contagion soon spread to Indonesia, Malaysia, the Philippines, and Russia.

The IMF prescribed its usual recessionary policies, which Thailand and Indonesia followed, and their economies contracted with dire material and political effects still evident. Malaysia, on the other hand, immediately imposed a twelve-month minimum for repatriating foreign portfolio investments, lowered interest rates, and lent its banks enough liquidity to withstand the worst of a credit crisis. South Korea, China, and India continued with their stringent currency controls, ignored IMF advice by putting capital into their banks, and weathered the Asian crisis of 1997–1998 fairly well.

The need to mitigate extreme swings in international exchange rates produced by massive movements of short-term speculative capital has not gone away. This concern, however, was eclipsed by the 2007–2008 beginnings of an international economic malaise known as the Great Recession, rooted not in speculative currency crises but in domestic financial speculation.

Thus we turn again to the financial sector, especially FIRE—the acronym for "Finance, Insurance, and Real Estate"—a grouping in the U.S. National Income and Product Accounts. FIRE grew vigorously from a little over 14 percent of GDP in 1970 to over 20 percent by 2009. This is a sector that produces nothing tangible and traditionally supported real production by accepting deposits and serving businesses and consumers by financing, insuring, and facilitating the purchase and sale of real property.

With the Fed's deliberate policy of low interest rates, however, banks, mortgage lenders, pension funds, endowment managers, insurance companies, and other financial institutions sought higher returns than were available by means of traditional levels of investment riskiness. The largest of the financial institutions morphed into juggernaut casinos where speculation in risky financial instruments that had little to do with producing and distributing goods and services became everyday occurrences. Not only did the tail begin to wag the dog, that tail has shown the capacity to be dangerous to the dog's health. Bruce Bartlett (2013) briefly reviews recent research on how the rapid growth of this sector has been linked to increasing income inequality, decline of wages and salaries as percentages of GDP, and reduced investment in producing sectors. And its role in creating the Great Recession is clear.

One trigger to the Great Recession was the U.S. housing bubble, fueled significantly by mortgage lenders venturing into more and more risky territories ("subprime mortgages") for higher returns. A second vulnerability was provided by innovations in deregulated financial markets. The new financial instruments were called **derivatives** because their value was derived from other assets, often cut-up pieces of multiple mortgages, that were claimed to reduce risk through diversification. There are many types of derivatives, but for clarity's sake, I will focus on mortgage-backed securities, which are in a sense the first layer, and thus avoid discussing derivatives based on other derivatives.

Issuing firms created and marketed these new mortgage-backed securities primarily to pension funds, hedge funds, insurance companies, and other financial enterprises, charging high fees for the service. Determining the riskiness of the underlying mortgages was an arduous and lengthy process, and issuing firms had them rated by one of three major credit-rating firms—Fitch Ratings, Standard & Poor's, and Moody's Investors Service, which are profitable oligopolies. The credit-rating firms were happy to keep their customers happy and loyal by doing what the customers wanted: quickly assigning top ratings (AAA or Aaa) to the securities without much in the way of expensive and time-consuming due diligence. This is a business model with unavoidable conflicts of interest.

Massive volumes of borrowed money financed much of the cost of creating and purchasing derivatives. Congress explicitly excluded the new financial instruments from regulation, and in 2004 the Securities and Exchange Commission (SEC), at the behest of the investment banks, relaxed a twelve-to-one debt-to-equity limit for the five largest investment banks—Goldman Sachs, Morgan Stanley, Lehman Brothers, Bear Stearns, and Merrill Lynch. The debt-to-equity ratios rapidly rose to what was euphemistically called "highly leveraged." The riskiest way to be highly leveraged is to have your debt in short-term borrowings while your assets, like derivatives, are long-term and of dubious liquidity.

As home prices rose, there was a wealth effect on consumers, many of whom withdrew the new equity by increasing their mortgages. The size of these new equity withdrawals (and debt increases) was huge: 7 percent of the 2007 GDP in the United States. In addition, the value of the stock components of people's defined-contribution retirement accounts, such as 401(k) accounts, also rose. The increased wealth propelled many people into a financial comfort zone that often included nonchalance about credit-card debt.

The continuing rise of housing prices underlay the entire system. Everyone, financial professionals and amateurs, "knew" that housing prices were going to continue to rise, and with few exceptions they all piled on. The prices of the overbuilt housing sector began to soften in 2007 (a bit earlier in some markets), and several financial institutions, notably Goldman Sachs, began betting against the mortgage-backed securities that they created and sold to their clients.

By 2008, the declines in house prices frightened investors so badly that the same herd instinct behind their earlier enthusiastic investments caused a stampede for the exits and exacerbated the collapse. Credit markets froze, and the value of mortgage-backed securities, always murky, dropped precipitously as the underlying mortgages became shakier and foreclosures spread from subprime mortgages to mortgages that initially were solid. With no markets for mortgage-backed securities, those holding them could not sell them in order to pay the debts incurred to buy them. There is some irony in the fact that many of the banks in the business of creating and selling mortgage-backed securities believed their own hyperbole (and that of their hired credit-rating agencies) and kept many of them on their own balance sheets.

Table 11.1 suggests how exciting September 2008 was. As you can tell from the companies' founding dates, many of these institutions were experienced and venerable. Nevertheless, both Bear Stearns and Lehman Brothers were leveraged to the point that their debt-equity ratios were around thirty to one, and even if not as spectacularly, other banks were also dangerously leveraged in debt.

U.S. GDP experienced an average of almost 4 percent per quarter of negative growth (that's really how they say it) from the second quarter of 2008 to the second quarter of 2009. Around eight million jobs were lost, unemployment rose to over 10 percent, and between October 2007 and the low point in March 2009, the prices of stocks listed on the New York Stock Exchange declined over 50 percent. Millions of homeowners found that the value of their houses had declined so precipitously that the houses' values were less than what homeowners owed on their mortgages ("underwater"), and foreclosure loomed. Foreign trade in goods and services declined 17 percent, making it the largest and fastest contraction in forty years. This is why this period is called the Great Recession, clearly an allusion to, but not quite, the Great Depression of the 1930s.

U.S. Policy Responses to the Great Recession

The Stimulus Act of February 2008 was the Bush administration's first effort to stem the downward spiral. The act cost around $152 billion, sending tax rebate checks to most taxpayers, who put at least half of the rebates into savings accounts or toward paying down previously contracted debt rather than stimulating demand for goods, services, and employment.

Secretary of Treasury Henry Paulson (another former head of Goldman Sachs) convinced Congress to pass the Emergency Economic Stabilization

Table 11.1. Selected Large Financial Institutions That Collapsed in 2008

Name of Financial Institution	Year Founded	Month of Collapse	Notes
Bear Stearns	1923	March	Investment bank; pioneered in creating mortgage-backed securities; acquired by JPMorgan Chase.
Lehman Brothers	1850	September	Investment bank; allowed to go through a regular bankruptcy and liquidation without federal help.
Merrill Lynch	1914	September	Investment bank and largest U.S. brokerage house; acquired by Bank of America.
American International Group	1919	September	Largest U.S. insurance firm, specializing in insuring financial instruments; federal government bailed out for more than $170 billion; a near-death experience.
Washington Mutual	1889	September	Largest U.S. savings and loan; acquired by JPMorgan Chase.
Federal National Mortgage Assn. (Fannie Mae)	1938	September	Guarantor and buyer of mortgages and seller of mortgage-backed securities; initially a government-sponsored company until it became a publicly held corporation in 1968; placed under conservatorship by the Federal Housing Finance Agency.
Federal Home Loan Mortgage Corp. (Freddie Mac)	1970	September	Guarantor and buyer of mortgages and seller of mortgage-backed securities; a government-sponsored private corporation; placed under conservatorship by the Federal Housing Finance Agency.
Wachovia	1879	December	One of the largest and most diversified financial services companies in the United States; acquired by Wells Fargo.

Act (October 3, 2008) in order to make bank bailout policy more expeditious, consistent, and coordinated. The act established the Troubled Asset Relief Program (TARP) with $700 billion to inject into financial institutions. In addition, the Federal Reserve was lending billions to the same banks, and the actual amounts and beneficiaries are now beginning to be known publicly.

Initially the Treasury funds were intended to buy toxic ("troubled") assets from the banks, but this strategy was soon changed to supply liquidity to the institutions by acquiring equity in the firms. So taxpayers became part owners of banks and other financial institutions rather than owners of useless financial assets. Despite this improvement, it was still obvious that resources were channeled to banks and bankers, the cause of the crisis, instead of toward the unemployed and homeowners in trouble, the victims of the crisis. This is yet another example of the ruptured Public Sector–citizen relationship.

Actions by the American International Group (AIG) provide an instructive tale. AIG was the nation's largest insurance company and had insured over $440 billion of derivatives. By September 2008, AIG ran out of cash and sources of credit until it received two federal bailouts of $85 billion apiece. Much of the money went directly to the investment banks that had insured AIG's holdings of derivatives, paying creditors 100 percent of what was owed them. Goldman Sachs received the largest share.

In addition to the size of its bailout, AIG was distinctive for its tone deafness and arrogance. Two weeks after the first $85 billion bailout, AIG threw a $440 million party at a ritzy California resort for its top executives. Moreover, just to underscore its obtuseness, AIG announced in early 2009 that it was awarding $165 million in bonuses to top executives to reward them for almost bringing down the firm.

Even when TARP money was used in more legitimate ways, there were problems. Instead of limiting financial institutions' size and scope so that bad decisions would not present a threat to the entire financial system, TARP encouraged stronger banks to take over shakier ones, thus, as noted in the previous chapter, promoting consolidation of the financial sector around even larger "too-big-to-fail" banks. And it was a gift to lawyers: shareholders of acquiring banks sued management, saying that the acquiring bank paid too much for the failing institutions; shareholders of the failed institutions claimed that the sale choreographed by the federal government severely undervalued their corporations; purchasers of mortgage-backed securities sued the issuers; and homeowners sued banks for illegal foreclosures.

The largest financial institutions are too big to fail, and they are also too politically connected to fail or to be broken up, and they have no incentive to change the behaviors that created the crisis. To the contrary, their executives now know that the federal government believes that they have to be bailed out when their moneymaking gambling does not work, and when those activities do work, there is lots of money to be made. Not a bad deal for them.

President Obama's American Recovery and Reinvestment Act (often simply called "the stimulus") of February 2009 weighed in at $786 billion, but unlike TARP, Treasury officials did not hand out money to friends, neighbors, and former colleagues. The stimulus expenditures went to transportation, education, energy, and health, which are intrinsically important to the economy and society. Although the expenditures were small compared with the Chinese government's response to the Great Recession, the nonpartisan Congressional Budget Office reported in 2010 that the stimulus, despite its size, had created or saved between 1 and 2.1 million jobs.

Each major period of unregulated market activity in the United States led to greater unevenness of the distribution of income, serious general economic downturns, and eventually periods of serious economic reform. As we have seen in chapters 4 through 8, the freewheeling Gilded Age of the 1870s and 1880s yielded to the Progressive Era with substantial reforms and regulations, and the Roaring Twenties ended with a whimper in the decade-long Great Depression of the 1930s with the new regulations and reforms of President Franklin Roosevelt's New Deal.

In the past thirty or so years, the pendulum of short memories swung back toward a faith in the beneficent operation of markets unfettered by government regulation, and by historical standards, the current political response to the crisis brought on by unregulated markets was tepid. The big banks funded by federal bailouts used some of those dollars to pay for heightened lobbying through such organizations as the American Bankers Association to fight any effort at reregulation. And President Obama's administration is already on record in favor of weakening the Sarbanes-Oxley Act passed in the wake of the corporate scandals in the early 2000s.

The Dodd-Frank Wall Street Reform and Consumer Protection Act, which underwent months of compromises, passed in July 2010. The act stipulated increased levels of financial reserves, restricted banks' use of their own (or borrowed) money for speculative investments ("proprietary trading"), established transparent markets for some derivatives trading, made ratings agencies accountable for mistakes, and protected financial-market investors. Even though full implementation is just beginning, the act in its current state is having a significant effect. The required levels of financial reserves and limits on proprietary trading have moved the big banks away from the riskiest trading activities toward those such as wealth management for pension funds, endowments, and individuals. The big banks' profits are still high, but mostly because of cost cutting.

There are fewer Wall Street employees, their average pay declined along with bonuses, and entire areas of activity were abandoned.

The Securities and Exchange Commission fined a number of big banks for bad behavior prior to and after the financial crisis and designed a couple of regulations for ratings agencies, a first for the industry. In early 2015, the Justice Department exacted a fine of $1.37 billion from Standard & Poor's, the largest of the rating agencies, for deliberately misleading rankings. But there is no movement toward reforming the preposterous business model. Despite uncertainty about the final shape of the Dodd-Frank Act and the vigor of its enforcement, the act continues to be fought against by bank lobbyists and bank-sponsored U.S. senators and representatives.

The big banks' postcrisis activities seriously damaged their reputations and made them vulnerable to stricter regulation. They are back in the business of selling derivatives and other dubious financial products, rigging interest-rate indexes, foreclosing illegally, dodging taxes, laundering money, and engaging in unbridled risk taking. They cannot resist. And they are also moving into nonfinancial activities that for most of the twentieth century were against the rules. Although the deregulation of the financial sector in the 1990s relaxed some of the restrictions, Goldman Sachs still had to get permission from the Federal Reserve to invest in the storage of aluminum. The bank figured out a way that involved moving tons of aluminum from one of its warehouses to another to avoid other rules and capturing high rents for storage, rents that increased the price of aluminum to producers and consumers. Think about this the next time you pop the top of a soda or beer can.

Goldman Sachs, Morgan Stanley, and JPMorgan Chase were also permitted to obtain oil refineries and pipelines in Oklahoma, Louisiana, and Texas, natural gas fields, utilities, tanker fleets, and loading docks that control port activities at Oakland, California, and Seattle. Financial sector?

Christine Lagarde (2014), managing director of the IMF, spoke at the Conference on Inclusive Capitalism in London on May 27, 2014. Among her other points, she outlined the functions of a financial system of stable providers of credit for businesses, governments, and consumers but said that instead, the financial system delivered "excess, in risk taking, leverage, opacity, complexity, and compensation."

Europe Grapples with the Great Recession

Early in the housing bubble, Fed chairman Alan Greenspan and his successor, Ben Bernanke, denied that the extreme price increases in housing needed attention. In the second stage, President George W. Bush, Ben Bernanke, and Treasury Secretary Henry Paulson denied in 2007 that the gathering problems in the mortgage-backed securities market would negatively affect the wider economy.

But mortgage-backed securities did tank, and their collapse grievously affected the wider U.S. economy and was also transmitted internationally. Table 11.2 conveys the patterns of recession in much of the world, comparing recent declines with the Great Depression to show that in several countries, the recent contraction of production and income was greater than in the 1930s. Europeans held almost a quarter of the risky financial instruments issued by U.S. financial institutions and were among those hit the hardest. But the Great Recession in the United States is not the entire story, since countries that experienced the most serious setbacks were those that managed to produce their own crises with little help from the United States.

Foreign countries and regions as disparate as Iceland, Ireland, Britain, Spain, eastern Europe, Cyprus, and India experienced rapid deflations of housing bubbles that hit their local banking sectors hard. The situation in Europe was made more complicated by twelve EU members establishing a common currency, the euro (€), in January 2002. They also formed the European Central Bank to monitor and smooth the transition. Eurozone members subsequently admitted seven more EU members into the

Table 11.2. Peak to Trough GDP Changes, 2007–2010 and 1928–1935 (Percentage of GDP Changes in Larger Economies)

	2007–2010	*1928–1935*		*2007–2010*	*1928–1935*
Ireland	−14.3	n.a.	Taiwan	−10.1	−6.2
Turkey	−12.8	n.a.	Singapore	−9.0	n.a.
Finland	−9.8	−4.0	Japan	−8.7	−7.3
Sweden	−7.5	−6.2	Hong Kong	−8.0	
Denmark	−7.3	−3.6	Thailand	−7.4	n.a.
Italy	−6.8	−5.5	Malaysia	−6.4	
Germany	−6.6	−24.5	South Korea	−4.6	−1.5
Britain	−6.4	−5.8	South Africa	−2.8	n.a.
Greece	−5.7	−6.5	Kenya	−2.7	n.a.
Netherlands	−5.2	−7.8	New Zealand	−2.6	−14.6
Austria	−5.0	−22.5	Mexico	−9.1	−20.8
Spain	−4.9	−6.1	Brazil	−4.7	−4.4
Belgium	−4.2	n.a.	Chile	−4.2	−30.0
France	−3.9	−14.7	United States	−4.1	−28.5
Portugal	−3.8	n.a.	Canada	−3.4	−29.6
Switzerland	−3.3	−8.0	Peru	−2.1	−25.8
Norway	−2.8	−7.8			

Sources: Floyd Norris, "In Great Recession, Other Nations Have Suffered More," *New York Times* (Sept. 18, 2010), B3; Angus Maddison, *Monitoring the World Economy, 1820–1992* (Paris: Development Centre, OECD, 1995), 69.

experiment with a common currency. Table 11.3 lists the twenty-eight countries currently in the EU, and asterisks indicate the nineteen that are in the eurozone.

Eurozone membership restricts the use of policies to recover from downturns. Members do not have the ability to devalue their national currencies in order to quickly lower wages and salaries across the board in terms of other currencies, thus stimulating their economies through increased exports and reduced imports. Nor can they increase their domestic money supplies to lower interest rates and encourage domestic investment and consumption. Devaluation and manipulating the domestic money supply require a national currency, and those in the eurozone do not have a national currency. They are welded into whatever is the value of the euro vis-à-vis other currencies, and they cannot expand their money supplies without borrowing.

In order to stabilize the banks in the nineteen-nation eurozone, the European Central Bank effected bailouts similar to those in the United States. The central banks of the nine non-eurozone members of the EU, notably Great Britain, also bailed out their banks when needed but imposed stricter conditions on them than in the United States. Moreover, since Great Britain was not a member of the eurozone, the British pound could depreciate and mitigate some of the negative effects on the British economy.

Ireland was an excellent example of turning a banking crisis into a fiscal crisis. The Irish government guaranteed its swollen and irresponsible

Table 11.3.   European Union Membership by Year of Admission

Belgium*	1957	Sweden	1995
France*	1957	Cyprus*	2004
Germany*	1957	Czech Republic	2004
Italy*	1957	Estonia*	2004
Luxembourg*	1957	Hungary	2004
Netherlands*	1957	Latvia*	2004
Denmark	1973	Lithuania*	2004
Great Britain	1973	Malta*	2004
Ireland*	1973	Poland	2004
Greece*	1981	Slovakia*	2004
Portugal*	1986	Slovenia*	2004
Spain*	1986	Bulgaria	2007
Austria*	1995	Romania	2007
Finland*	1995	Croatia	2013
Candidate Countries: Iceland, Macedonia, Turkey			

* Indicates members of the eurozone.

Source: "Member Countries," *European Union,* http://europa.eu/about-eu/countries/
member-countries (accessed July 5, 2013).

banking sector's liabilities owed to the banks' depositors and creditors. This move transferred the entire financial burden to Irish taxpayers. As a consequence, it transformed a banking problem into a fiscal crisis with a public debt several times the size of Ireland's GDP, which declined 10 percent between 2007 and 2009. For the first time in decades Irish voters rejected the ruling political party, with its unsavory connections to banks and bankers. The Irish economy continues to be in bad shape.

In contrast, there is a set of eurozone countries in which genuine fiscal crises created dire effects on local banks. In the 1990s and 2000s, the introduction of the euro and low interest rates encouraged heavy borrowing by governments with weaker economies, and money poured in from German banks and banks in other low-interest-rate countries looking for better returns. Goldman Sachs and Morgan Stanley helped Greece and Italy use exotic financial instruments to hide the extent of their national debts from investors and the European Central Bank. The irresponsible borrowing (and lending) led to a German export boom, but the end of real-estate bubbles sharply reduced borrowing governments' tax revenues and ability to repay the loans.

No matter whether crises originated in banking systems or fiscal overreach, the stringent conditions accompanying new loans from the so-called Troika—the European Central Bank (eurozone), the European Commission (EU), and the International Monetary Fund—made bad situations worse where they have been applied. In addition, each loan is contested and uncertain until executed. This uncertainty is not conducive to an orderly recovery, and it affects even U.S. stock markets.

Austere Politics in Europe and the United States

In the eurozone, fiscal austerity is the principal policy strategy, enforced as conditions for lending by the three cooperating multinational financial institutions. The three have approved lending billions of euros, especially to Greece, Spain, Portugal, and Cyprus. Belgium and Italy ("too big to fail, and too big to bail out") had similar but less dire problems. The conditions for these loans resemble the IMF and Washington Consensus programs for Latin America in the 1980s, programs responsible for the lost decade and the erosion of organized labor's political and economic standing. One principal difference was that the IMF this time was less stringent in its demands, but the other two were steadfast in their insistence on severe cuts in public expenditures.

The general idea of the austerity policy is to cut back government spending and reduce government debt sufficiently to establish a degree of financial stability that can be the basis of future economic growth, encourage foreign investment, and reassure actual and potential foreign creditors that the borrowing governments' bonds are creditworthy. Favorite types of budget cutting are to reduce the numbers of Public-Sector workers and shrink wages, salaries, health benefits, job security, and pensions for remaining Public-Sector workers while increasing working hours and minimum retirement ages.

Such policies can degenerate into a situation similar to chasing one's own tail in a downward spiral. Severe cuts in government spending depress the economy and thus tax receipts, undermining the original deficit target that was the reason for expenditure cuts. So more expenditure reductions must be implemented, further depressing economic activity and tax receipts, and the target level of deficit reduction is once again undercut. And so on. With one minor exception, the ministrations of the Troika have caused the national debts of Greece, Portugal, Italy, Ireland, and Spain to increase as a proportion of their respective GDPs every year since 2008.

In both Europe and the United States, an obsession with fiscal debt frequently accompanies calls to lower national labor costs for greater export competitiveness. The two policies are complementary rationales for an assault on workers' rights and protections, thus identifying employers' interests as the national interest. Policies leading to domestic recessions and high rates of unemployment can accomplish lower labor costs, but these are not circumstances that encourage foreign investors.

The more general question is whether such policies can stimulate the economies that are implementing them. The standard Keynesian advice to stimulate a national economy is to increase deficit expenditures by the central government along with low interest rates to encourage borrowing for investment and consumption. The logic of curtailing government purchases of goods and services as a cure for recession is dubious, the historical record says no, and recent events vote against it. None of the five nations noted above has recovered per-capita GDP to 2008 levels.

Even the stronger European economies have felt the effects of misguided policies. The Conservative government of Great Britain, not a member of the eurozone, implemented an austere budget in the name of fiscal responsibility and succeeded in slowing Britain's already slow recovery from the fourth quarter of 2010.

Germany, the largest economy and population in the eurozone and EU, is the leader of the eurozone austerity campaign. Although the German economy took a substantial hit from the 2008–2009 financial crises and the decline in export demand, it rebounded well in most of 2010 with the help of a modest government stimulus and by managing to export almost half of its industrial production. The stimulus ran out at the end of 2010, and the initial postrecession bounce soon lost its momentum. Even so, the German leadership is relentless in pushing for reduced government expenditures to the point that the IMF sounds uncharacteristically soft, particularly on fiscal-deficit limits and occasionally on controls of speculative capital movements.

The 2014 elections in Greece brought an anti-austerity leftist government to power which immediately began calling for honoring only a negotiated portion of its foreign-held national debt. Greece began defaulting on its debt at the end of June 2015, and if it continues to default, Spain, Portugal, and other highly indebted governments would be under powerful popular pressure to follow Greece. This would be anathema to the creditor nations, including Germany and other northern EU creditors whose governments and populace already resent the subsidies sent to the south. One result could be a substantial surge of already strong right-wing nationalist and xenophobic parties and movements in several EU members. This would tear apart the eurozone and perhaps the EU.

In the United States, there are politically significant factions that push similar fiscal policies. U.S. **net national debt**, which is the total of Treasury bonds held by the public, foreign and domestic, was a bit more than 70 percent of GDP at the end of 2012, and at the same time, the **gross national debt**, which includes the net debt and adds in all the bonds held

---

TWO NOTES ON GERMANY

In the past decade, Germany pioneered backing away from western Europe's traditionally generous worker benefits and social safety nets. Shrinking social safety nets is always difficult, and demographic trends work against doing so. In the 1950s there were seven workers for every retiree in economically advanced societies, but by 2050, the ratio in the EU will be 1.3 to 1. The aging of the European population will shrink tax revenues at the very time that the demand for social expenditures will rise. Europeans' unwelcoming attitude toward immigrants limits the extent to which young workers from outside the EU can offset the trend. This will be especially difficult in France, where public social expenditures are currently over 30 percent of the GDP, the highest in Europe. The United States, a bit easier on immigrants, is in a similar but less extreme position.

German criticism of the countries that cannot get their fiscal houses in order never mentions that careless lending by German banks helped create the **sovereign debt** crises in the eurozone or that Germany's export successes have in part been due to the eurozone's weaknesses and uncertainties. These problems dragged the value of the euro below what it otherwise would have been in respect to the Japanese yen, enabling German machine and automakers to undersell their most serious competitors. The euro's decline in respect to the U.S. dollar also helped Germany, especially since China's renminbi is tied to the U.S. dollar.

by federal agencies like the Social Security Administration and the Fed, was a bit over 100 percent of GDP.

Changes in net national debt move markets, but it is worth looking at the evolution of the gross debt over the years. At the end of World War II, it was 120 percent of U.S. GDP, and despite a couple of minor bump-ups due to the Korean War and recessions, it declined steadily through the Truman, Eisenhower, Kennedy, Johnson, Nixon, Ford, and Carter administrations, until it weighed in at about 30 percent of GDP in 1980.

In President Reagan's two terms and President George H. W. Bush's single term, the debt as a percentage of GDP shot up to well over 60 percent of GDP. Years later, David Stockman, President Reagan's budget director, confirmed rumors that the administration deliberately increased federal debt through tax cuts and expenditure increases in order to frighten the citizenry into sharply curtailing the government's ability to craft and implement effective policy—a tactic they called "starving the beast."

President Clinton's two terms resulted in the gross national debt falling back below 60 percent of GDP, but President George W. Bush's two terms saw the percentage rise to almost 90 percent. President Obama took office in 2009 as the economy was sliding into the Great Recession, and the decline in tax revenues and the spending to ameliorate the disaster brought the debt to over 100 percent.

The so-called deficit hawks, many of whom were complicit in the run-up of the debt during President George W. Bush's administration, have predicted for years that the U.S. debt is so high that investors' confidence in U.S. Treasury bonds is going to plummet, forcing the bonds' interest rates to rise sharply, creating turbulence in credit markets and another serious recession. Years have gone by, and no such thing has happened; foreign and domestic investors' appetite for U.S. debt remains strong, and interest rates stay at record lows.

An indication of the current strength of foreign confidence in the U.S. government's financial stability is that, in the words of a 2012 Federal Reserve research report by Ruth Judson (2012), "half or a bit more than half of U.S. currency circulates abroad." Most of the value of foreign holdings of U.S. currency is in one-hundred-dollar bills, the largest denomination since the Fed began retiring larger denominations—five-hundred-dollar, one-thousand-dollar, five-thousand-dollar, ten-thousand-dollar, and the never publicly circulated one-hundred-thousand-dollar bills—in 1969.

Employing the starve-the-beast strategy, deficit hawks try to scare U.S. citizens about the burden of such a heavy debt for our children and grandchildren. First of all, the U.S. national debt is denominated in U.S. dollars, the volume of which is controlled by the U.S. government—the Fed and Treasury. If push came to shove, some debt retirement is possible through expanding the U.S. money supply, and a little deliberately manipulated inflation would reduce the real value of the national debt. The idea that Greece and Detroit offer a cautionary tale for the United States is badly informed.

In addition, arguments about the debt burden to future generations ignore the fact that draconian cuts in federal expenditures will create a more onerous type of burden: broken school systems, dangerous and inefficient transportation and sanitation infrastructures, reduced levels of public safety, weakened judicial systems, environmental degradation, unemployment, and ineffective provisions for global warming. Like deregulation and other antigovernment sentiments, such a strategy pleases those who wish to have few restrictions on the use of their resources, have an underdeveloped sense of community, and are able and willing to stay in the private sector for such services as health, education, security of persons and property, transportation, and recreation. Free markets mean freedom for capital to operate without considering anything other than private gain and are liberating for those whose wealth and exercise of power were constrained by government policy. On the other hand, free markets can be debilitating for those whose standards of living depend on the availability of jobs, workers' rights, and the provision of public services.

As a final note, it may surprise you to find that federal deficits have been declining for several years, due to increased tax revenue from a slowly growing economy and to reckless cuts in expenditures, which President Obama called "mindless austerity." It is difficult to find news about these deficit reductions. Nobel Prize laureate Paul Krugman (2014) notes that the lack of such news resembles news about the Affordable Care Act ("Obamacare"), which is all about its problems and seldom mentions that ten million more people are now insured (not counting young people enrolling on their parents' plans), costs have gone down, and the proportion of adult Americans under the age of sixty-five without health insurance declined from 16.4 percent to 11.3 percent. In the twenty-six states that expanded Medicaid coverage, the proportions went from 15 percent to 9 percent, and in the states that refused Medicaid expansion, the proportions went from 18 percent to 14 percent. Among the groups making the biggest gains were people between the ages of eighteen and thirty-four, rural residents, and lower-income people. This is a triumph, and the U.S. House of Representatives wasted time and energy voting to repeal it more than fifty times over the past three years.

So why have declining federal deficits been such a secret, not trumpeted by those most concerned about federal deficits—the deficit hawks? Behind hysterical exhortations about fiscal crises, inflation, burdening our children and grandchildren, and so on, deficit hawks' goal is less about federal deficits than about further contracting unemployment insurance, food stamps, health insurance subsidies, and other safety-net programs for the poor. The notorious budgets put together by Representative Paul D. Ryan (Republican, Wisconsin, and former vice presidential candidate) are egregious illustrations of this aspiration.

Although the EU and the eurozone are often compared to the United States, there is a key difference: there is no central political body in the EU or eurozone with the political and fiscal authority of the U.S. federal government. The transfer of tax dollars from one U.S. state to another, even if noticed, is not a hot political issue, but as the textbox shows, it is substantial. But in the loose collection of semi-independent nations of the EU and eurozone, with diverse histories, levels of prosperity, and interests, nationalist feelings are still strong after years of economic integration.

WHO GETS HOW MUCH FROM
THE FEDERAL GOVERNMENT?

The Tax Foundation, using 2005 data, and *The Economist* magazine with data from 1990–2009 have produced different calculations of the net flows from each state to and from the federal government, and they are surprisingly similar in ranking the states. Both sets of data show that Mississippi, Alaska, Louisiana, Alabama, Kentucky, Montana, Oklahoma, South Carolina, Missouri, Idaho, Arizona, and Wyoming were states where residents received more from the federal government than the state governments and residents paid in federal taxes and fees. In this list, Mississippi received the highest return per dollar paid to the federal government—$2.02 and $2.46, and Wyoming received the least—$1.11 and $1.37. (The Tax Foundation's estimates are listed first, and those from *The Economist* are listed second.)

Why highlight these eleven states? Because they all contain strong strains of anti-federal-government sentiment, and not unexpectedly, they all voted for Mitt Romney and Paul Ryan in the 2012 presidential election. Such criteria ought to include Texas, where the possibility of peaceful secession is an active and noisy issue. Texas's returns from the federal government per $1.00 paid to the federal government were $0.94 and $0.86, and for the purposes of comparisons with three relatively liberal states, California's numbers were $0.78 and $0.92, New York's were $0.79 and $0.71, and Massachusetts's were $0.82 and $0.86.

Sources: "Federal Taxes Paid vs. Federal Spending Received by State, 1981–2005," Tax Foundation, http://taxfoundation.org/article/federal -taxes-paid-vs-federal-spending-received-state-1981-2005 (accessed June 25, 2013); "America's Fiscal Union: The Red and the Black," *Graphic Detail* (blog), *The Economist*, August 1, 2011, http://www.economist.com/blogs/ dailychart/2011/08/americas-fiscal-union (accessed June 25, 2013).

The eurozone does have the European Central Bank, which decided to follow the example of the U.S. Fed, engaging in a policy called quantitative easing—buying eighty-five billion dollars of Treasury bonds and mortgage-backed securities per month—to ease credit and propel the economy. The U.S. Fed quadrupled its holdings of these financial instruments to four trillion dollars, a larger amount than expected from the European Central Bank. But even if eurozone members were to agree on a coherent monetary policy and a set of common banking rules, monetary policy in Europe, as in the United States, is not enough; political roadblocks in both places prevent a forceful fiscal policy to promote economic growth and reduce unemployment.

Monetary policy has generally been considered to be more effective in calming down an overheated economy (inflation) than in stimulating an economy in recession. Monetary policy can make credit scarcer and more expensive, thus discouraging borrowing. But more available and less expensive credit cannot stimulate new economic activity if borrowers do not see good investment opportunities. One of the aphorisms about monetary policy is "You can lead a horse to water, but you cannot make it drink."

With the uncertainty of European and U.S. governments' ability and willingness to apply effective antirecession policies, some leaders, such as finance ministers and central bankers of the twenty leading economies at their G20 meetings—which represent 90 percent of global GDP—had expressed the hope that China would be the principal source of the tide needed to lift all boats (yachts?). After all, China is the world's second-largest economy, behind the United States, and it has demonstrated the ability to grow at astounding rates for more than a decade at a time.

Energized by massive public investments in infrastructure projects, China's economy is indeed rebounding, but depending on China's economy has some issues, apart from the political. As odd as it sounds, China is beginning to experience a labor shortage, having to raise wages, improve working conditions, and deal with labor strikes. One factor is that there are fewer fifteen- to twenty-five-year-old workers, due in good part to China's one-child policy that began affecting family sizes a little more than twenty years ago.

China has responded by sending some production to lower-wage areas, such as Vietnam, and shifting export production in the direction of up-market and more complex products where profit margins are greater. This includes building major bridges in San Francisco and New York City. If this trend continues, China will be competing more with South Korea instead of Thailand and Indonesia, thus replicating the experience of post–World War II Japan and South Korea.

A third strategy would be to expand China's domestic markets for its goods. Although this strategy is politically riskier than working up the export food chain, it appears to have support among China's leadership. Recent reports say that the Chinese leadership is discussing shifting 250 million rural residents to new and existing metropolitan areas. The idea is to curtail these folks' access to subsistence agriculture and to integrate them into commercial life as sellers of labor services and buyers of consumer goods. Several twenty-story towers to house these new urbanites have been completed, and more are under way.

Finally, the gradual appreciation of the renminbi and the recent decision to back off unlimited supplies of loanable funds to its banking system suggest that the leadership believes it would not be in China's interest to continue to grow at such a breakneck pace that it threatens social and political control and the natural environment. China's economic resurgence helped recovery in the East and Southeast Asian economies and was felt throughout the world's resource-based exporters, including Russia, Canada, New Zealand, Australia, Indonesia, Latin America, and Africa. And the new determination seems to have worked: the Chinese economy grew 7.5 percent in 2014, the lowest rate of growth since 1990, and the exchange rate of the renminbi has weakened. The Chinese government appeared a bit unnerved by these numbers and moved to ease credit restrictions.

The attendant slowdown of the Chinese demand for raw materials (petroleum, agricultural products, and a wide range of minerals) cooled off the recent commodities boom, and Latin American and African governments have felt the brunt of the change. Not that the commodity boom was all that beneficial for exporters' economies. Buoyant commodity export markets along with large Chinese investments in Latin American and African transportation raised the prices of the raw-material exporters' currencies. So the raw-material exporters' industrial sectors, which already had trouble competing with low-price manufacturing imports from China, suffered a double blow: the rise in exchange rates made their manufacturing exports less competitive and manufacturing imports from China even cheaper.

As noted more than once, the export of raw materials is not an adequate platform for general economic expansion if guided by markets. Latin America, where the recent commodity boom caused deindustrialization, found this out several times in the past two centuries, and Russia is discovering the power of this generalization.

China is unlikely to serve as a savior of the global economy. And unless the EU and the United States stimulate their economies in systematic and coordinated ways, it is unclear how they will regain the path to steady growth and tolerable levels of unemployment. It was heartening to hear that in recent meetings of the G20, there was an almost unanimous call for a vigorous fiscal policy to reduce unemployment. It came across as a more important priority than earlier concerns about deficits and debts, although the new emphases did not impress those who want President Obama to fail at any price to the nation.

One exception to Republican intransigence about President Obama's initiatives is granting the president so-called fast-track authority that enables the president to negotiate trade treaties and restricts Congress's role to a yes-or-no vote without amendments. President Obama and his agents are negotiating an agreement called the Trans-Pacific Partnership to reduce trade barriers among twelve Pacific nations, from Canada and Japan to western South America and Australia, but excluding China. The president is also in an earlier stage of negotiating a similar pact with the European Union—The Transatlantic Trade and Investment Partnership.

NAFTA casts a deep shadow over the Trans-Pacific negotiations. When President George H. W. Bush designed NAFTA, he did not include provisions to protect workers and the environment, but President Clinton, over the strenuous opposition of the Mexican government, did add some of those protections before sending the agreement to Congress for ratification. The provisions were ineffective, and the agreement is associated with the sharp concentration of U.S. income at the expense of the middle range of U.S. income receivers. Since the negotiations for the Trans-Pacific pact have been held in secret, there is doubt about how much better it is than NAFTA. Both NAFTA and the Trans-Pacific treaties are Republican-backed projects supported by a Democratic president against his party, and they are generally unpopular outside corporate circles. The Trans-atlantic negotiations raise a different question: since the EU has stricter consumer, worker, and environmental protections than the United States, is the United States interested in weakening European protections (race to the bottom) or increasing them in the United States in order, as treaty advocates repeatedly say, "to level the playing field"? (See comparative advantage in the glossary.)

THREE WORRISOME TRENDS

I conclude the book with three topics that are important concerns. The three—the distribution of income, the economic ascendancy of service production over manufacturing, and climate change—are general trends with little likelihood of being ameliorated by U.S. policy.

The Distribution of Income

In the previous chapter, I described changes in the distribution of wage and salary incomes, important in any discussion of income distribution.

Nevertheless, too many studies of income distribution focus exclusively on wage and salary patterns. Much of the income of the very rich comes from property ownership in the form of profits, dividends from stock ownership, rent (from real estate), interest (from loans, including federal government bonds), and **capital gains** (from selling assets such as stocks, bonds, and real estate for more than their purchase prices). The last source is seldom included in income distribution data, but capital gains are like the others on the list in that they all derive from ownership of real and financial capital. Since property ownership is much more concentrated than income, income from these sources accrues to limited ranges of well-to-do income receivers. In 2007, just before the Great Recession, net capital gains income (minus capital losses) equaled just under one trillion dollars, and capital gains are taxed at lower rates than ordinary income.

Property income is more volatile and sensitive to cyclical fluctuations than wages and salaries, and the Great Recession caused the proportions of income in the top income groupings to decline between 2006 and 2008. But save your sympathy; by 2012, the top income receivers' percentages had bounced back. Pavlina Tcherneva (2014) found that in 1949 to 1953—the economic recovery from the first recession after World War II—20 percent of the increased income from the recovery went to the top 10 percent of income receivers and 80 percent to the remaining 90 percent of income receivers. In eight of the nine recoveries from the other postwar recessions, the gains to the top 10 percent from the recoveries successively rose at the expense of the 90 percent. In the most recent recovery, 2009 to 2012 (Tcherneva's most recent data), the top 10 percent of income recipients gained 116 percent of the increased income, which meant that the 90 percent lost income equal to 16 percent of the gains from the recovery.

Gini coefficients are the standard summary statistics of income concentration, and as you can see from the last column of table 11.4, the coefficients rose almost 21 percent between 1970 and 2013. The first five columns of table 11.4 present more information than the Gini coefficient. Statisticians array income-receiving households from the poorest to the richest, count out the first (and poorest) 20 percent (one-fifth, or a quintile) of households, and calculate the percentage of total income received by that 20 percent. In 2000 and 2013, the percentage of income received by that first 20 percent was 3.6 and 3.2 percent of total income. And so on for the next 20 percent, accounting for each fifth and also the highest 5 percent, included in the top 20 percent. And since income from capital gains is not included, table 11.4 underreports the income of the very rich.

Table 11.4 shows that the top 5 percent and top 20 percent (including the top 5 percent) of income recipients are the segments to have increased their proportions of total income since 1970. The greatest loss in percentage points was in the middle fifth, which dropped from 17.4 to 14.4 per-

Table 11.4.   Distribution of Aggregate Income among Households

Year	Percent Distribution of Personal Income						Gini Ratios
	Lowest Fifth	Second Fifth	Middle Fifth	Fourth Fifth	Highest Fifth	Top 5 Percent	
1970	4.1	10.8	17.4	24.5	43.3	16.6	0.394
1980	4.2	10.2	16.8	24.7	44.1	16.5	0.403
1990	3.8	9.6	15.9	24.0	46.6	18.5	0.428
2000	3.6	8.9	14.8	23.0	49.8	22.1	0.462
2013	3.2	8.4	14.4	23.0	51.0	22.2	0.476

Source: U.S. Census Bureau, "Historical Income Tables: Households," U.S. Census Bureau, 2014, http://www.census.gov/hhes/www/income/data/historical/household (accessed Feb. 2, 2015).

centage points. The middle of income receivers (a.k.a., the middle class) earned between forty thousand dollars and eighty thousand dollars in 2015 prices, and thirty years ago, 25 percent of this group were manufacturing production workers in the Core Sector. Today, 13 percent of middle-income earners are in manufacturing, contributing to the erosion, or "hollowing out," of this middle-income segment.

Occupational changes in this group of middle-income receivers of forty thousand to eighty thousand dollars have implications for gender composition and education. Manufacturing production jobs were and are dominated by men, and by men with at most a high school diploma. Nowadays, two out of three of leading occupations in this mid-income range are registered nurses and elementary school teachers, occupations in which women are the majority. The entire range of health-care services, accountants and auditors, social work, financial advisers and managers, legal assistants and aides, secretaries and office managers are also majority women middle-income occupations that require at least some college: In 2015, 38 percent of women in their late twenties and early thirties have college degrees, while 31 percent in the same cohort of men have college degrees, and the rates of college completion continue to diverge. While men hold 70 percent of jobs earning eighty thousand dollars or more, women have moved from 25 percent of middle-income earners in 1980 to 44 percent now.

In sharp contrast to middle-income receivers, the highest fifth of income recipients increased their proportion of personal income from 43.3 percent in 1970 to 51 percent in 2013, an increase of 7.7 percentage points. In the same time period, the top 5 percent of income recipients increased their share of total income from 16.6 percent to 22.2 percent, or 5.6 percentage points. This means that those in the top 5 percent of recipients received 73 percent of the increased proportions of income accruing to the entire top 20 percent of income recipients between 1970 and 2013.

Another way to indicate how concentrated income was, even within the top groups, is to see that of the 2013 income received by the top 20 percent (one-fifth) of income recipients, 43.5 percent of that income went to the top 5 percent, while in 1970, the corresponding proportion was 38.3 percent. Going one step further and beyond the table, the top 1 percent of income recipients accounted for 22 percent of total income and 95 percent of total income increases during the recovery from the Great Recession.

The concentration of income, for which the foundation was laid in the 1980s, does not mean that everyone else is receiving less in absolute amounts. The absolute numbers and percentages of families and individuals existing below the official poverty line began to decline in the mid-1990s. By the end of the decade, the percentages were lower than in 1980, but they turned upward in 2004 and again rose to their highest point since the beginning of the Great Recession.

The top 1 percent of income receivers, whether from Wall Street, Silicon Valley, the energy industry, casinos, inheritance, or somewhere else, includes the billionaires who own at least one thousand millions of dollars in assets. As individuals, they have the resources to move politics. In addition, since the Supreme Court's ruling in *Citizens United v. Federal Election Commission* (2010), corporations can spend freely and advocate loudly for and against candidates as long as they do not contribute to an official campaign or a political party. The written opinion by the majority treated unions as entities parallel to corporations, with the same rights, restrictions, and political potentials, demonstrating an unsuspected sense of humor among the conservative jurists.

The *Citizens United* decision did uphold the requirement to disclose an advertisement's sponsor. This is why there are so many bland-sounding nonprofit front organizations in politics. Learning that a nasty advertisement was funded by, say, Citizens United does not tell us whether the organization is the vehicle of a very rich person, a group of corporations, or something else.

In this world populated by rich and powerful individuals and corporations unrestrained in exercising political influence, these patterns of income and wealth have implications that go beyond who gets to buy more toys. Who benefits most from the idea that raising taxes is an abomination? Who benefits from a smaller, even crippled federal government? The answers are: the very rich, who do not need public services, dislike restrictions on their treatment of employees, and would likely pay a disproportionate amount of any higher taxes.

And there is another cost from extreme income inequality. As people move from smaller cities and towns into large metropolitan areas or move around inside large metropolitan areas, they have gathered into neighborhoods and suburbs that are more and more homogeneous in terms of income and therefore homogeneous along other characteristics such as occupation, education, ethnicity, and race. For the rich and fairly prosperous, this clustering is by choice, but for the majority, it is a matter of affordability. An important aspect of the ghettoization of the rich, the upper middle classes, lower middle classes, and on down the income rankings is that poor and struggling communities support poor and struggling schools and other public services, and unlike in small towns, the children from each community are isolated from those of other communities, although interschool athletic competitions are a minor offset.

Sure, the really rich can send their children to hotshot private schools no matter where they live, but the children of the prosperous but not really rich will go to their community's public schools and meet children of their prosperous but not really rich neighbors, an isolation that characterizes each community. Each community reproduces itself with its advantages or lack thereof through the public schools, libraries, parks, events, public health (for example, sewers and potable water), and other facilities. Overall, the likelihood of U.S. children of parents in the bottom two quintiles of income receivers moving up a quintile or so is lower than for children in Australia, Canada, France, Germany, and Japan. Within the United States, the likelihood of moving up from the poorest quintile is lowest in the Southeast and industrial Midwest and highest in the Northeast, Great Plains, and West. On the other hand, the likelihood that children of affluent parents will themselves be affluent is much higher than for those moving up, and those rates are remarkably uniform throughout the nation.

As it becomes clear that the economic and political system produces such skewed results, showering such extreme benefits on such a small proportion of the population, the legitimacy of the system suffers. Political disaffection and alienation rise among the majority, and even more dangerous, the conditions generate an increasing disregard, even contempt for rules and laws that produce such outcomes.

Manufacturing and Services

Radical shifting in the composition of employment and production in the U.S. economy is another general long-run trend that has affected the economy and the nature of work, recorded in table 11.5. I mentioned the agricultural transformation in chapter 9, and as you can see, agricultural employment continued to decline after the 1970s.

Manufacturing also experienced employment declines, but not as dramatic as in agriculture. Manufacturing employment was volatile in the six decades after 1950, but even with its ups and downs, it is clear that manufacturing employment peaked in 1988 at almost twenty million workers. From there, it continued to fluctuate from year to year until 1998, when it began to decline consistently. The number of manufacturing workers hit a bottom in 2009 and 2010—and then grew slowly over the next five years.

Outsourcing U.S. manufacturing production to foreign sites plays a role in this employment reduction, and a number of familiar manufactures have ceased to be produced in the United States: incandescent lightbulbs, cell phones, laptop computers, minivans, stainless steel flatware (knives, spoons, and forks), stainless steel rebar, vending machines, and canned sardines. Moreover, the proportion of imported components of U.S. manufactured output rose from 17 percent in 1997 to around 25 percent more recently.

Outsourcing within the United States also played a role. As large manufacturing corporations reorganized ("restructured" or "downsized"), they

Table 11.5. Employment and GDP by Major Industry Groups, 1950, 2000, 2012 (Percentages of Total Employment and of GDP)

	1950	1950 GDP by Industry Group	2000	2012	2012 GDP by Industry Group
Goods Production	**51.5**	**44.4**	**18.5**	**14.2**	**26.9**
Agriculture, forestry, fishing	18.0	7.3	1.6	1.5	1.5
Mining	1.6	3.2	0.5	0.6	1.9
Construction	4.3	4.5	4.6	3.9	3.6
Manufacturing	27.6	29.4	11.8	8.2	19.9
Services Production	**48.3**	**54.8**	**73.8**	**79.7**	**68.3**
Transportation and utilities	7.3	9.1	3.4	3.4	4.5
Wholesale trade	4.8	5.9	3.8	3.9	4.7
Retail trade	12.2	12.2	10.4	10.2	4.9
Finance, insurance, real estate	3.4	10.8	5.5	5.4	13.4
Other services	9.7	8.5	36.4	41.8	28.6
Federal government	3.5	4.6	2.0	1.9	4.3
State and local government	7.4	3.7	12.3	13.1	7.9
Total (percentages)	99.8	99.2	92.3	93.9	95.2
Total (1,000,000 people)	55.1		146.2	163.7	142.3

Notes: 2000 and 2012 percentage totals are less than 100 because some self-employed and unpaid family workers are not distributed by industry group.
In the heterogeneous "Other services" category, professional, business, and information services (research and development, management, administration, lawyers, accountants, information technicians, and so on) made up half of the category, and health workers were around a fourth of the total. Leisure-hospitality (including zoos and museums as well as hotels, restaurants, and theaters) made up close to 10 percent. The remaining 20 percent of the category is made up by nonpublic schools, membership organizations (churches, Sierra Club, NAACP, unions), auto repair, car washes, beautician services, mortuaries, laundries, and other disparate service activities.

"Federal government" does not include the men and women in the military.
Education is about half of "State and local government" employment.

Sources: Economic Report of the President (Washington, DC: Government Publishing Office, 2001), 328; U.S. Census Bureau, *Historical Statistics of the United States: Colonial Times to 1970*, Part 1 (Washington, DC: Government Printing Office, 1975), 233; Bureau of Labor Statistics, "Employment by Major Industry Sector," *Monthly Labor Review* (December 2013), http://www.bls.gov/emp/ep_table_201.htm (accessed Feb. 2, 2015); Bureau of Labor Statistics, "Industry Employment and Output Projections to 2022," *Monthly Labor Review* (December 2013), http://www.bls.gov/opub/mlr/2013/article/industry-employment-and-output-projections -to-2022-2.htm (accessed Feb. 4, 2015); Teresa L. Gilmore, Edward T. Morgan, and Sarah B. Osborne, "Annual Industry Accounts: Advance Statistics on GDP by Industry for 2010," *Survey of Current Business* 91, no. 5 (May 2011): 14.

contracted out for a range of services that they had previously done in-house with their own employees. For example, let's say that an automobile firm employed people to provide such services as security, accounting, cleaning, hauling, and advertising. After encountering strong foreign and domestic competition, however, the firm became leaner and meaner by firing all of those folks and contracting out for the five sets of services with independent and specialized firms that are likely to pay lower wages to nonunionized workers and provide less in the way of health and pension benefits. People formerly performing the five sets of services were counted as working in the automobile manufacturing sector, but when the services were outsourced to specialized firms, bean counters in the Bureau of Labor Statistics considered the workers performing those same functions for the same firm as being in different parts of the service sector. But this type of outsourcing does not account for all that much of the decline in manufacturing employment, which is real and large.

But let's not panic. While there were fewer workers in manufacturing in 2012 than in 1950, labor productivity in manufacturing increased substantially over those years. As a result, the **real value** of U.S. manufacturing production, corrected for inflation, grew rather steadily after World War II while employing fewer people, and it increased more than two and one-half times between 1970 and 2007 (before the self-inflicted Great Recession). Among the eight largest manufacturing economies, only the rate of China's industrial growth outpaced that of the United States. So while the manufacturing workforce and manufacturing's proportion of total production have declined, the absolute value of U.S. manufacturing has grown, and grown at higher levels than in six of the seven other largest manufacturing economies. The rise in labor productivity enabled downsizing while increasing output (but not wages), and other sectors have grown more rapidly.

In contrast to employment in firms making goods, services expanded to the point that in 2012, services made up almost 80 percent of employment and almost 70 percent of the GDP. As noted earlier, services are intangibles, produced and consumed simultaneously, such as child care, a haircut, a live concert, lawn care, and a restaurant meal. These examples are all familiar consumer services, but many in the service sector provide business services and sell legal counsel, management consulting, research and development, information technology, telecommunications, accounting, personnel recruitment, advice on CEO salaries, advertising, security, and so on to business firms and various layers of government. By their nature, services are often nontradable products.

The two principal explanations for the rapid rise of the service sector involve, on one hand, changes in demand and, on the other, some odd properties of service production. The demand side explanations are straightforward, arguing that the growth of demand for business services can be attributed to the use of increasingly complex technologies in production, complicated corporate structures, and the need to navigate among myriad rules and regulations from three levels of government.

Also from the demand side, the shift toward consumer services is seen to be the result of rising prosperity that enabled some consumers to increase their consumption of services such as travel, golf, yacht, and country club activities; cosmetic surgery; concert, film, and theater attendance; private school attendance; and so on. This demand-side explanation encompasses a trend that has been going for over a century: consumers in general have been substituting market purchases for goods and services that had been produced in the household outside the market. Soap, clothes, and furniture are examples of goods now typically purchased rather than made within households.

From the second half of the twentieth century, the substitution of market purchases for household production has been strongly oriented toward services: prepared food in restaurants and stores; child and elder care; tax preparation; and maintenance and cleaning of houses, yards, and autos. In single-parent households and where both parents work full time, the turn to service providers in the market expresses genuine imperatives beyond simply consumer preferences.

The supply-side explanation is a bit more complicated. The argument, often called the "cost disease" theory, contends that some, if not all, service production is characterized by low, if any, increases in labor productivity. Meanwhile, productivity gains are routine in manufacturing—a progressive sector. The conventional assumption from economic theory is that increased productivity raises wages of those workers and can do so without raising product costs and prices. Let's suspend our skepticism about this myth and take one further step: assume that the higher wages in the progressive sector exert irresistible pressure to raise wages in the stagnant sector, not 100 percent of wage increases in the progressive sector but more than warranted by low or nonexistent productivity gains. Over time, costs and prices in the stagnant sector rise, compared to those in manufacturing, mining, and agriculture, and are registered as output growth.

The elusive character of service provision that yields no measureable physical products makes it difficult to measure productivity changes. For instance, service production is often just the time spent with the customer—a half-hour appointment with a physician, a professor's lecture, two hours of a plumber's time, an hour with a sex worker. Adam Smith, the author of *The Wealth of Nations* (1776) and the founder of modern economics, acknowledged these issues by distinguishing between "productive labor"—fabricating tangible products like a table—and "unproductive labor"—providing personal services to an elite with lots of leisure. Such a sharp dichotomy is no doubt overstated for the twentieth and twenty-first centuries, but it underscores how long people have struggled with the issue of services.

While questions about productivity gains in services continue to have uncertain answers, it appears that we can expect continuing cost increases in labor-intensive activities not likely to experience cost-reducing technological advances or competitive pricing from imports.[1] In addition to the services listed above, the list includes wholesale and retail trade, finance-insurance-real estate (FIRE), most business services, and health care, education, research and development, police and fire protection, mail delivery, construction and maintenance of bridges, roads, and public buildings, and sanitation, legal, beautician, and funeral services. Many of these are provided wholly or partially through different levels of government, suggesting that in the long run, taxes are not going to decline in a graying United States population without massive cuts in public services.

In this list, research and development is interesting. Much of our invention, innovation, and technology applications that lead to productivity gains come from private and especially public sources of research funding. But the anomaly is that the activity is very labor intensive and offers little hope of experiencing significant productivity increases and cost declines.

Similar to agriculture, much of whatever productivity gains that occurred in services have resulted from applying new manufactured products such as copiers, fax machines, calculators, computers, bar code scanners, pharmaceuticals, CAT scanners, and so on. One concern about the declining prominence of manufacturing in the U.S. economy is that there will be a concomitant reduction in productivity-enhancing domestic research and development. And even if it does not lead to such a diminution, economic growth in the United States will continue to increase the absolute and relative size of service activities less likely to generate rising living standards.

Climate Change

Two respected groups recently issued reports that concluded that the climate is becoming warmer and that human activity is a major cause.

The Intergovernmental Panel on Climate Change, a United Nations group, issued the *Fifth Assessment Report on Climate Change* (2013–2014). The report emphasizes that ice caps are melting at increased rates, water supplies are coming under stress, heat waves and heavy rains are intensifying, coral reefs are dying, and fish and other species are migrating toward the poles. If the amount of greenhouse gases doubles by the end of the century, average temperatures will rise from 2.7 to 5.0 degrees Fahrenheit. Although the United States and other more prosperous countries have cut some greenhouse gas emissions, the amount is overwhelmed by increased emissions from China, India, and other "middle-income" nations. On the other hand, the poorest nations have contributed least to climate change but will suffer the most from the warming trends.

The U.S. National Oceanic and Atmospheric Administration (NOAA), *Third U.S. National Climate Assessment* (May 23, 2014) described that already in the United States water was scarcer in dry regions, torrential rains increased in wet regions, wildfires grew worse, heat waves became more common and severe, forests were assaulted by heat-resistant insects, and sections of some coastal cities were experiencing regular flooding. All these occurrences resulted from less than a two degree Fahrenheit increase in average temperatures in the past century. If greenhouse gas emissions continue to escalate at current rates, temperatures could rise ten degrees by the end of the century.

In the face of such a dire situation, it is reasonable to proceed on two fronts: reduce greenhouse gas emissions worldwide and make adaptive changes. Alternative energy sources, such as wind, solar, ocean tides, and geothermal power are becoming more reliable and economical, and hydrogen fuel cells and nuclear fusion (not fission) have the potential to join the list. Nevertheless, reducing greenhouse gas emissions would entail a daunting political struggle. In the United States, fossil fuels have been the bases of immense family fortunes that wield much political clout, and hundreds of thousands and their families depend on producing and distributing these fuels for their livings. And on the world stage, it is doubtful that any country, especially the poorest, would be willing to compromise its efforts to become more prosperous.

On the defensive side, the politics are equally daunting. The Erie Canal, transcontinental railroad, Panama Canal, St. Lawrence Seaway, and interstate highway system are familiar examples of large-scale infrastructure projects that needed governments to organize, finance, and construct, and an effective mitigation of climate change in the United States would be at least as massive as any two of them. Such an effort would require an increase in the scale and authority of the federal government that would be somewhere between extremely unlikely and impossible in today's political mood, even apart from climate-change deniers.

U.S. Presidents

The presidents are arrayed in chronological order, followed by the years of their presidencies (not of their elections), and an asterisk (*) indicates death in office. The final notation reports political party affiliation. Presidents Jefferson through John Quincy Adams were members of the Democratic-Republican (D-R) Party, but when it split after J. Q. Adams's election, Adams's followers were identified as National Republicans. In the 1830s, the National Republicans along with assorted other groups formed the Whig Party. The Union Party was composed of War Democrats and Republicans united against secession in the U.S. South.

1. George Washington (1789–1797) None
2. John Adams (1797–1801) Federalist
3. Thomas Jefferson (1801–1809) D-R
4. James Madison (1809–1817) D-R
5. James Monroe (1817–1825) D-R
6. John Quincy Adams (1825–1829) D-R
7. Andrew Jackson (1829–1837) D
8. Martin Van Buren (1837–1841) D
9. William Henry Harrison (1841–1841*) Whig
10. John Tyler (1841–1845) Whig
11. James Polk (1845–1849) D
12. Zachary Taylor (1849–1850*) Whig
13. Millard Fillmore (1850–1853) Whig
14. Franklin Pierce (1853–1857) D
15. James Buchanan (1857–1861) D
16. Abraham Lincoln (1861–1865*) R
17. Andrew Johnson (1865–1869) Union
18. Ulysses S. Grant (1869–1877) R
19. Rutherford B. Hayes (1877–1881) R
20. James Garfield (1881–1881*) R
21. Chester A. Arthur (1881–1885) R
22. Grover Cleveland (1885–1889) D
23. Benjamin Harrison (1889–1893) R
24. Grover Cleveland (1893–1897) D
25. William McKinley (1897–1901*) R
26. Theodore Roosevelt (1901–1909) R
27. William Howard Taft (1909–1913) R
28. Woodrow Wilson (1913–1921) D
29. Warren Harding (1921–1923*) R
30. Calvin Coolidge (1923–1929) R
31. Herbert Hoover (1929–1933) R
32. Franklin D. Roosevelt (1933–1945*) D
33. Harry S. Truman (1945–1953) D
34. Dwight D. Eisenhower (1953–1961) R
35. John F. Kennedy (1961–1963*) D
36. Lyndon B. Johnson (1963–1969) D
37. Richard M. Nixon (1969–1974) R
38. Gerald R. Ford (1974–1977) R
39. James E. Carter (1977–1981) R
40. Ronald W. Reagan (1981–1989) R
41. George H. W. Bush (1989–1993) R
42. William J. Clinton (1993–2001) D
43. George W. Bush (2001–2008) R
44. Barack M. Obama (2008–2017) D

Glossary

When the text uses terms included in the glossary, those terms will be in **bold type**.

Arbitrage is buying a good or service in one market and selling it at a higher price in another. Simultaneously buying and selling foreign currency in two markets and simultaneously borrowing and lending in two different markets are common examples that help to keep prices uniform across different markets.

Army worms are small caterpillars, the larvae of a moth that has a prodigious appetite for cotton plants.

Backward linked, in this book, means the connection between an export and those back down the chain of suppliers. When an export experiences a surge of demand, it will stimulate all of its suppliers.

Balance of payments is the most comprehensive accounting for international transactions of an individual nation and includes two principal accounts. The first part is the current account, of which payments for exports and imports (the **balance of trade**) are components. The current account also contains unilateral transfers (for example, U.S. government grants to foreign militaries and private U.S. residents' remittances to the folks in the old country) as well as repatriated earnings from foreign investment. The last are profits from foreign-owned enterprises operating in the United States sent out of the country and profits from U.S.-owned foreign enterprises brought into the country. The second part is the capital account, which records the financial transactions involved in both **foreign portfolio investment** and **foreign direct investment**.

Balance of trade is the balance of payments for a nation's exports and imports of goods and services, and it is the principal component of the current account.

Bretton Woods Conference was held in Bretton Woods, New Hampshire, in 1944 as World War II began to look as though it was ending. The conference's purpose was to create a new international financial framework robust enough to support postwar international trade and investment, which had declined precipitously during the 1930s Depression and subsequent war. Forty-three Allies, one neutral country (Argentina), and several European colonies attended. The resulting agreement created the **dollar-exchange standard** and the International Bank for Reconstruction and Development (now known as the **World Bank**) and the **International Monetary Fund** to monitor and regulate the new system.

Capital controls are national regulations on foreign investments and purchases and sales of domestic currencies.

Capital gains result from selling such assets as stocks, bonds, and real estate for more than their purchase prices.

Capital goods are manufactured products used in further production. Factories, machinery, and equipment are examples. Automobiles and furniture are products that can be either capital or consumer goods, depending on owner and use.

Capitalism is the social organization of production and distribution that has three integral features: the wage association between employees and employers (capital-labor relationship); profit-motivated private firms are the principal source of products and services, competing with each other in product markets to realize profits (the capital-capital relationship); and the first two relationships are set in a national political framework with shifting public sector–citizen interactions (the public sector–citizen relationship). While capitalism requires markets in goods and services, active commodity markets can exist in a wide variety of social relationships of production that are not capitalist—for example, slavery.

Carpetbagger is a derogatory label for northerners who moved to the South after the Civil War, primarily to pursue economic and political opportunities or to teach and "missionize" black southerners.

Cartels are formal agreements among firms operating in an **oligopolistic** market to coordinate members' prices and production decisions.

Comparative advantage, in most introductory economics textbooks, assures you that the benefits from international specialization and trade among nations are parallel to the argument that specialization among individuals within a nation leads to mutually beneficial exchange. The theory of comparative advantage treats nations as indivisible units, comparable to an individual. But the reality is that nations are not harmonious collections of individuals; they are filled with groups with often conflicting and contradictory interests. This means that a nation does not benefit or lose through international commerce but rather that some groups in the nation benefit at the expense of others. To deny such complexity is to risk conclusions that serve some groups and disadvantage other groups. While winners may gain enough to compensate losers and still be ahead, it is unlikely that political mechanisms able to achieve such compensation would be tolerated. Arithmetic models based on relative prices and national units are not adequate for a rigorous analysis of the benefits and losses from international trade.

Consumer Price Index (CPI) is an index created by the Bureau of Labor Statistics, U.S. Department of Labor, to measure changes in the prices of a fixed market basket of goods and services important for typical urban consumers.

Convertibility is the ability to convert paper currency into specie—gold and silver.

Corporations are business firms owned by those holding the corporation's **stocks** (or shares)—certificates of equity (ownership). Those owners cannot lose any more money than what they have paid for the stocks, even if the corporation goes through bankruptcy, leaving many unpaid creditors.

Crowding out usually refers to federal government policies that "crowd out" spending by other sectors.

Deflation is a general decrease of prices, benefiting lenders and disadvantaging borrowers.

Demand deposits are checking accounts.

Derivatives are financial instruments whose value is derived from other assets. Derivatives based on pieces of different mortgages were common before the Great Recession.

Deregulation in this book refers to lifting government-imposed restrictions and limitations on actions by firms. It comes in two forms: overt, which is announced and promoted as formal policy, and covert, which is simply to appoint regulatory agencies' leaders who are strongly opposed to the agencies' missions while seriously underfunding them.

Devaluation occurs when the price of country A's currency denominated in country B's currency declines.

Discretionary spending is that part of consumer spending that is above what is considered necessary for basics such as food, clothing, housing, water, and other utilities.

Disposable income is a family's income after taxes.

Dividends are payments to corporations' shareholders from profits.

Dollar-exchange standard is the adjustment mechanism established by the **Bretton Woods Conference**, and it was closer to the **gold standard** than to a flexible exchange rate system even though the volume of gold held by a national treasury no longer determined the volume of money circulating in its national economy. The U.S. dollar became the new key currency—an international legal tender—to which all other currencies were pegged and defended by their governments. For foreign central banks and only foreign central banks, dollars were convertible to gold at thirty-five dollars per ounce. Unlike the **gold standard** and a **flexible exchange-rate system**, the dollar-exchange standard focused exclusively on deficits and required adjustments only on the deficit nations.

Dumping occurs when a firm, usually by means of a government subsidy, sells its exports at lower prices than those same goods in the exporter's home market.

Durable goods are expected to last several years. Durable consumer goods are those likely to last three years or more.

Economies of scale occur when higher levels of a firm's output allow for new efficiencies that reduce average (per-unit) costs.

Exchange rate is the price of one nation's currency in another nation's currency. At this writing, the price of the English pound (£) in U.S. dollars is around $1.66. To express the same ratio in a different manner, the price of $1.00 U.S. is £0.60. Both numbers are exchange rates.

Factors of production are usually considered to be labor, capital, and land (including cultivating, mining, drilling, and so on). Each factor has its markets with individual characteristics.

Fiscal deficit is a shortfall between government revenues and expenditures in a year.

Fiscal policy is the deliberate use of the federal government's budget to stimulate or dampen the rate of economic growth. For example, if the economy is growing so rapidly that it threatens serious inflation, raising taxes and reducing expenditures, together or alone, is likely to reduce growth and stabilize prices. The other side of the same policy is to stimulate a sluggish economy by lowering taxes and increasing expenditures (unless Congress is paralyzed by gridlock).

Fixed costs must be paid no matter how much is produced and sold. These are a firm's costs associated with the land, buildings, and capital equipment as well as other overhead costs such as contracted insurance, loans, and Internet services.

Flexible exchange-rate systems operate through international currency markets, raising the price of a balance-of-trade surplus nation's currency in respect to other currencies—its **exchange rate**—and reducing a balance-of-trade deficit nation's exchange rate. As a consequence, prices of the surplus nation's exports rise in foreign markets and import prices decline in its home market, both reducing exports and increasing imports and thereby contributing to a reduced surplus. On the other hand, the reduction of the price of a deficit-nation's currency leads to lower prices of the deficit-nation's exports in foreign markets and rising prices of imports in the home market, thus increasing exports, reducing imports, and moving toward a balance. The expectation, then, is that both deficit and surplus nations will be propelled closer to balance. Most exchange-rate flexibility is among leading currencies, and most other exchange rates are pegged to one or another major currency.

Foreign direct investment (FDI) occurs when an investor in country A sets up or buys a plant, mine, farm, plantation, bank, or other productive activity in country B or when that foreigner buys more than 10 percent of a country B enterprise. Either way, the country A investor has a substantial stake and considerable control in a productive activity located in country B, and FDI has been a major cause of conflict between foreign investors and local elites. Contrast with **foreign portfolio investment**.

Foreign portfolio investment (FPI) occurs when a country A investor buys bonds from country B's government or private companies or purchases less than 10 percent of a particular country B corporation. The idea is that this is a purely financial investment adding to a portfolio in the hope that the investment will yield good returns but with little or no interest in or ability to control the foreign government or firm.

Forward link, in this book, refers to the process by which an export can become an input for a new domestic industry. Shippers of lumber establish domestic furniture companies; sugar exporters begin to use some of their sugar in new candy factories. Both are examples of a forward-linked stimulus.

Gini coefficient is the most commonly used measure of income inequality. Its theoretical limits are 0.0 (perfect equality) to 1.0 (perfect inequality).

Gold standard required convertibility of currencies fixed in terms of gold. A surplus-trade nation would experience an inflow of gold and convertible currencies, expanding the amount of domestic currency, leading to inflation, reducing its exports' international competitiveness, and increasing the attractiveness of imports. A deficit-trade nation experienced the mirror image: loss of gold; reduced currency in circulation; deflation; more competitive exports; and reduced imports. Changes in exports and imports reduced trade surpluses and trade deficits. The actual operation of the nineteenth-century gold standard was uneven, but even when the process worked with textbook tidiness, it produced inflation in the economies with export surpluses and deflation in economies importing more than they exported. Neither made a government popular with citizens.

Gross domestic product (GDP) is the most comprehensive measure of the value of a nation's total output of goods and services over a year. Its major categories are consumer expenditures, business investment expenditures for inventories, plant, and equipment, the value of governments' spending and production, and the value of exports minus the value of imports. In 1991, the U.S. government began to use GDP rather than **gross national product (GNP)** to be consistent with most of the rest of the world. The principal difference between them is that the GNP counts all production within the U.S. borders irrespective of whether domestic residents or foreign residents receive the profits, while the GDP does not include profit flows from U.S. production to foreign residents or profit flows from foreign production to U.S. owners. The size of the difference between the two measures is small.

Gross national debt is the total value of all U.S. federal debt (bonds), while **net national debt** excludes all federal debt held by agencies of the federal government.

Gross national product (GNP) is described at **gross domestic product (GDP)** above.

Horizontal integration occurs when firms take over competitors engaged in the same lines and stages of production, as in when competing railroads merge.

Income is the amount of net receipts over a given period of time—month, year. Income therefore is a flow variable (over time) rather than a stock variable. *See* **wealth.**

Human capital is considered parallel to physical capital. At the level of the national workforce or of an individual, investments in training, education, and health can yield higher future incomes.

Inflation is a general rise in prices, benefiting borrowers and disadvantaging lenders.

Import-substituting industrialization was the strategy of most countries trying to become industrial economies in the 1950s through the 1970s. The idea was to erect substantial tariffs and **capital controls** in order to stimulate local industrial growth. This strategy is not unlike how the United States industrialized so rapidly through the nineteenth century.

Inputs are the materials, fuels, and intermediate products used in the process of production.

International Monetary Fund (IMF) and the **World Bank** were created by the **Bretton Woods Conference** to monitor and stabilize the international trade and payments system. The IMF's principal responsibility was to deal with imbalances considered to be of a short-term, cyclical nature by lending hard currency (for example, U.S. dollars) to a nation running a deficit in its international payments. Borrowing beyond a certain point, however, often required the borrowing government to agree to certain conditions—the IMF's "conditionality." Similar to the medicine of the gold standard, the IMF's standard prescriptions to reduce a balance-of-trade deficit were to enact deflationary domestic policies, emphasizing reductions in government expenditures such as social services and subsidized urban food and transportation. In addition, the IMF pressured nations to abolish government regulations such as workers' protections and controls over domestic and international merchandise and financial transactions, seeing these protections and controls as impeding the operation of efficient markets. Under the current leadership of Christine Lagarde, the eleventh managing director, the IMF's conditionality has become less rigid and less harsh.

Legal tender is a currency that by law has to be accepted in payment "for all debts public or private." Look for that phrase on any denomination of our current paper money.

Less-developed countries (LDCs) is a descriptive phrase with a history. The "third world" was a term coined at an Indonesian conference of African and Asian leaders in the 1950s to denote nations that were neither allied with the United States and western Europe nor the Soviet and Chinese in the Cold War. The rubric always represented a very diverse group of nations in Africa, Asia, and Latin America, and beginning in the 1970s and 1980s, the rapid economic growth of some East and Southeast Asian economies, the wealth of Middle East oil exporters, the economic stagnation of Africa, and uneven economic achievements in Latin America increased the nations' heterogeneity, reduced their common interests, and made any collective name of dubious value. The disappearance of the Soviet Union and communist Eastern Europe, a good piece of the "second world," led to the use of "emerging markets" for some of the nations experiencing relatively rapid economic growth or recently using markets rather than central planning. For example, BRIC is shorthand for Brazil, Russia, India, and China, and often an *S* is attached for South Korea or South Africa. Given the lack of attractive alternatives, I will continue to use the bland term "less-developed countries" (LDCs) because it is relatively clear and familiar.

Macroeconomic policy is federal policy designed to affect the growth rate of the entire economy, hence "macro"—the whole works. **Fiscal policy** and **monetary policy** are the most commonly used tools to affect the levels of economic activity across the board.

Market structure concerns the number of firms in an industry and the degree of competition among them. Common categories are monopoly (one seller), **oligopoly** (a few interdependent firms), and highly competitive (a rather large number of firms that are, relative to industry size, small).

Monetary policy is the deliberate use of the cost and availability of credit to stimulate a sluggish economy or dampen an economy in danger of overheating and generating inflation. The Federal Reserve System (Fed) sets and implements policy, and the U.S. Treasury Department can affect credit markets by changing its deposits in commercial banks. Monetarism is the belief that credit is the major influence of economic activity, although many (perhaps most) economists suspect that the Fed's effect on the economy is much stronger on the restraint side rather than stimulus. ("You can lead a horse to water, but you cannot make it drink.")

National debt, sometime called public debt, is the accumulation of all deficits. That is, it is the amount of government bonds in the hands of creditors. *See also* **gross national debt** and **net national debt**.

Net national debt is the total value of all U.S. federal debt (bonds) minus all federal debt held by agencies of the federal government.

Oligopoly is a market organization with few producers and sellers who recognize their interdependence and dislike price wars. The term corresponds to the more familiar political term: oligarchy—rule by the few.

Piecework is the arrangement by which an individual worker is paid by the number of units he or she produces.

Primary products are raw materials with little or no processing from agriculture, mining, fisheries, and forestry.

Producer goods, also known as intermediate goods, are sold to firms and government agencies as inputs for further production. They can be either **capital goods**, such as machinery, or raw materials to be used in further processing.

Progressive taxes mean that taxpayers pay higher *rates* of taxation at higher income levels. If those with higher incomes pay greater absolute amounts of tax than poorer people, the tax could be progressive, regressive, or proportional; it's a matter of *proportions* of income paid in taxes.

Real value is monetary value corrected for inflation.

Regressive taxes impose higher tax *rates* on people with lower incomes. As in the case of **progressive taxes**, it is a matter of *proportions* of income paid.

Scalawag was a derogatory label for white Southerners who worked with the Republicans in post–Civil War Reconstruction. Many had opposed secession and the war.

Secondary products are manufactured goods.

Sovereign debt is often used interchangeably with **national debt**, but occasionally the meaning is more precise. When a nation issues bonds denominated in a currency other than its own, as when Greece issues bonds in euros, it might be called sovereign debt.

Stagflation is the simultaneous appearance of inflation and low or negative economic growth and increased rates of unemployment.

Stocks (shares) are certificates of equity (ownership) in a corporation and usually traded on an organized market, such as the New York Stock Exchange and the NASDAQ exchange.

Tariffs are taxes on imports.

Tertiary products are services.

Transnational corporations (a.k.a. multinational corporations) are corporations with substantial activities in two or more nations.

Value added for a firm is its total sales minus purchases of goods and services from other firms. What is left are wages, salaries, and profits—what that firm's activities have added to overall product value. Farmers sell wheat to millers, millers sell flour to bakers, and bakers sell bread. The value added in each stage is calculated by subtracting purchase price from selling price. Adding up all three selling prices yields a hodgepodge number.

Variable costs are costs to firms that vary with the levels of production. Wages, fuel, and raw material inputs are common examples.

Vertical integration occurs when a firm merges backward (that is, with suppliers of inputs) or forward to marketing and distribution. When steel firms bought iron ore mines in the Mesabi Iron Range in Minnesota, it was **backward-linked** vertical integration. **Forward-linked** vertical integration occurred when firms making complex products such as mechanical reapers and sewing machines established retail outlets in order to provide the necessary training for customers and maintenance and repair services.

Wealth is the value of a person's, firm's, or nation's assets at a particular point in time, say, December 31, 2016. Because of this point-in-time aspect, wealth is a stock variable. Income, measured over a period of time, is a flow variable.

World Bank (formerly known as the International Bank for Reconstruction and Development) and the **International Monetary Fund (IMF)** were created by the **Bretton Woods Conference** to monitor and stabilize the international trade and payments system. The World Bank made long-term loans to countries where chronic balance-of-payments deficits were seen to be due to the structure of the deficit nation's economy.

Notes

CHAPTER 1: MERCANTILISM, BRITISH COLONIALISM, AND INDEPENDENCE

1. The frequent problem with the powerful standing army was that it could easily be a threat to the authority of the political elites in the imperial center, and continual expansion was often a way to keep the army occupied and away from the political center. Julius Caesar's crossing the Rubicon showed that this strategy did not always work.

2. I refer to "England" when I am speaking about specifically English issues but to "Britain" or "Great Britain" when I mean the entire political unit that includes England, Scotland, Wales, Northern Ireland, and, at different times, all of Ireland.

3. The large Mayan cities of Guatemala and southern Mexico had dissolved centuries before the Spaniards arrived, but the dispersed communities in the Guatemalan highlands retained enough organization to be useful to the conquerors.

4. Even agricultural settlers often admired Indian women's work discipline in cornfields and villages while remaining disdainful of the men's hunting and fishing as real work.

5. In this usage, the word "servant" is not limited to domestic help. It includes workers in a wide range of occupations in agriculture, commerce, trades, and so on.

6. Non-English constituted almost 20 percent of the white colonial population at the time of the revolution, and they included Irish and Scots, German immigrants to Pennsylvania, and the New York Dutch, whom the British conquered in 1664.

CHAPTER 2: DEFINING THE NEW NATION

1. Spain and France had passed New Orleans and related territories back and forth over centuries, and without the due diligence of a title search, it is not clear Napoleon had the right to sell them. Supposedly secret treaties notwithstanding, Napoleon had substantial influence over Spain even before installing his brother, Joseph, on the Spanish throne in 1808.

2. These estimates assume that age and gender compositions are roughly the same in the black and white populations.

3. There is an active cottage industry of people claiming the essentially religious (read: Protestant) nature of the document, but since the words of the Constitution do not support the contention, they are left with having to channel the founding fathers for their intentions.

4. By the 1850s, foreign investors were investing directly into railroad companies rather than buying state and local government bonds that the governments then channeled into transportation projects.

5. The power to select post office locations, employ thousands of employees, and place contracts for carrying the mail made the U.S. postmaster one of the most desirable positions in the presidential cabinet.

6. "Wage goods" is a bit of a misnomer because much of the cotton produced by black slaves was sent to the North to be turned into cotton apparel, some of which was bought by planters for their slaves. "Slave goods" and "goods for workers" do not sound quite right, so we will stick to wage goods.

7. Armaments and ship fittings were exceptions to the prominence of wage goods, just as breweries and shipbuilding were exceptions to the small size of manufacturing firms.

8. This did not mean, however, that industrialists all spurned the values of the landed aristocracy. Many successful industrialists bought land and strove to become accepted by traditional aristocratic society. These strivings were a favorite subject of contemporary novelists, who had diverse opinions about such aspirations.

9. The Gallagher and Robinson article and a selection of the resulting controversy are included in Louis (1976).

10. "Steal" is a more apt term than "borrow." England had laws against the export of machinery or the emigration of skilled mechanics to foreign lands, which the United States became after independence.

11. It is ironic that the availability of women working outside their own homes was necessary for the development of a cult of domesticity among well-to-do families.

12. A telling example of the sectors' separateness is apparent in Daniel R. Hundley's (1860) popular travelogue that portrays the South to northern readers as a very strange, alien place.

13. In a manner similar to market outcomes, policies affecting the patriarchic family were also regarded as illegitimate.

CHAPTER 3: REGIONS, SECTIONS, AND CIVIL WAR

1. My typology of linkages is derived from what is called the staple theory, although it is more a typology than a true theory. The original formulation is credited to the Canadian historian Harold Innes in the 1930s, and Douglass C. North (1966) is a highly respected application of the staple theory to U.S. history.

2. Conforming to standard practice in the United States, the planters sold rather than freed their surplus slaves. Because freeing slaves was often limited to dodging responsibility for caring for the old and ill, the U.S. proportion of free African Americans, always low compared with other slave societies in the Americas, declined in these years until it was less than 11 percent in 1860.

3. Fifteen years after leaving the presidency, John Tyler was elected to the Confederate legislature.

4. Abraham Lincoln was not ambivalent. In a speech on June 26, 1857, at Springfield, Illinois, Lincoln said that the authors of the Declaration of Independence "did not declare men equal in *all* respects," but claimed them to be "equal in certain inalienable rights, among which are life, liberty, and the pursuit of happiness. This is what they said and this they meant." Quoted in Kenneth M. Stampp (1990: 106).

5. Lincoln was not on the presidential ballots of ten of the fifteen slave states, and the South Carolina legislature picked presidential electors.

6. The U.S. government compensated slave owners for freeing their slaves only in the District of Columbia. A few months before the Emancipation Proclamation, the U.S. government abolished slavery there and compensated slaveholders an average of around three hundred dollars per slave on condition of their taking a loyalty oath.

CHAPTER 4: WARTIME LEGISLATION, WESTERN EXPANSION, AND RECONSTRUCTION

1. The federal government gave eastern states, which contained little or no federal land, grants of land in the West.

2. Mississippi made slavery illegal by changing its state constitution in 1865 but did not ratify the Thirteenth Amendment until 1995.

3. The amendment also was subsequently important in order for corporations to be considered persons with Bill of Rights protections.

4. The fifteenth amendment was unpopular in the West, where Asians and Mexican Americans were significant minorities. Oregon ratified the amendment in 1959 and California in 1962.

5. The back-to-Africa sentiment was revived by Marcus Garvey (1887–1940) and his Universal Negro Improvement Association that he brought to New York from his native Jamaica in 1917.

CHAPTER 5: CHANGING FORMS
OF INDUSTRIAL DEVELOPMENT

1. Cotton textiles are technically intermediate products, but we use the term throughout the text as shorthand to designate "heavy" intermediate products.

2. Oligopoly means a few sellers and corresponds to the more familiar political term: oligarchy—rule by the few.

3. Quoted by Susan Strasser (2004: 212).

4. Patricia Nelson Limmerick (1987: 27) is too dismissive of eastern nativism when she writes: "In race relations, the West could make the turn-of-the-century Northeastern urban confrontations between European immigrants and American nativists look like a family reunion."

CHAPTER 6: SOCIAL CHANGE, POLITICS, AND REFORM

1. Louisiana was so enthusiastic about shutting schools that its rate of white literacy declined between 1880 and 1900.

2. It was not until the 1930s that Congress enlarged the ICC's scope to other types of interstate transportation. After years of deregulation and reducing ICC authority, Congress abolished the ICC in 1995.

CHAPTER 7: THE UNITED STATES IN THE WORLD

1. As I described in chapter 2, this limited ambition corresponded to Britain's free-trade imperialism of the early nineteenth century.

CHAPTER 8: WAR, DEPRESSION, WAR

1. Nanking was the capital of Nationalist China, and Japanese soldiers, over a six-week period, raped, pillaged, murdered, and burned anyone and anything in sight. Estimates of the death toll range from one hundred thousand to three hundred thousand.

CHAPTER 9: POST–WORLD WAR II
RECOVERY AND MODERN TIMES, 1945–1980s

1. I use the term "Modern Times" for the mass production–mass consumption social formation rather than Fordism, postwar social structures of accumulation, monopoly capitalism, late capitalism, labor segmentation, embedded liberalism, and welfare capitalism. Each of these alternatives is from authors who present a

picture generally consistent with what I have called Modern Times, and I have
learned from them all.

2. I use the measure of the federal debt that excludes debt holdings by federal
agencies—net national debt.

3. These three decisions became lumped together under the misleading rubric
of "one man, one vote," and more recently it has been known as "one person, one
vote."

4. The U.S. Constitution fixes the apportionment of the U.S. Senate as two senators per state, which means that recent constituent numbers per U.S. senator for
California were 18,300,000 and 282,000 for Wyoming.

5. Despite decades of worry about illegal residents in the United States, official
estimates were not undertaken until the late 1980s and 1990s, and those estimates
were that there were three million to five million immigrants who had illegally
entered the United States or overstayed their entry permits.

6. When the U.S. Supreme Court struck down school segregation in 1954, seventeen states by law required that public schools be racially segregated. In 1967,
the Supreme Court declared that laws prohibiting interracial marriages were not
constitutional, and the decision affected the sixteen states that had such laws.

7. These acts are usually celebrated as triumphs of American values, but occasionally writers and speakers acknowledge that it was a disgrace that it took one
hundred years to guarantee basic citizenship rights to all citizens.

8. Gary Becker (1971) was one of the best-known sources of the economic
argument. These economic arguments did not notice that white employers used
workplace discrimination to control and discipline their white workers.

CHAPTER 10: THE DISSOLUTION OF U.S. MODERN
TIMES, 1980s INTO THE TWENTY-FIRST CENTURY

1. The IMF, the World Bank, the Inter-American Development Bank, and the
U.S. Treasury are located in Washington, DC, thus the appropriateness of the
"Washington Consensus," coined by John Williamson (1990).

2. These trends have increased. In 2012, 80 percent of the value of the Honda
Accord and 20 percent of the value of the Ford Fusion were made in the United
States (Canadian production is considered to be of the United States, but do not
tell the Canadians).

3. The year 2008 is the beginning of the Great Recession, and I use it because
export figures had yet to decline and thus still represented the peak of a long-term
trend.

4. Cuba has the potential for a similar disaster. If the same institutional "reforms" are wreaked on Cuba, as many prominent in U.S. politics would have it,
the Cuban Revolution's unusual degree of income equality (already weakening)
and world-class health and education systems would be out the window.

5. I am grateful to Damien W. S. Weaver for forcing the importance of these
connections on me.

6. Republicans' confidence in winning in 2012 was illustrated by the overflow of parking for private jets at Logan Airport, Boston, as Romney supporters came to join him in celebrating his victory.

CHAPTER 11: THE GREAT RECESSION, AUSTERITY, AND THREE WORRISOME TENDENCIES

1. Using an imaginative set of indirect indices, Edward N. Wolff (2002) suggests that transportation, communications, and public utilities have demonstrated some labor productivity gains but that generally productivity in service-sector firms is stagnant.

References and Recommendations

Aglietta, Michel. 1979. *The Theory of Capitalist Regulation: The U.S. Experience*. London: New Left.

Alden, Dauril. 1984. *Colonial Roots of Modern Brazil*. Berkeley: University of California Press.

Anderson, Benedict. 1983. *Imagined Communities: Reflections of the Origin and Spread of Nationalism*. New York: Verso.

Anderson, Fred. 2005. *The War That Made America: A Short History of the French and Indian War*. New York: Viking.

Appleby, Joyce. 1987. "The American Heritage: The Heirs and the Disinherited." *Journal of American History* 74: 789–813.

Atack, Jeremy, Fred Bateman, and William N. Parker. 2000. "The Farm, the Farmer, and the Market." In *The Cambridge Economic History of the United States*, Vol. 2: *The Long Nineteenth Century*, edited by Stanley L. Engerman and Robert E. Gallman, 245–84. New York: Cambridge University Press.

Averitt, Robert T. 1968. *The Dual Economy: The Dynamics of American Industry Structure*. New York: Norton.

Axtell, James. 1981. *The European and the Indian: Essays in the Ethnohistory of Colonial North America*. New York: Oxford University Press, esp. the third, ninth, and tenth essays.

Bair, Sheila. 2012. *Bull by the Horns: Fighting to Save Main Street from Wall Street and Wall Street from Itself*. New York: Free Press.

Bartlett, Bruce. 2013. "'Financialization' as a Cause of Economic Malaise." *Economix* (blog), *New York Times*, June 11. http://economix.blogs.nytimes.com/2013/06/11/financialization-as-a-cause-of-economic-malaise.

Becker, Gary. 1971. *The Economics of Discrimination*. 2nd ed. Chicago: University of Chicago Press.

Benson, Susan Porter. 1968. *Counter Cultures: Saleswomen, Managers, and Customers in American Department Stores*. Urbana: University of Illinois Press.

———. 2007. *Household Accounts: Working Class Family Economics in the Interwar United States*. Ithaca, NY: Cornell University Press.

Bergier, J. F. 1973. "The Industrial Bourgeoisie and the Rise of the Working Class, 1700–1914." In *The Fontana Economic History of Europe*, Vol. 3, pt. 1, edited by Carlos Cipolla, 397–451. London: Fontana.

Berlin, Ira. 2010. *The Making of African America: The Four Great Migrations*. New York: Viking Penguin.

Bernstein, Michael A., and David E. Adler, eds. 1994. *Understanding American Economic Decline*. New York: Cambridge University Press.

Blight, David W. 2001. *Race and Reunion: The Civil War in American Memory*. Cambridge, MA: Belknap.

Blinder, Alan S. 2012. *After the Music Stopped: The Financial Crisis, the Response, and the Work Ahead*. New York: Penguin.

Block, Fred L. 1977. *The Origins of International Economic Disorder: A Study of the United States International Monetary Policy from World War II to the Present*. Berkeley and Los Angeles: University of California Press.

Blumin, Stuart M. 2000. "The Social Implications of U.S. Economic Development." In *The Cambridge Economic History of the United States*, Vol. 2: *The Long Nineteenth Century*, edited by Stanley L. Engerman and Robert E. Gallman, 813–64. New York: Cambridge University Press.

Braverman, Harry. 1974. *Labor and Monopoly Capital: The Degradation of Work in the Twentieth Century*. New York: Monthly Review.

Brenner, Robert. 2006. *The Economics of Global Turbulence: The Advanced Capitalist Economies from Long Boom to Long Downturn, 1945–2005*. New York: Verso.

Bureau of Labor Statistics. 2013. "Employment by Major Industry Sector." *Monthly Labor Review* (December). http://www.bls.gov/emp/ep_table_201.htm.

———. 2013. "Industry Employment and Output Projections to 2022." *Monthly Labor Review* (December). http://www.bls.gov/opub/mlr/2013/article/industry-employment-and-output-projections-to-2022-2.htm.

Chandler, Alfred D. 1977. *The Visible Hand: The Managerial Revolution in American Business*. Cambridge, MA: Belknap.

Cohen, Lizabeth. 2004. *A Consumer's Republic: The Politics of Mass Consumption in Postwar America*. New York: Vintage.

Cohen, William. 1991. *At Freedom's Edge: Black Mobility and the Southern White Quest of Racial Control, 1861–1915*. Baton Rouge: Louisiana State University Press.

Coontz, Stephanie. 1992. *The Way We Never Were: American Families and the Nostalgia Trap*. New York: Basic.

Coyle, Diane. 2014. *G.D.P.: A Brief but Affectionate History*. Princeton, NJ: Princeton University Press.

Crafts, N. F. R., S. J. Leybourne, and T. C. Mills. 1991. "Britain," in *Patterns of European Industrialization: The Nineteenth Century*, edited by R. Sylla and G. Toniolo, 109–52. New York: Routledge.

Crouzet, F. 1972. *Capital Formation in the Industrial Revolution*. New York: Barnes and Noble.

Davis, Ralph. 1973. *The Rise of the Atlantic Economies*. London: Weidenfeld.

Delfino, Susanna, and Michele Gillespie, eds. 2005. *Global Perspectives on Industrial Transformation in the American South*. Columbia: University of Missouri Press.

Dochuk, Darren. 2011. *From Bible Belt to Sun Belt: Plain-Folk Religion, Grassroots Politics, and the Rise of Evangelical Conservatism*. New York: Norton.

Dorris, Jonathan Truman. 1953. *Pardon and Amnesty under Lincoln and Johnson: The Restoration of the Confederates to Their Rights and Privileges, 1861–1898*. Chapel Hill: University of North Carolina Press.

Du Bois, W. E. B. 1896. *The Suppression of the African Slave Trade to the United States of America, 1638–1870*. Harvard Historical Series 1. Cambridge, MA: Harvard University Press.

Economic Report of the President. 2001. Washington, DC: Government Publishing Office.

Economist. 2011. "America's Fiscal Union: The Red and the Black." *Graphic Detail* (blog), *The Economist*, August 1. http://www.economist.com/blogs/dailychart/2011/08/americas-fiscal-union.

Edelstein, Michael. 2000. "War and the American Economy in the Twentieth Century." In *The Cambridge Economic History of the United States*, Vol. 3: *The Twentieth Century*, edited by Stanley L. Engerman and Robert E. Gallman, 329–406. New York: Cambridge University Press.

Engerman, Stanley L. 2000. "Slavery and Its Consequences for the South in the Nineteenth Century." In *The Cambridge Economic History of the United States*, Vol. 2: *The Long Nineteenth Century*, edited by Stanley L. Engerman and Robert E. Gallman, 329–66. New York: Cambridge University Press.

Engerman, Stanley L., and Kenneth L. Sokoloff. 2000. "Technology and Industrialization, 1790–1914." In *The Cambridge Economic History of the United States*, Vol. 2: *The Long Nineteenth Century*, edited by Stanley L. Engerman and Robert E. Gallman, 367–402. New York: Cambridge University Press.

Engerman, Stanley L., and Robert E. Gallman, eds. 2000. *The Cambridge Economic History of the United States*. 3 vols. New York: Cambridge University Press.

Fenichel, Allen H. 1966. "Growth and Diffusion of Power in Manufacturing, 1838–1919." In *Output, Employment, and Productivity in the United States After 1800*, edited by Dorothy S. Brady, 443–78. New York: Conference on Research in Income and Wealth, National Bureau of Economic Research.

Fogel, Robert William. 2003. *The Slavery Debates, 1952–1990: A Retrospective*. Baton Rouge: Louisiana State University Press.

Foner, Eric. 1989. *Reconstruction: America's Unfinished Revolution*. New York: Harper & Row.

Fones-Wolf, Elizabeth A. 1994. *Selling Free Enterprise: The Business Assault on Labor and Liberalism, 1945–60*. Urbana: University of Illinois Press.

Fowler, William M. Jr. 2005. *Empires at War: The French and Indian War and the Struggle for North America, 1754–1763*. New York: Walker.

Fraser, Steve. 2015. *The Age of Acquiescence: The Life and Death of American Resistance to Organized Wealth and Power*. New York: Little, Brown.

Frieden, Jeffrey A. 2006. *Global Capitalism: Its Fall and Rise in the Twentieth Century*. New York: Norton.

Friedland, William H., Amy E. Barton, and Robert J. Thomas, eds. 1981. *Manufacturing Green Gold: Capital, Labor, and Technology in the Lettuce Industry*. New York: Cambridge University Press.

Gadrey, Jean, and Faiz Gallouj, eds. 2002. *Productivity, Innovation and Knowledge in Services: New Economic and Socio-Economic Approaches*. Northampton, MA: Edward Elgar.

Galambos, Louis. 2002. "The U.S. Corporate Economy in the Twentieth Century." In *The Cambridge Economic History of the United States*, Vol. 3: *The Twentieth Century*, edited by Stanley L. Engerman and Robert E. Gallman, 927–68. New York: Cambridge University Press.

Galenson, David W. 1996. "The Settlement and Growth of the Colonies: Population, Labor, and Economic Development." In *The Cambridge Economic History of the United States*, Vol. 1: *The Colonial Era*, edited by Stanley L. Engerman and Robert E. Gallman, 135–208. New York: Cambridge University Press.

Gallagher, John, and Ronald Robinson. 1976. "The Imperialism of Free Trade." In *Imperialism: The Robinson and Gallagher Controversy*, edited by William Roger Louis, 53–72. New York: New Viewpoints. Originally published in *Economic History Review*, second series 6 (1953).

Gatrell, V. A. C. 1977. "Labour, Power, and the Size of Firms in Lancashire Cotton in the Second Quarter of the Nineteenth Century." *Economic History Review* 30: 95–139.

Gallman, Robert E. 2000. "Economic Growth and Structural Change in the Long Nineteenth Century." In *The Cambridge Economic History of the United States*, Vol. 2: *The Long Nineteenth Century*, edited by Stanley L. Engerman and Robert E. Gallman, 1–56. New York: Cambridge University Press.

Gerschenkron, Alexander. 1943. *Bread and Democracy in Germany*. Berkeley and Los Angeles: University of California Press.

———. 1966. "Economic Backwardness in Historical Perspective." In *Economic Backwardness in Historical Perspective*, edited by Alexander Gerschenkron, 5–30. Cambridge, MA: Harvard University Press.

Gilmore, Teresa L., Edward T. Morgan, and Sarah B. Osborne. 2011. "Annual Industry Accounts: Advance Statistics on GDP by Industry for 2010." *Survey of Current Business* 91, no. 5 (May): 8–24.

Go, Julian. 2008. *American Empire and the Politics of Meaning: Elite Political Cultures in the Philippines and Puerto Rico during U.S. Colonialism*. Durham, NC: Duke University Press.

Gordon, Colin. 1994. *New Deals, Business, Labor, and Politics in America, 1920–1935*. New York: Cambridge University Press.

Gordon, Donald M., Richard Edwards, and Michael Reich. 1982. *Segmented Work, Divided Workers: The Historical Transformation of Labor in the United States*. New York: Cambridge University Press.

Greenberg, Amy S. 2005. *Manifest Manhood and the Antebellum American Empire*. New York: Cambridge University Press.

Gregory, James N. 2005. *The Southern Diaspora: How the Great Migrations of Black and White Southerners Transformed America*. Chapel Hill: University of North Carolina Press.

Gregory, Mary, Wiemer Salverda, and Ronald Schettkat. 2007. *Services and Employment: Explaining the U.S.-European Gap.* Princeton, NJ: Princeton University Press.

Haines, Michael R. 2000. "The Population of the United States, 1790–1920." In *The Cambridge Economic History of the United States,* Vol. 2: *The Long Nineteenth Century,* edited by Stanley L. Engerman and Robert E. Gallman, 143–206. New York: Cambridge University Press.

Hayden, Dolores. 2003. *Building Suburbia: Green Fields and Urban Growth, 1820–2000.* New York: Pantheon.

Heim, Carol. 2000. "Structural Changes: Regional and Urban." In *The Cambridge Economic History of the United States,* Vol. 3: *The Twentieth Century,* edited by Stanley L. Engerman and Robert E. Gallman, 83–190. New York: Cambridge University Press.

Henretta, James A. 1988. "The War of Independence and American Economic Development." In *The Economy of Early America: The Revolutionary Period, 1763–1790,* edited by Ronald Huffman and John J. McCusker, 45–87. Charlottesville: University Press of Virginia.

Howe, Daniel Walker. 2007. *What Hath God Wrought? The Transformation of America, 1815–1848.* New York: Oxford University Press.

Howenstine, Ned G., and William J. Zeile. 1994. "Characteristics of Foreign-Owned U.S. Manufacturing Establishments." *Survey of Current Business* 74, no. 1 (Jan.): 34–59.

Hughes, J. R. T. 1976. *Social Control in the Colonial Economy.* Charlottesville: University Press of Virginia.

Hundley, Daniel Robert. 1860. *Social Relations in Our Southern States.* New York: Henry B. Price.

Innis, Harold Adams. 1927. *The Fur-Trade of Canada.* Toronto: University of Toronto Press.

Irwin, Neil. 2014. "A Big Safety Net and Strong Job Market Can Coexist: Just Ask Scandinavia." *New York Times,* Dec. 17, B2.

Jaynes, Gerald David. 1986. *Branches without Roots: Genesis of the Black Working Class in the American South, 1862–1882.* New York: Oxford University Press.

Judson, Ruth. 2012. "Crisis and Calm: Demand for U.S. Currency at Home and Abroad from the Fall of the Berlin Wall to 2011." International Finance Discussion Paper 1058, Board of Governors of the Federal Reserve System, Washington, DC.

Kalman, Laura. 2010. *Right Star Rising: New Politics, 1974–1980.* New York: Norton.

Kammen, Michael. 1970. *Empire and Interest: The American Colonies and the Politics of Mercantilism.* New York: Lippincott.

Kanstroom, Daniel. 2007. *Deportation Nation: Outsiders in American History.* Cambridge, MA: Harvard University Press.

Keynes, John Maynard. (1923) 1971. *A Tract on Monetary Reform.* London: Macmillan. Reprint, London: Macmillan; New York: St. Martin's.

———. 1936. *A General Theory of Employment, Interest, and Money.* New York: Harcourt, Brace.

Keyssar, Alexander. 2000. *The Right to Vote: The Contested History of Democracy in the United States.* New York: Basic.

Kimmel, Michael. 2013. *Angry White Men: American Masculinity at the End of an Era.* New York: Nation.

Kindleberger, Charles P. 1973. *The World in Depression, 1929–1939.* Berkeley and Los Angeles: University of California Press.

Klein, Herbert S. 2012. *A Population History of the United States.* 2nd ed. New York: Cambridge University Press.

Kotz, D. M., T. McDonough, and M. Reich, eds. 1994. *Social Structures of Accumulation: The Political Economy of Growth and Crisis.* Cambridge: Cambridge University Press.

Krugman, Paul. 2014. "Secret Deficit Lovers." *New York Times,* October 10.

Kruse, Kevin M. 2015. *One Nation under God: How Corporate America Invented Christian America.* New York: Basic.

Lamoreaux, Naomi R. 2000. "Entrepreneurship, Business Organization, and Economic Concentration." In *The Cambridge Economic History of the United States,* Vol. 2: *The Long Nineteenth Century,* edited by Stanley L. Engerman and Robert E. Gallman, 403–33. New York: Cambridge University Press.

Landes, David S. 1965. "Japan and Europe: Contrasts in Industrialization." In *State and Economic Enterprise in Japan,* edited by W. W. Lockwood, 93–182. Princeton, NJ: Princeton University Press.

———. 1969. *The Unbound Prometheus.* Cambridge: Cambridge University Press.

Lagarde, Christine. 2014. "Economic Inclusion and Financial Integrity—An Address to the Conference on Inclusive Capitalism." London, May 27. https://www.imf.org/external/np/speeches/2014052714.htm.

Langley, Lester D. 1996. *The Americas in the Age of Revolution, 1750–1850.* New Haven, CT: Yale University Press.

Larson, John Lauritz. 2009. *The Market Revolution in America: Liberty, Ambition, and the Eclipse of the Common Good.* New York: Cambridge University Press.

Lepore, Jill. 2013. "Long Division: Measuring the Polarization of American Politics." *New Yorker,* Dec. 2, 75–79.

Limmerick, Patricia Nelson. 1987. *The Legacy of Conquest: The Unbroken Past of the American West.* New York: Norton.

Linklater, Andro. 2002. *Measuring America : How an Untamed Wilderness Shaped the United States and Fulfilled the Promise of Democracy.* New York: Walker.

Lipsey, Robert E. 2000. "U.S. Foreign Trade and the Balance of Payments." In *The Cambridge Economic History of the United States,* Vol. 2: *The Long Nineteenth Century,* edited by Stanley L. Engerman and Robert E. Gallman, 685–732. New York: Cambridge University Press.

Lipsitz, George. 1994. *Rainbow at Midnight: Labor and Culture in the 1940s.* Urbana: University of Illinois Press.

Louis, William Roger, ed. 1976. *Imperialism: The Gallagher and Robinson Controversy.* New York: New Viewpoints.

Louky, James, Jeanne Armstrong, and Larry J. Estrada, eds. 2006. *Immigration in America Today: An Encyclopedia.* Westport, CT: Greenwood.

Love, Eric T. 2004. *Race over Empire: Racism and U.S. Imperialism, 1865–1900.* Chapel Hill: University of North Carolina Press.

Lynch, John. 1986. *The Spanish American Revolutions, 1808–1826.* 2nd ed. New York: Norton.

Maddison, Angus. 1995. *Monitoring the World Economy, 1820–1992*. Paris: Development Centre, OECD.

Maier, Pauline. 2010. *Ratification: The People Debate the Constitution, 1787–1788*. New York: Simon and Schuster.

Main, Jackson Turner. 1966. "Government by the People: The American Revolution and the Democratization of the Legislatures." *William and Mary Quarterly* 23: 391–407.

———. 1965. *The Social Structure of Revolutionary America*. Princeton, NJ: Princeton University Press.

Mantoux, Paul. 1962. *The Industrial Revolution in the Eighteenth Century*. Rev. ed. New York: Harper & Row.

Marglin, Stephen A., and J. B. Schor, eds. 1990. *The Golden Age of Capitalism: Reinterpreting the Postwar Experience*. Oxford: Clarendon.

Marx, Karl. (1857–1858) 1974. *Grundrisse*. Edited and translated by M. Nicolous. Reprint, New York: McGraw-Hill.

May, Robert E. 2002. *Manifest Destiny's Underworld: Filibustering in Antebellum America*. Chapel Hill: University of North Carolina Press.

———. 2013. *Slavery, Race, and Conquest in the Tropics: Lincoln, Douglas, and the Future of Latin America*. New York: Cambridge University Press.

McCusker, John J., and Russell R. Menard. 2010. "The Origins of Slavery in the Americas." In *The Oxford Handbook of Slavery in the Americas*, edited by Robert L. Paquette and Mark Smith, 275–92. New York: Oxford University Press.

McDonough, Terrence, Michael Reich, and David M. Kotz, eds. 2010. *Contemporary Capitalism and Its Crises: Social Structure of Accumulation Theory for the 21st Century*. New York: Cambridge University Press.

McElvaine, Robert S. 1993. *The Great Depression, America, 1929–1941*. New York: Times Books.

McWhirter, Cameron. 2011. *Red Summer: The Summer of 1919 and the Awakening of Black America*. New York: Henry Holt.

Meier, August. 1964. *Negro Thought in America, 1880–1915: Racial Ideologies in the Age of Booker T. Washington*. Ann Arbor: University of Michigan Press.

Milkman, Ruth. 1987. *Gender at Work: The Dynamics of Job Segregation by Sex during World War II*. Urbana: University of Illinois Press.

Mokyr, Joel. 1985. "The Industrial Revolution and the New Economic History." In *The Economics of the Industrial Revolution*, edited by Joel Mokyr. Totowa, NJ: Rowman and Allenheld.

Montgomery, David. 1987. *The Fall of the House of Labor: The Workplace, the State, and American Worker Activism, 1865–1925*. New York: Cambridge University Press.

Nash, Gary B. 2005. *The Unknown American Revolution: The Unruly Birth of Democracy and the Struggle to Create America*. New York: Viking.

Nedelsky, Jennifer. 1982. "Confining Democratic Politics: Federalists, Anti-Federalists, and the Constitution." *Harvard Law Review* 96: 342–362.

Norris, Floyd. 2010. "In Great Recession, Other Nations Have Suffered More." *New York Times*, Sept. 18, B3.

North, Douglas C. 1966. *The Economic Growth of the United States, 1790 to 1860*. New York: Norton.

O'Connor, James. 1973. *The Fiscal Crisis of the State*. New York: St. Martin's.

Olson, Alison Gilbert. 1991. *Making the Empire Work: London and American Interest Groups, 1690–1790*. Cambridge, MA: Harvard University Press.

Opdyke, Sandra. 2000. *The Routledge Historical Atlas of Women in America*. New York: Routledge.

Padgen, Anthony. 1990. *The Fall of Natural Man: The American Indian and the Origins of Comparative Ethnology*. New York: Cambridge University Press.

———. 1994. *European Encounters with the New World*. New Haven, CT: Yale University Press.

———. 1995. *Lords of All the World: Ideologies of Empire in Spain, Britain, and France c. 1500–c. 1800*. New Haven, CT: Yale University Press.

Paul, Rodman Wilson, and Elliott West. 2001. *Mining Frontiers of the Far West, 1848–1880*. Albuquerque: University of New Mexico Press.

Pérez, Louis A. 1998. *The War of 1898: The United States and Cuba in History and Historiography*. Chapel Hill: University of North Carolina Press.

Polanyi, Karl. 1957. *The Great Transformation*. Boston: Beacon.

Quigley, David. 2004. *Second Founding: New York City, Reconstruction, and the Making of American Democracy*. New York: Hill and Wang.

Ransom, Roger L., and Richard Sutch. 2001. *One Kind of Freedom: The Economic Consequences of Emancipation*. New York: Cambridge University Press.

Richardson, Heather Cox. 2014. *West from Appomattox: The Reconstruction of America after the Civil War*. New Haven, CT: Yale University Press.

Roark, James L. 1977. *Masters without Slaves: Southern Planters in the Civil War and Reconstruction*. New York: Norton.

Rolle, Andrew F. 1965. *The Lost Cause: The Confederate Exodus to Mexico*. Norman: University of Oklahoma Press.

Salisbury, Neal. 1996. "The History of Native Americans from before the Arrival of the Europeans and Africans until the American Civil War." In *The Cambridge Economic History of the United States*, Vol. 1: *The Colonial Era*, edited by Stanley L. Engerman and Robert E. Gallman, 1–52. New York: Cambridge University Press.

Sanders, Elizabeth. 1999. *Roots of Reform: Farmers, Workers and the American State, 1877–1917*. Chicago: University of Chicago Press.

Schulman, Bruce J., and Julian E. Zelizer, eds. 2008. *Rightward Bound: Making America Conservative in the 1970s*. Cambridge, MA : Harvard University Press.

Semmel, Bernard. 1970. *The Rise of Free Trade Imperialism: Classical Political Economy, the Empire of Free Trade, and Imperialism, 1750–1850*. New York: Cambridge University Press.

Silbey, Joel H. 2005. *Storm over Texas: The Annexation Controversy and the Road to Civil War*. New York: Oxford University Press.

Smith, Adam. (1776) 1927. *An Inquiry into the Nature and Causes of the Wealth of Nations*. London: W. Strahan. Reprint, New York: Modern Library.

Smith, Alan K. *Creating a World Economy: Merchant Capital, Colonialism, and World Trade, 1400–1825*. Boulder, CO: Westview, 1991.

Stampp, Kenneth M. 1990. *America in 1857: A Nation on the Brink*. New York: Oxford University Press.

Standing, Guy. 1989. "Global Feminization through Flexible Labor." *World Development* 17: 1077–95.

Stansell, Christine. 1987. *City of Women: Sex and Class in New York, 1789–1860*. Urbana: University of Illinois Press.

Stiglitz, Joseph. 2013. *The Price of Inequality: How Today's Divided Society Endangers Our Future*. New York: Norton.

Stokes, Melvin, and Stephen Conway, eds. 1987. *The Market Revolution in America: Social, Political, and Religious Expressions, 1800–1880*. Charlottesville: University Press of Virginia.

Stolper, Gustav. 1967. *The German Economy, 1870 to the Present*. New York: Harcourt, Brace and World.

Strasser, Susan. 2004. *Satisfaction Guaranteed: The Making of America's Mass Market*. Washington, DC: Smithsonian.

Strom, Sharon Hartman. 1992. *Beyond the Typewriter: Gender, Class, and the Origins of Modern American Office Work, 1900–1930*. Urbana: University of Illinois Press.

———. 2001. *Political Woman: Florence Luscomb and the Legacy of Radical Reform*. Philadelphia: Temple University Press.

———. 2003. *Women's Rights*. Westport, CT: Greenwood.

———. 2006. "Labor, Race and Colonization: Imagining a Post-Slavery World in the Americas." In *The Problem of Evil: Slavery, Race and the Ambiguities of American Reform*, edited by Steven Mintz and John Stauffer, 260–70. Amherst, MA: University of Massachusetts Press.

Strom, Sharon Hartman, and Frederick Stirton Weaver. 2011. *Confederates in the Tropics: Charles Swett's Travelogue of 1868*. Jackson: University Press of Mississippi.

Stromquist, Shelton. 2006. *Reinventing "The People": The Progressive Movement, the Class Problem, and the Origins of Modern Liberalism*. Urbana: University of Illinois Press.

Sylla, Richard. 2000. "Experimental Federalism: The Economics of American Government." In *The Cambridge Economic History of the United States*, Vol. 2: *The Long Nineteenth Century*, edited by Stanley L. Engerman and Robert E. Gallman, 483–541. New York: Cambridge University Press.

Tax Foundation. 2007. "Federal Taxes Paid vs. Federal Spending Received by State, 1981–2005." http://taxfoundation.org/article/federal-taxes-paid-vs-federal-spending-received-state-1981-2005.

Tcherneva, Pavlina R. 2014. "Reorienting Fiscal Policy: A Bottom-Up Approach." *Journal of Post Keynesian Economics* 37: 43–66.

Thompson, Edward P. 1963. *The Making of the English Working Class*. New York: Vintage.

Thurow, Lester. 1975. *Generating Inequality: Mechanisms of Distribution in the U.S. Economy*. New York: Basic.

Tilly, Richard. 1991. "Germany." In *Patterns of European Industrialization: The Nineteenth Century*, edited by R. Sylla and G. Toniolo, 175–96. New York: Routledge.

Ueda, Reed. 1994. *Postwar Immigrant America: A Social History*. Boston: Bedford.

U.S. Census Bureau. 1975. *Historical Statistics of the United States: Colonial Times to 1970*, Part 1. Washington, DC: Government Printing Office.

———. 2014. "Historical Income Tables: Households." U.S. Census Bureau. http://www.census.gov/hhes/www/income/data/historical/household.

U.S. Department of Commerce. 1962. *U.S. Commodity Exports and Imports as Related to Output, 1960 & 1959*. Washington, DC: Government Printing Office.

———. 1979. *U.S. Commodity Exports and Imports as Related to Output, 1976 & 1975*. Washington, DC: Government Printing Office.

Vatter, Harold G. 1985. *The U.S. Economy in World War II*. New York: Columbia University Press.

Vaughn, Alden T. 1982. "From White Man to Redskin: Changing Anglo-American Perceptions of the American Indian." *American Historical Review* 87: 917–53.

Walther, Eric. 2003. *The Shattering of the Union: America in the 1850s*. Lanham, MD: Rowman & Littlefield.

Weaver, Frederick S. 2011. *Economic Literacy: Basic Economics with an Attitude*. 3rd ed. Lanham, MD: Rowman & Littlefield.

Wells, Wyatt. 2003. *American Capitalism, 1945–2000: Continuity and Change from Mass Production to the Information Society*. Chicago: Ivan R. Dee.

White, Richard. 1991. *"It's Your Misfortune and None of My Own": A History of the American West*. Norman: University of Oklahoma Press.

———. 2011. *Railroaded: The Transcontinentals and the Making of Modern America*. New York: Norton.

Williams, David. 2008. *Bitterly Divided: The South's Inner Civil War*. New York: New Press.

Williamson, John. 1990. "What Washington Means by Policy Reform." In *Latin American Adjustment: How Much Has Happened?*, edited by John Williamson, 5–20. Washington, DC: Institute for International Economics.

Wilson, William Julius. 1978. *The Declining Significance of Race: Blacks and Changing American Institutions*. Chicago: University of Chicago Press.

Wolff, Edward N. 2002. "How Stagnant Are Services?" In *Productivity, Innovation and Knowledge in Services*, edited by Jean Gadrey and Faiz Gallouj, 3–25. Northampton, MA: Edward Elgar.

Woodruff, William. 1966. *Impact of Western Man: A Study of Europe's Role in the World Economy*. New York: St. Martin's.

Wright, Gavin. 2013. *Sharing the Prize: The Economics of the Civil Rights Revolution in the American South*. Cambridge, MA: Belknap.

Zunz, Olivier. 1990. *Making America Corporate, 1870–1920*. Chicago: University of Chicago Press.

Index

veterans: African American, 155; land
   grants to, 18, 26; pensions for, 129
Vietnam, 204
Vietnam War, 183, 195
violence: anti-labor, 113, 121; racial,
   83–87, 110, 155–56, 187–89; in West,
   74–78
Virgin Islands, 137, 142*t*, 145
voter suppression, 60, 78–79, 82, 84–85,
   110; and immigrants, 122–23
Voting Rights Act, 189

wage labor, 42; Marx on, 37–38; in
   South, 81
Wake Island, 145
Walker, William, 59
Wallace, George C., 190
War Capitalism, 165–67
War of 1812, 33, 40
wars, paying for, 18, 151, 151*t*, 166, 214
Washington, Booker T., 86
Washington, George, 32
Washington Consensus, 197, 263n1
waterpower, 42
wealth, definition of, 257
welfare, 188, 212
Wells, Ida B., 86–87
West: expansion in, 48–49; and
   government, 130; population, 50*t*,
   73*t*; settling, 72–78, 73*t*
whites: and civil rights movement,
   189–91; and Civil War, 62, 81;

definition of, 104; in Hawaii, 138–
   39; migration of, 105; and politics,
   82–85; and Reconstruction, 109; and
   slavery, 53
Wilson, Woodrow, 129, 150, 152,
   154–55, 157
Wolff, Edward N., 264n1
woman suffrage, 29, 55, 84–85, 121–23,
   152; early, 153*t*
women: and labor movement, 112;
   and reform, 121–22, 152; and
   Revolution, 19–20; in West, 78
women's work: clerical, 118; in
   colonies, 16; department stores
   and, 101; foreign assembly and,
   202; industrialization and, 40,
   43–44; postwar, 175, 185; and
   wages, 115
working class, 111–18, 111*t*
World Bank, 171; definition of, 257
world position of U.S.: early federal
   government and, 33–34; prewar,
   131–46
World Trade Organization (WTO), 203
World War I, 149–54; aftermath of,
   154–59; paying for, 151, 151*t*
World War II, 165–67; paying for,
   151, 151*t*, 166; postwar recovery,
   169–78

yields, 127, 185–86
Young, Brigham, 48